Nevada: A History of Changes

DANGBERG HISTORICAL SERIES
Donald Dickerson, Editor

Cover design and original art by Bill Barker
Text design and production by Nickie Price
Typesetting by Valerie Isham, Nevada Typesetting
Printed by Cal Central Press

Nevada: A History of Changes is typeset in Garth Graphic
Roman and Italic for text matter, Univers 75 for subheads, and
Triumvirate Compressed for chapter headings.

Second Printing, May 1987
Third Printing, Sept. 1989

Library of Congress Catalog No. 86-82332
ISBN 0-913205-09-5

ACKNOWLEDGEMENTS

The author, the editor, and the Grace Dangberg Foundation gratefully acknowledge the assistance of the following individuals and organizations: Nickie and Bill Price, Monica Newell, Bill Barker, Leontine Bennet, Gary Elam, Bill Germino, Gary BeDunnah, Ken Bedrosian; the Nevada Historical Society: Eslie Cann, Lee Mortensen, Ann Spencer, Eric Moody, Phil Earl; Special Collections of the University of Nevada Reno Library: Tim Gorelangton, Lee Kosso, Robert E. Blesse; the Nevada State Museum: Bob Nylen; Special Collections of the University of Nevada Las Vegas Library; the late Joseph Anderson; John M. Townley; the Huntingdon Library; the Elko County School District; the Nevada Department of Transportation: Bob Davis, Robin Holabird; the Nevada Commission on Tourism: Richard Moreno; Summa Corporation, the Tropicana Hotel, the Stardust Hotel, Bally's Grand Hotel, Harvey's, the Lake Tahoe Visitors Authority, the Reno-Sparks Chamber of Commerce, the Reno News Bureau, and the Las Vegas News Bureau.

*To the memory of
Grace M. Dangberg (1896–1985)*

Nevada: A History of Changes

By David Thompson

A Publication of
The Grace Dangberg Foundation

Contents

CHAPTER 1

The Indians

For thousands of years before the first white intruders entered the Great Basin, American Indians were the only people who lived in Nevada. Most of them led a wandering life, migrating in small groups of families, or bands. These native Americans left no written histories for us to read. We know about them only through the discoveries of archaeologists and the writings of the first explorers, trappers, soldiers, and settlers who passed through the Great Basin.

The oldest known Indian sites in the State date from about 5000 to 10,000 B.C. One of the earliest places where the Indians lived, worked, and died was discovered in 1933 at Tule Springs in southern Nevada. The archaeologists who excavated this site found man-made items or artifacts used perhaps twelve thousand years ago. There have also been discoveries of ancient Indian objects that were nearly as old at other locations in Elko, Lander, and Pershing Counties.

ANCIENT LIFEWAYS

These prehistoric Nevadans had a stone age culture, that is, their tools were made from stone and bone. In the southern part of Nevada along the Colorado River, an ancient people called the Anasazi built a sophisticated civilization under stone age conditions, with fields of crops, mines, and villages. These Indians, who mysteriously disappeared from Nevada about 1150 A.D., lived in houses like those of the Pueblo Indians of Arizona and New Mexico.

The migratory bands of northern Nevada and the Indians who replaced the Anasazi lived close to nature. They depended upon the weather and their knowledge of the land for survival. These bands of Indians were self-sufficient. Their culture was based upon the necessity of living in a delicate balance with their environment. Their world, their habits, and their religious ideas were derived from several thousands of years of experience in living off the land. The realities of their existence made the Indian culture very conservative and resistant to radical change.

There are four major tribal groups in Nevada: the Washo, Shoshone, northern Paiute, and southern Paiute Indians. With the exception of the two Paiute groups, the tribes speak different languages. In the beginning of the nineteenth century, these Indian tribes were living in much the same way as their ancestors had lived for the past thousand years. Bands of families moved from place to place, following the seasons as food became available. Food was critically important to them. Many of the bands had names indicating their main food, such as cui-ui eaters, trout eaters, rabbit eaters, ground squirrel eaters, and so on.

These bands and tribal groups had their own territory over which they roamed, but they had no formal boundaries like our modern counties and states. They had no formal structure of government but lived in accordance with their social customs and the decisions of the elders and principal men of the community. They had neither elections nor bureaucracies.

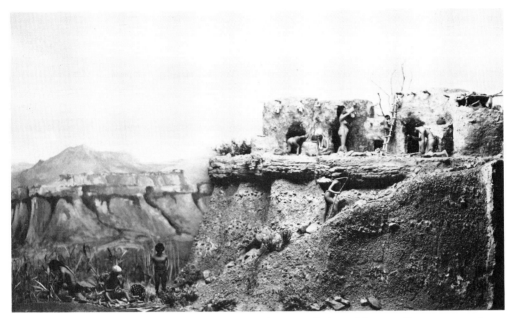

Ancient Anasazi villages, such as the one shown in this Nevada State Museum diorama, were the most sophisticated settlements in the Great Basin during prehistoric times. These villages were able to accumulate food surpluses by growing crops along river beds, and this allowed a large number of people to be able to live in a small area for a long time. The stored food was kept in fortified villages where it could be protected from nomadic, predatory Indians. The Anasazi dominated southern Nevada until their culture mysteriously disappeared from the region in about A.D. 1150.

Courtesy of Nevada State Museum

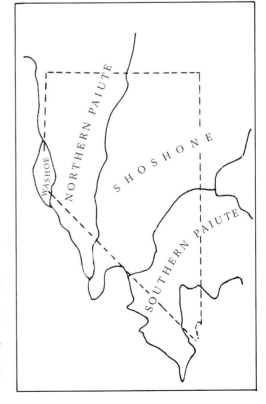

Indians of Nevada. This chart shows the distribution of the major American Indian linguistic groups in the State, as well as the approximate boundaries of tribal territory, as of 1863. Note that the tribal areas, which conform to the geographic outlines of the western part of the Great Basin, have nothing in common with Nevada's political boundaries which were arbitrarily established by the United States Congress.

One of the rare first-hand accounts of Indian life during the years before the coming of white culture was written by Sarah Winnemucca, whose Indian name was Thocmetony ("Shell Flower"). Born about 1844, she was the grand-daughter of Truckee, the paramount chief of the northern Paiutes at the time the whites were first seen. Her father, Winnemucca, later succeeded Truckee as leader of the northern Paiutes. She wrote about her experiences in *Life Among the Paiutes: Their Wrongs and Claims,* first published in 1883. This account shows what Indian society was like in northwestern Nevada:

> The chief's tent is the largest tent, and it is the council-tent, where everyone goes who wants advice. In the evenings the head men go there to discuss everything, for the chiefs do not rule like tyrants; they discuss everything with their people, as a father would in his family. Often they sit up all night. They discuss the doings of all, if they need to be advised. If a boy is not doing well they talk that over, and if the women are interested they can share in the talks. If there is not room enough inside, they all go out of doors, and make a great circle. The men are in the inner circle, for there would be too much smoke for the women inside. The men never talk without smoking first. The women sit behind them in another circle, and if the children wish to hear, they can be there too. The women know as much as the men do, and their advice is often asked. We have a republic as well as you. The council-tent is our Congress, and anybody can speak who has anything to say, women and all.

In the Indian society, the leaders had different duties and responsibilities than political leaders have today, and the people of the bands had a greater sense of unity, as Sarah Winnemucca noted:

> The chiefs do not live in idleness. They work with their people, and they are always poor for the following reason. It is the custom with my people to be very hospitable. When people visit them in their tents, they always set before them the best food they have, and if there is not enough for themselves they go without.
>
> The chief's tent is the one always looked for when visitors come, and sometimes many come the same day. But they are all well received. I have often felt sorry for my brother, who is now the chief, when I saw him go without food for this reason. He would say, "We will wait and eat afterwards what is left." Perhaps little would be left, and when the agents did not give supplies and rations, he would have to go hungry.
>
> At the council, one is always appointed to repeat at the time everything that is said on both sides, so that there may be no misunderstanding, and one person

Little Paiute girls display their doll and toy cradle in this sun-lit shot of a happy moment in their lives.

Courtesy of Nevada Historical Society

at least is present from every lodge, and after it is over, he goes and repeats what is decided upon at the door of the lodge, so all may be understood. For there is never any quarrelling in the tribe, only friendly counsels. The sub-chiefs are appointed by the great chief for special duties. There is no quarrelling about that, for neither sub-chief or great chief has any salary. It is this which makes the tribe so united and attached to each other, and makes it so dreadful to be parted. They would rather all die at once than be parted.

The main events in the life of the Indians were in many respects similar to modern Nevada society, but the Indian culture took on many different forms. Sarah Winnemucca's account continues:

The grandmothers have the special care of the daughters just before and after they come to womanhood. The girls are not allowed to get married until they have come to womanhood; and that period is recognized as a very sacred thing, and is the subject of a festival, and has peculiar customs. The young woman is set apart under the care of two of her friends, somewhat older, and a little wigwam, called a teepee, just big enough for the three, is made for them, to which they retire. She goes through certain labors which are thought to be strengthening, and these last twenty-five days. Every day, three times a day, she must gather, and pile up as high as she can, five stacks of wood. This makes fifteen stacks a day. At the end of every five days the attendants take her to a river to bathe. She fasts from all flesh-meat during these twenty-five days, and continues to do this for five days in every month all her life. At the end of the twenty-five days she returns to the family lodge, and gives all her clothing to her attendants in payment for their care. Sometimes the wardrobe is quite extensive.

It is thus publicly known that there is another marriageable woman, and any young man interested in her, or wishing to form an alliance, comes forward. But the courting is very different from the courting of the white people. He never speaks to her, or visits the family, but endeavors to attract her attention by showing his horsemanship, etc. As he knows that she sleeps next to her grandmother in the lodge, he enters in full dress after the family has retired for the night, and seats himself at her feet. If she is not awake, her grandmother wakes her. He does not speak to either young woman or grandmother, but when the young woman wishes him to go away, she rises and goes and lies down by the side of her mother. He then leaves as silently as he came in. This goes on some-

Outfitted for a cold weather hunt, this Southern Paiute warrior was photographed at Moapa Valley by John Wesley Powell's Colorado River exploring expedition of 1871–72. Dressed in a fringed buckskin suit, he holds a bow and several arrows. He keeps more arrows on his back in a quiver made of fox or bobcat skin, which shows his skill at hunting. His belt and moccasins are made of leather.

Courtesy of Nevada Historical Society

times for a year or longer, if the young woman has not made up her mind. She is never forced by her parents to marry against her wishes. When she knows her own mind, she makes a confidant of her grandmother, and then the young man is summoned by the father of the girl, who asks him in her presence, if he really loves his daughter, and reminds him, if he says he does, of all the duties of a husband. He then asks his daughter the same question, and sets before her minutely all her duties. And these duties are not slight. She is to dress the game, prepare the food, clean the buckskins, make his moccasins, dress his hair, bring all the wood, — in short, do all the household work. She promises to "be himself," and she fulfils her promise. Then he is invited to a feast and all his relatives with him. But after the betrothal, a teepee is erected for the presents that pour in from both sides.

At the wedding feast, all the food is prepared in baskets. The young woman sits by the young man, and hands him the basket of food prepared for him with her own hands. He does not take it with his right hand; but seizes her wrist, and takes it with the left hand. This constitutes the marriage ceremony, and the father pronounces them man and wife. They go to a wigwam of their own, where they live till the first child is born. This event also is celebrated. Both father and mother fast from all flesh, and the father goes through the labor of piling the wood for twenty-five days, and assumes all his wife's household work during that time. If he does not do his part in the care of the child, he is considered an outcast. Every five days his child's basket is changed for a new one, and the five are all carefully put away at the end of the days, the last one containing the navel-string, carefully wrapped up, and all are put up into a tree, and the child put into a new and ornamented basket. All this respect shown to the mother and child makes the parents feel their responsibility, and makes the tie between parents and children very strong. The young mothers often get together and exchange their experiences about the attentions of their husbands; and inquire of each other if the fathers did their duty to their children, and were careful of their wives' health. When they are married they give away all the clothing they have ever worn, and dress themselves anew. The poor people have the same ceremonies, but do not make a feast of it, for want of means.

Our boys are introduced to manhood by their hunting of deer and mountain-sheep. Before they are fifteen or sixteen, they hunt only small game, like rabbits, hares, fowls, etc. They never eat what they kill themselves, but only what their father or elder brothers kill. When a boy becomes strong enough to use larger bows made of sinew, and arrows that are ornamented with eagle-feathers, for the first time, he kills game that is large, a deer or an antelope, or a mountain-sheep. Then he brings home the hide, and his father cuts it into a long coil which is wound into a loop, and the boy takes his quiver and throws it on his back as if he was going on a hunt, and takes his bow and arrows in his hand. Then his father throws the loop over him, and he jumps through it. This he does five times. Now for the first time he eats the flesh of the animal he has killed, and from that time he eats whatever he kills but he has always been faithful to his parents' command not to eat what he has killed before. He can now do whatever he likes, for now he is a man, and no longer considered a boy.

Seasonal Migrations

The Indians had to move constantly to hunt and gather food. Many of the Indians built temporary shelters, called wickiups, out of grass, tules, cattails, sagebrush, willows, or pine boughs. Large willow branches were placed in a circle and the tops bent over to form a dome. The poles were then covered with brush or grass to keep out most of the wind and cold. In winter the shelter was warmed by a small fire; an opening in the top let the smoke out. When the bands moved on to another area in search of fish, game, or seeds, they abandoned the old wickiups and built new ones wherever they camped.

In eastern Nevada, the Shoshone Indians built tepees instead of wickiups. More typical of the Plains Indians than of those living in the Great Basin, the Shoshone summer tepees were made from interwoven rushes and willow branches. They used these light structures in warm weather and lived in tepees made of sewn hides in the winter.

The most important food gathering activity of the migratory Indians was the pine nut harvest from the pinon pine trees. To the Indians of the Great Basin, the pine nuts

A Wickiup Constructed and Furnished in the Ancient Way. The inset photograph shows what the frame of the wickiup looks like before the roof and sides are thatched. In the main illustration, the woven willow frame has been covered with swatches of woven grass to make a semi-permanent house. A freshly laid campfire is in the foreground, and a shady veranda shelters the occupants from the sun. Bits of dried meat and fish hang from the rafters of the sunshade, well above the reach of camp dogs and varmints. Against the wickiup, a conical burden basket, a fine-woven winnowing tray, a willow water jug, and a small individual serving bowl are visible. A luxuriant rabbitskin blanket is draped over the sunshade and out of the way, ready to keep its owner warm in cold weather. Photos by Margaret Wheat

were as important as wheat is to us or rice is to the Chinese; it was their staple food which could be stored for future use. This made the crop vitally important to the Indians, for in a bad harvest year or when the weather cut down on the food that could be obtained by fishing or hunting, the band's supply of stored food could mean the difference between life and death. In such a society without money or commerce, stored food was the main form of wealth.

Men armed with long poles knocked the pine cones from the branches of the pinon pines to the ground. The women and children collected the cones and separated the nuts, which were placed into cone-shaped burden baskets for transportation or storage. The nuts could then be carried or stored near camp until they were ready to be eaten.

After the nuts were separated from the cones, they were roasted in their shells. Then women ground them between stones, as they would with a mortar and pestle or *metate.* The women then separated the crushed shells from the nuts by tossing the mixture in a winnowing basket. The lightweight shells were fanned out, and the pine nuts were put into cooking baskets. Sometimes the nuts were eaten whole, and sometimes they were ground into flour.

The flour was used to make a thick soup or porridge. The cooking started with a fire made of sagebrush and greasewood, which was used to heat a number of rocks. The Indian women used cooking baskets, woven from natural fibers with such skill that they were watertight, to hold the mixture of pine nut flour and water. The women put the hot rocks from the fire into the cooking basket until the mixture began to boil. If the flour and water mix was especially thick, it could be scooped up and plunged into cold water to form a loaf of pine nut bread.

The Indians celebrated the annual pine nut harvest with dances and parties. The

Washo Indians, for example, celebrated their rites at Double Springs in Douglas County. A pine nut dance was an all-night affair which started at sunset. Shoulder to shoulder, the Indian dancers formed a tight circle around a pine nut tree. When the Man-Who-Knows-Many-Songs started to sing, the dancers began moving in unison to their left with a slow, shuffling step.

The Indians had parties and festivals on other occasions too, such as this celebration described by Sarah Winnemucca:

Many years ago, when my people were happier than they are now, they used to celebrate the Festival of Flowers in the spring. I have been to three of them only in the course of my life.

Oh, with what eagerness we girls used to watch every spring for the time when we could meet with our hearts' delight, the young men, whom in civilized life you call beaux. We would all go in company to see if the flowers we were named for were yet in bloom, for almost all the girls are named for flowers. We talked about them in our wigwams, as if we were the flowers, saying, "Oh, I saw myself today in full bloom!" We would talk all the evening in this way in our families with such delight, and such beautiful thoughts of the happy day when we should meet with those who admired us and would help us to sing our flower-songs which we made up as we sang. But we were always sorry for those that were not named after some flower, because we knew they could not join in the flower-songs like ourselves, who were named for flowers of all kinds.

At last one evening came a beautiful voice, which made every girl's heart throb with happiness. It was the chief, and every one hushed to hear what he said to-day.

"My dear daughters, we are told that you have seen yourselves in the hills and in the valleys, in full bloom. Five days from to-day your festival day will come. I know every young man's heart stops beating while I am talking. I know how it was with me many years ago. I used to wish the Flower Festival would come every day. Dear young men and young women, you are saying, 'Why put

Pine Nut Harvest. Washo women show what it takes to harvest a heavy crop of nuts from the pinon pine groves of western Nevada. The sticks are used to fell the pine cones, which burst open like flowers when ripe. The pine nuts are caught, accumulated, and winnowed in the large flat trays the women are carrying. Once harvested, the nuts were carried back to camp in woven burden baskets like that worn by the woman in the center. Their shawls shelter the women from the sun.

Courtesy of Nevada Historical Society

Dat-so-la-lee, the famous Washo Indian basket maker, produced woven work of the finest quality. Here she stands beside two masterpieces of degikup—finely coiled and braided fiber baskets of elegant traditional design. Dat-so-la-lee became a legend in her own lifetime for the great beauty and careful craftsmanship of her basketry.

Courtesy of
Nevada State Museum

Sarah Winnemucca (c. 1844–1891). The first Paiute Indian to have written an account of her people, Sarah spoke to large crowds at lectures in San Francisco, Baltimore, Boston, and other major cities, trying to educate the public on the problems of the reservation system. Elaborately attired for the lecture circuit, Sarah sports complex shell and beadwork accessories in this studio photograph from about 1883. Her short-sleeved and star-spangled gown, gathered at the waist, reaches to the knee in several tiers of patterned fringe. Ornamented moccasins, leggings, and a handsome necklace complete the costume. The purse is made of velvet, fringed with beads and embroidered with a figure of Cupid.

Courtesy of Nevada Historical Society.

Summer Harvest of Indian Grass, July, 1897. These Paiutes are cutting large swaths of grass and carrying them to the threshing ground—a bare, flat, sunbaked area—where older women singe the little black seeds to separate them from the stems. In the background, other women are cleaning the roasted seeds with the help of winnowing baskets. The seeds were carried back to camp in burden baskets, to be later husked and ground between stones to make flour or meal.

Courtesy of Nevada Historical Society

it off five days?" But you all know that is our rule. It gives you time to think, and to show your sweetheart your flower."

All the girls who have flower-names dance along together, and those who have not go together also. Our fathers and mothers and grandfathers and grandmothers make a place for us where we can dance. Each one gathers the flower she is named for, and then all weave them into wreaths and crowns and scarfs, and dress up in them.

Some girls are named for rocks and are called rock-girls, and they find some pretty rocks which they carry; each one such a rock as she is named for, or whatever she is named for. If she cannot, she can take a branch of sage-brush, or a bunch of rye-grass, which have no flower.

They all go marching along, each girl in turn singing of herself; but she is not a girl any more, — she is a flower singing. She sings of herself, and her sweetheart, dancing along by her side, helps her sing the song she makes.

I will repeat what we say of ourselves. "I, Sarah Winnemucca, am a shell-flower, such as I wear on my dress. My name is Thocmetony. I am so beautiful! Who will come and dance with me while I am so beautiful? Oh, come and be happy with me! I shall be beautiful while the earth lasts. Somebody will always admire me; and who will come and be happy with me in the Spirit-land? I shall be beautiful forever there. Yes, I shall be more beautiful than my shell-flower, my Thocmetony! Then, come, oh come, and dance and be happy with me!" The young men sing with us as they dance beside us.

Our parents are waiting for us somewhere to welcome us home. And then we praise the sage-brush and the rye-grass that have no flower, and the pretty rocks that some are named for; and then we present our beautiful flowers to these companions who could carry none. And so all are happy; and that closes the beautiful day.

The Indians also gathered other seeds and natural foods, which they prepared for eating in much the same way as the pine nuts. As each of the crops were harvested, the Indians knew just where the next one was ripening. After the harvest, the Indians

Antelope Drive. This Nevada State Museum diorama demonstrates how the Indian hunters herded their prey into the killing circle, where the antelope were slaughtered with arrows, spears, and rocks.
Courtesy of Nevada State Museum

moved away to another food-gathering area, carrying their baskets, water jugs, and babies on their backs.

Hunting and Fishing

Hunting was another principal source of food. It was carried out with stone age weapons by hunters moving on foot; the Indians of the Great Basin, as elsewhere in North America, had no horses until the arrival of the white intruders. The antelope, deer, and mountain sheep were extremely important to the Indians. They used every part of the animal to provide food or some necessity of life. Various portions of the prey were used to make clothing, footwear, tools, weapons, ornaments, string, and rope.

These larger animals were killed when hunters herded them along sagebrush or rock fences into a pen, where waiting Indians slaughtered them with rocks, spears, and arrows. In *Life Among the Paiutes: Their Wrongs and Claims,* Sarah Winnemucca described just such an antelope hunt:

> My people capture antelopes by charming them, but only some of the people are charmers. My father was one of them, and once I went with him on an antelope hunt.
> The antelopes move in herds in the winter, and as late in the spring as April. At this time there was said to be a large herd in a certain place, and my father told all his people to come together in ten days to go with him in his hunt. He told them to bring their wives with them, but no small children. When they came, at the end of ten days, he chose two men, who he said were to be his messengers to the antelopes. They were to have two large torches made of sage-brush bark, and after he had found a place for his camp, he marked out a circle around which the wigwams were to be placed, putting this own in the middle of the western side, and leaving an opening directly opposite in the middle of the eastern side, which was towards the antelopes.
> The people who were with him in the camp then made another circle to the east of the one where their wigwams were, and made six mounds of sage-brush and stones on the sides of it, with a space of a hundred yards or more from one mound to the next one, but with no fence between the mounds. These mounds were made high, so that they could be seen from far off.

The women and boys and old men who were in the camp, and who were working on the mounds, were told to be very careful not to drop anything and not to stumble over a sage-brush root, or a stone, or anything, and not to have any accident, but to do everything perfectly and to keep thinking about the antelopes all the time, and not to let their thoughts go away to anything else. It took five days to charm the antelopes, and if anybody had an accident he must tell of it.

Every morning early, when the bright morning star could be seen, the people sat around the opening to the circle, with my father sitting in the middle of the opening, and my father lighted his pipe and passed it to his right, and the pipe went round the circle five times. And at night they did the same thing.

After they had smoked the pipe, my father took a kind of drum, which is used in this charming, and made music with it. This is the only kind of musical instrument which my people have, and it is only used for this antelope-charming. It is made of a hide of some large animal, stuffed with grass, so as to make it sound hollow, and then wound around tightly from one end to the other with a cord as large as my finger. One end of this instrument is large, and it tapers down to the other end, which is small, so that it makes a different sound on the different parts. My father took a stick and rubbed this stick from one end of the instrument to the other, making a penetrating, vibrating sound, that could be heard afar off, and he sang, and all his people sang with him.

After that the two men who were messengers went out to see the antelopes. They carried their torches in their right hands, and one of them carried a pipe in his left hand. They started from my father's wigwam and went straight across the camp to the opening; then they crossed, and one went around the second circle to the right and the other went to the left, till they met on the other side of the circle. Then they crossed again, and one went round the herd of antelopes one way and the other went round the other way, but they did not let the antelopes see them. When they met on the other side of the herd of antelopes, they stopped and smoked the pipe, and then they crossed, and each man came back on the track of the other to the camp, and told my father what they saw and what the antelopes were doing.

This was done every day for five days, and after the first day all the men and women and boys followed the messengers, and went around the circle they were to enter. On the fifth day the antelopes were charmed, and the whole herd followed the tracks of my people and entered the circle where the mounds were, coming in at the entrance, bowing and tossing their heads, and looking sleepy and under a powerful spell. They ran round and round inside the circle just as if there was a fence all around it and they could not get out, and they staid there until my people had killed every one. But if anybody had dropped anything, or had stumbled and had not told about it, then when the antelopes came to the place where he had done that they threw off the spell and rushed wildly out of the circle at that place.

For the larger animals and human enemies, the Indians also had a more powerful weapon than the bow and arrow: the atlatl and dart. The atlatl was a wooden, hand-held catapult which increased the range, speed, and force of the short spear or dart it threw. The dart had a point of carefully chiselled flint rock or glasslike black obsidian.

Arrow and projectile-point making was a man's job. The points were carefully shaped by chipping (also called knapping). Hunters would often fashion their points while waiting for their prey along game trails. One well-known source of projectile points was located near Steamboat Springs in southern Washoe County, where hunters could find beautiful and superior scinter and basalt rock.

Smaller animals, such as rabbits and ground squirrels, were trapped by snares or nets and then skinned. Rabbits were abundant in the Great Basin desert. They were hunted in large community drives. Each family in the band contributed a net made of woven hemp. The mesh of the net was designed to be just large enough to catch a rabbit behind the ears when it tried to force its way through. Some of the Indians stretched the nets out across a wash, or dry river bed, while the others fanned out in the desert, forming a moving wall to frighten the rabbits into running towards the nets. The captured rabbits were clubbed to death and skinned. The meat was then either roasted and eaten or dried for storage as winter food. The rabbit pelts — the skin and fur — were

The Rabbit Drive. In this Nevada State Museum diorama, Indians with clubs stand by a large woven net stretched across a dry creek bed, while other members of the band beat the brush in the distance to drive the rabbits into the trap. A successful hunt produced both food and clothing for the hunters and their families.

Courtesy of Nevada State Museum

The Atlatl and Dart. This southern Nevada Indian is ready to kill man or beast with his formidable throwing tool. The deadly combination of spear and sling was popular for hundreds of years in the Great Basin, until it was replaced by firearms.

Courtesy of Southwest Museum, Los Angeles

Spear Fishing in Northwestern Nevada. This beautiful photograph by E. S. Curtis shows how it was done along the rivers, streams, and lakes of the State. Spearing fish required great individual skill, cunning, and agility. The Indians also caught fish with nets and traps, and often invited their friends to share the catch.

Courtesy of the Library of Congress

In this winter photograph taken in about 1920, Washoe Indian couple John and Wama Anthony wear warm and luxurious rabbitskin robes, made in the traditional style, as their well-behaved dog sits a respectful distance away.

Courtesy of Nevada Historical Society

cut into strips, sewn together, twisted into ropes, and hung up to dry. When they were completely cured, the ropes of soft fur were woven with cordage into a soft cape which could be worn over the shoulders during the day and used as a blanket at night. A man's blanket required about one hundred rabbit skins, while a child's blanket needed only about forty.

Birds such as mudhens (coots) were also hunted in the fall, in "drives" similar to those which have been discussed. They were skinned before roasting, and the Indians used their feathers to make warm blankets and capes.

The Indians also fished to get food. Pyramid and Walker Lakes, Lake Tahoe, and the rivers of northern and western Nevada provided a variety of fish to those patient enough to spear or net them. If they weren't eaten immediately, the fish were dried on a rack and then stored for winter use. The dried fish could also be ground with stones into a meal and cooked to make a nourishing soup.

Zenas Leonard, a trapper traveling with Joseph Walker down the Humboldt River in 1833, described the Shoshone Indians he saw fishing there:

> "They subsist upon grass-seed, frogs, fish, &c. — Fish, however, are very scarce — their manner of catching which, is somewhat novel and singular. They take the leg-bone of a sandhill crane, which is generally about 18 inches long, this is fastened in the end of a pole — they then, by means of a raft made the rushes, which are very plenty — float along the surface of these lakes, and spear the fish. They exhibit great dexterity with this simple structure — sometimes killing a fish with it at a great distance.
>
> They also have a kind of hook by which they sometimes are very successful, but it does not afford them as much sport as the spear. This hook is formed of a small bone, ground down on a sandstone, and a double beard cut in it with a flint — they then have a line made of wild flax. This line is tied nearest the beard end of the hook, by pulling the line the sharp end with the beard, catches, and turns the bone crossways in its mouth."

INTRUSION AND CHANGES

For a thousand years before the appearance of white intruders, the Indians of Nevada maintained a culture which was superbly adapted to their natural situation. Largely self-sufficient, these Indian bands were able to exist as social and economic units free of the massive interdependence which characterizes our modern society. Indian life was shattered, however, when it came into contact with the technology, materialism, and turbulent individualism of white civilization.

The First Whites

The first white intruders, with their guns and horses, burst into the settled ways of the Indians like "men from Mars". To the Indians, the whites looked strange, acted even stranger, and owned material possessions beyond the wildest dreams of the first Nevadans. It took less than two generations — only about forty years — to almost completely destroy the Indians' way of life.

Few Indian accounts of the first intruders have survived the passage of time. One of the most extensive was written by Sarah Winnemucca:

> I was a very small child when the first white people came into our country. They came like a lion, yes, like a roaring lion, and have continued so ever since, and I have never forgotten their first coming. My people were scattered at that time over nearly all the territory now known as Nevada. My grandfather was chief of the entire Piute nation, and was camped near Humboldt Lake, with a small portion of his tribe, when a party travelling eastward from California was seen coming. When the news was brought to my grandfather, he asked what they looked like? When told that they had hair on their faces, and were white, he jumped up and clasped his hands together, and cried aloud, —
>
> "My white brothers, — my long-looked for white brothers have come at last!"
>
> He immediately gathered some of his leading men, and went to the place where the party had gone into camp. Arriving near them, he was commanded to halt in a manner that was readily understood without an interpreter. Grandpa at once made signs of friendship by throwing down his robe and throwing up his arms to show them he had no weapons; but in vain, — they kept him at a distance. He knew not what to do. He had expected so much pleasure in welcoming his white brothers to the best in the land, that after looking at them sorrowfully for a little while, he came away quite unhappy. But he would not give them up so easily. He took some of his most trustworthy men and followed them day after day, camping near them at night, and travelling in sight of them by day, hoping in this way to gain their confidence. But he was disappointed, poor dear old soul!
>
> Seeing they would not trust him, my grandfather left them, saying, "Perhaps they will come again next year." Then he summoned his whole people, and told them this tradition:
>
> "In the beginning of the world there were only four, two girls and two boys. Our forefather and mother were only two, and we are their children. You all know that a great while ago there was a happy family in this world. One girl and one boy were dark and the others were white. For a time they got along together without quarrelling, but soon they disagreed, and there was trouble. They were cross to one another and fought, and our parents were very much grieved. They prayed that their children might learn better, but it did not do any good; and afterwards the whole household was made so unhappy that the father and mother saw that they must separate their children; and then our father took the dark boy and girl, and the white boy and girl, and asked them, 'Why are you so cruel to each other?' They hung down their heads, and would not speak. They were ashamed. He said to them, 'Have I not been kind to you all, and given you everything your hearts wished for? You do not have to hunt and kill your own game to live upon. You see, my dear children, I have power to call whatsoever kind of game we want to eat; and I also have the power to separate my dear children, if they are not good to each other.' So he separated his children by a word. He said, 'Depart from each other, you cruel children; — go across the mighty ocean and do not seek each other's lives.'"

"So the light girl and boy disappeared by that one word, and their parents saw them no more, and they were grieved, although they knew their children were happy. And by-and-by dark children grew into a large nation; and we believe it is the one we belong to, and that the nation that sprung from the white children will some time send some one to meet us and heal all the old trouble. Now, the white people we saw a few days ago must certainly be our white brothers, and I want to welcome them. I want to love them as I love all of you. But they would not let me; they were afraid. But they will come again, and I want you one and all to promise that, should I not live to welcome them myself, you will not hurt a hair on their heads, but welcome them as I tried to do."

How good of him to try and heal the wound, and how vain were his efforts! My people had never seen a white man, and yet they existed, and were a strong race. The people promised as he wished, and they all went back to their work.

The Indians generally stayed away from the intruders. This was easy in the first years of contact, when the white trapping parties were small and didn't stay long. The overland emigrants presented a different problem. Their cattle, mules, and horses ate up all the grass along the California Trail, and the emigrants cut and burned all the wood for fuel. Game animals were either hunted down or fled. The Indians along the Humboldt River in particular were affected by the devastating passage of the whites, which destroyed the delicate ecological balance of Indian life and cut off their regular food supply.

Strife on the Roads

Armed conflict soon followed along the emigrant road. The thousands of emigrants who came down the Humboldt with their cattle, oxen, horses, and mules gave the Indians the opportunity to take animals from the white intruders for food or for greater speed and mobility in traveling. Ambushes of small parties of travelers provided the Indians with firearms, which could also be acquired by barter. Unscrupulous station keepers along the California Trail often worked with local Indians to attack and rob small parties of emigrants, and they provided these favored bands with guns and ammunition.

Both the Indians and the emigrants retaliated when acts of violence and thievery

Winnemucca (c. 1880–1882), the paramount chief of the Northern Paiutes, poses for a portrait photographer in a Virginia City studio. Embodying both religious and military authority, he wears a fur hat topped with feathers and the tunic of an officer in the United States Army. Winnemucca also sports a carved and decorated wooden nose plug as an additional mark of rank and distinction.

Courtesy of Nevada Historical Society

took place. The innocent were murdered when the guilty could not be found. Along the Humboldt River section of the California Trail, white men and Indians fought and killed each other in bloody warfare that lasted through the 1850's.

William Hickman was a pioneer of Utah who traveled overland to California in the fall of 1851. In his autobiography, entitled *Brigham's Destroying Angel,* he gave a horrifying description of the slaughter on the trail:

> All moved off nicely, until we got about four hundred miles on our road, and were traveling down the Humboldt River. There we began to see where wagons had been burned, and also skeletons of men, women and children, their long and beautiful hair hanging on the brush; and sometimes a head with as beautiful locks of hair as I ever saw, and sometimes those of little children, with two or three inches of flaky hair, either lying by or near them, the wolves having eaten the flesh off their bones. But all the bodies of the men, women and children that were found had a portion of the skin taken off the tops of their heads. They had all been scalped, and the savages, in all probability, as we talked of it, were then in the mountains having war-dances with the whoops and yells of demons, over these scalps of honesty and innocence.

> Some of the boys began to get terribly riled up, and wanted to stop and hunt the Indians. Our train traveled snugly together and camped on clear ground, tying our horses at night, and corraling our cattle, always keeping out a strong guard. About this time we met the train coming back that had started ahead of us, having fought the Indians several days, lost nearly half of their stock, and twelve or thirteen of their men. They advised us to turn back, assuring us there was no show to get through. We thought differently, and some of the boys laughed at them. Finding out we were determined they turned to go with us, but told us they had traveled and fought Indians all day only three days before. As we journeyed, with the new company in our rear, all at once there was a dash, a hoot and a yell from the brush about three hundred yards off. The train was halted; twenty-five of my men in less than a minute had their guns, about half of us mounted our horses, the balance on foot, and instead of waiting for them to circle and fight we went for them, telling at the same time the other company to remain still and take care of the teams.

> The Indians had made no arrangements for a retreat, but ran into the willow brush on the river, which was fordable anywhere, and after them we went. They took a fright like a gang of wild antelopes, and ran in all directions. We popped them right and left until all were out of sight. I flew around on my horse to see the boys, fearing I had lost some of them, but all were safe. Two were slightly wounded. All swore they would scalp the Indians, and have a war-dance over their scalps. I told them to do as they pleased. They got thirty-two scalps off of the Indians killed on the ground, and what gave my men increased anger, one of the Indians was found with the scalps of two women, cured and dried, and another had the scalp of a child, I should think not more than three or four years of age. I need not tell you — you may guess the feeling that existed.

Both Indians and whites tried to stop the reprisals. On August 7, 1855, a Treaty of Friendship between the United States and the western Shoshone Indians of northeastern Nevada was signed at Haws' ranch in Elko County by Indian Agent Garland Hurt and ten principal men of the western Shoshone tribe. This treaty was doomed, however, by the failure to Congress to ratify or officially recognize the document. Indian Agent Hurt and other government officials had promised the Indians food and gifts as part of the peace agreement. The food and gifts were never delivered as promised, and many Shoshones became embittered.

Heavy attacks by Indians upon the overland emigrants followed, and the majority of these fights took place along the Humboldt River. By 1862, the United States was in the middle of its Civil War. The Indian attacks along the Humboldt and the Central Overland Route, opened four years earlier, endangered the security of the transcontinental telegraph lines and the overland mail. Because this was a national concern, the United States Army sent strong forces from California to bring peace to the region. Throughout 1862, the Indian raiding parties, as well as peaceful bands along the Humboldt, were attacked by soldiers and driven from the area. On January 29, 1863, troops commanded by General Patrick E. Connor made a forced march in the dead of winter into Idaho. The soldiers attacked a large hostile Indian encampment across the frozen Bear River in Cache Valley and defeated the Indians completely. This battle broke the power of the Shoshone tribes of north-eastern Nevada and effectively ended the problem of Indian raids along the California Trail. The western Shoshones formally made peace on October 1, 1863, when twelve chiefs and principal men of the Indian tribe signed a treaty with the United States at Ruby Valley, in Elko County. This treaty, later ratified by Congress, brought the troubles with the western Shoshone to a close.

The Goshute Indians, a branch of the western Shoshone tribe, lived in eastern Nevada along the Central Overland Route. When large numbers of emigrants began to pass through their territory after 1859, the Indians found it difficult to feed themselves. In the spring of 1860, the Goshutes attacked a number of Pony Express stations along the route, and in 1863, Goshute Indians led by Chief White Horse attacked and burned seven overland mail stations. Captain S.P. Smith and units of California volunteer cavalry defeated the Goshutes in a series of fights at Duck Creek, Spring Valley, and Steptoe Valley, and the Goshute War was over by autumn, 1863.

War and Peace with the Paiutes

In western Nevada, the northern Paiutes were the first tribe of Indians to become involved in armed conflict with the white intruders. The first battle between Indians and white trappers, discussed elsewhere, took place in 1833. Afterwards, Chief Truckee counselled his people to remain at peace with the whites, and there were generally good relations between the white settlers of western Nevada and the Paiutes. As Sarah Winnemucca remembered, "We lived together, and were as happy as could be. There was no stealing, no one lost their cattle or horses. . . ."

Chief Winnemucca, who followed Truckee as the paramount chief of the northern Paiutes, signed a Treaty of Friendship with the settlers in 1855. The terms of the treaty provided that Paiute tribal justice would punish Indians shown to have been killing or robbing the whites. Likewise, white men who killed or stole from the Indians were to be punished by the settlers' government. The treaty expressly disapproved of random acts of revenge or reprisal. While this treaty was not ratified by Congress, the Indians and settlers both lived up to it, and it kept things friendly between the Indians and the settlers until the discovery of the rich silver deposits of the Comstock Lode, in the hills of northwestern Nevada.

Patrick E. Connor (1820–1891) of Ireland. A businessman, lawman, soldier, and pioneer of Texas and California, Connor was a veteran of three different wars. As a general in the United States Army, he decisively defeated the last hostile bands of Shoshone Indians in the Great Basin at the battle of Bear Lake in 1863, ending attacks upon emigrants traveling along the California Trail.

Courtesy of the Church of Latter-day Saints

Numaga, Northern Paiute chieftain at Pyramid Lake at the time of the 1860 Pyramid Lake Paiute War. His name, meaning "the Giver," came from his generosity towards others. Numaga was a constant advocate of a peace policy with the whites. During a tribal war council, he had this to say: "You would make war upon the whites. I ask you to pause and reflect. The white men are like the stars over your heads. You have wrongs, great wrongs, that rise up like those mountains before you; but can you, from the mountain tops, reach and blot out those stars? Your enemies are like the sands in the bed of your rivers; when taken away they only give place for more to come and settle there. Could you defeat the whites in Nevada, from over the mountains in California would come to help them an army of white men that would cover your country like a blanket. What hope is there for the Paiute? From where is to come your guns, your powder, your lead, your dried meats to live upon, and hay to feed your ponies with while you carry on this war? Your enemies have all of these things, more than they can use. They will come like the sand in a whirlwind and drive you from your homes. You will be forced among the barren rocks of the north, where your ponies will die; where you will see the women and old men starve, and listen to the cries of your children for food. I love my people; let them live; and when their spirits shall be called to the Great Camp in the southern sky, let their bones rest where their fathers were buried." Numaga's words were prophetic — the chiefs who remained hostile after the end of the 1860 war were hunted down with their followers and killed by troops from Nevada and California. Numaga died of tuberculosis in 1871 at Wadsworth and was greatly mourned by Indians and whites alike.

Courtesy of Nevada Historical Society

A formidable-looking Paiute warrior cradles his carbine for the camera, about 1875. He is richly dressed for this studio portrait by photographer E.P. Butler and displays the sort of resolute pride that helped defeat Major Ormsby's expedition to Pyramid Lake in 1860.

Courtesy of Nevada Historical Society

That discovery changed everything. The Indians of Nevada were never very numerous; in 1859, Indian Agent Frederick Dodge reported that there were only about 3,750 people in the twelve principal bands of the northern Paiutes, while the three bands of the Washo tribe numbered only about one thousand Indians altogether. At that time — just before the rush to the Comstock Lode — there were just five hundred to one thousand whites living in the area. Thousands of new settlers began to pour into western Nevada in the spring of 1859, and they just kept coming. Many, if not most, of these new settlers did not know or did not care about the 1855 Treaty of Friendship with the Paiutes. They did not live up to the terms of the treaty and, even worse from the Indian point of view, began to live in areas that the Paiutes considered to be their exclusive territory.

Pyramid Lake War

Early in May, 1860, several white men at Williams Station on the big bend of the Carson River kidnapped some Indian girls. Shortly thereafter, Indians burned the station and killed the white men there. Major Ormsby and other settlers organized a volunteer militia force and marched to Pyramid Lake. On May 12, the white force was ambushed, and Ormsby and many of his force were killed. The leader of the Indians in this battle was Numaga, a relative of their paramount chief, Winnemucca. After the defeat of Ormsby, the whites organized a military expedition of over 500 men from California, commanded by Colonel John C. Hays. This force engaged the Paiutes in a skirmish on June 2, 1860, at Pyramid Lake, near the scene of the Ormsby disaster. The Paiutes

Major William Ormsby, a businessman and pioneer of Carson City, led a volunteer force of white miners and settlers into calamitous defeat in the first battle of Pyramid Lake.
Ormsby's militiamen were routed with heavy casualties, and Ormsby was killed, when Northern Paiute warriors ambushed them along the Truckee River in 1860.
Courtesy of Nevada Historical Society.

Captain Edward Storey of Virginia City was one of the few white casualties of the Second Battle of Pyramid Lake in 1860, where the Indians were forced to withdraw from their traditional encampments and move into the less fertile valleys north of Pyramid Lake. Storey County was named after him.
Courtesy of Nevada Historical Society.

withdrew to the north. The U.S. Army then built Fort Churchill on the Carson River to keep peace in the territory.

On May 25, 1862, Governor James W. Nye met with the principal chiefs of the Northern Paiute Indians, including Winnemucca and Numaga, at the big bend of the Truckee River, near present-day Wadsworth. At this meeting, as a sign of peace and friendship, the Indians and whites exchanged gifts. Numaga gave away his war cap made of a whole otter skin trimmed with large eagle plumes, his pipe of peace, tomahawk, and a magnificent bow, arrows, and quiver; these articles had been worn by him in all his battles. This meeting united most of the Northen Paiute leaders in a policy of peace with the whites.

Black Rock, Paradise Valley, and Quinn River Wars

Lieutenant Colonel Charles McDermit, the Commanding Officer of the Military District of Nevada, was one of the leading figures of the 1865 war against hostile Indian bands in northern Nevada. These bands were led by Paiute Chief "Black Rock Tom," who did not support the 1862 peace agreement between Winnemucca and Governor Nye. Trouble began in early 1865, with attacks on the Black Rock Desert stretch of the National Wagon Road. Fighting spread to Paradise Valley in April, and to the Quinn River Valley in August. Colonel McDermit was ambushed and killed on Quinn River August 7, 1865. "Black Rock Tom" was captured and shot August 11, near Unionville. The hostile Indian bands were broken up after January, 1866, ending warfare between the Northern Paiutes and the whites.

United States Army Colonel Charles McDermit, a former county sheriff from California, commanded the troops fighting hostile Indians north of Pyramid Lake during the Civil War. Although McDermit was killed by Indians who ambushed him in August of 1865, his Paiute opponent "Black Rock Tom" was captured and shot within a week. Paiute resistance in Paradise Valley, Quinn River Valley, and on the Black Rock Desert ended with the death of "Black Rock Tom," and the area was rapidly settled by ranchers.

Courtesy of Nevada Historical Society

Fort Churchill, about 1861. Established in 1860, Fort Churchill was the first permanent military base in Nevada.

Courtesy of Nevada Historical Society

The battles with the Indians on the Truckee and the Humboldt resulted in the United States Army setting up Fort Churchill in 1860, Fort McDermitt [McDermit] in 1865, Camp Winfield Scott in 1866, and other posts to protect travelers on the California Trail. A drawing of Fort Churchill shows how one of these forts looked. The barracks, stables and administrative buildings are around the fort's parade ground, where several companies of soldiers are assembled for drill. Cavalry horses are in their corrals in the foreground, near the tents where visiting troops are camped. Like other army forts in Nevada, there was no stockade wall surrounding the post. The Army abandoned these forts late in the nineteenth century, and some of them became Indian reservations.

RESERVATIONS, ALLOTMENTS, AND COLONIES

Once the tribes were pacified, the policy of the federal government was to persuade Nevada's Indians to give up their wandering way of life. Instead, the Indians were supposed to take up cattle raising and agriculture. The theory was that the Indians were to live on tracts of land, called reservations, which had been set aside especially for them by the United States Department of the Interior. The Indians would stay on these reservations, and the rest of the land could be opened up to white settlement. On the reservations, the Indian Agents who supervised the Indians would see that the Indians learned how to farm. While they were learning, the government would provide enough resources to feed and clothe the Indians until they could fend for themselves. This policy was only partly successful and resulted in much bad feeling.

The first of these establishments was a farm established for the western Shoshones at Ruby Valley by Indian Agent William "Uncle Billy" Rodgers. It was later abandoned after a brief period of operation. Two large tracts of land surrounding Pyramid Lake and Walker Lake were also set aside in 1859, to serve as reservations for the northern Paiutes. Actual reservations were not established there until the early 1860's. Other reservations were created by the United States Department of the Interior between 1870 and 1890, such as Camp McCarry and Moapa (1872), Duck Valley and Carlin Farm (1877), and Fort McDermit (1889). A few other reservations and most of the urban

Indian colonies were founded in the twentieth century.

Many Indians, however, shunned the reservations and took jobs as laborers or domestic help on white ranches. Others lived in the towns, and were employed cutting wood.

By 1862, the miners on the Comstock were using lumber from the Sierra forests and firewood from the neighboring pinon forests on the foothills near Virginia City. The Indians were hired to cut trees, and the newly arrived white intruders afforded them a market for their pine nuts. Mark Twain thought the nuts were delicious, claiming that he had learned to like them so much in his days as a newspaper man on the Comstock that he still wanted to enjoy them years later. As he expressed it in 1876: "Once a Piute [Paiute] always a Piute." By 1868 and 1869, barely ten years after the opening of the mines, the Indians were involved in a commercial enterprise and shipped about 75,000 pounds of nuts to markets away from their pine nut lands.

A reporter observed in 1881, that by selling pine nuts to the whites and buying beef with the money, the Indians "could get five times . . . the grub" they would have if they ate the nuts. This observer did not recognize the fact that the pine nuts were the staple food of the Indians. They continue to gather and prepare them in the ancient way, even today.

However, once the ecological balance between the Indian and nature was broken, the Indian way of life was gone forever. The game was all gone. The pine nut trees were cut down and burned to power the steam equipment of the whites. The grass-seed never ripened for food, because the ranchers cut the grass for hay while it was still green. The fertile land was taken by white ranchers and townsmen. All this caused a crisis in Indian society. Many tribal leaders were assassinated by their own people or hunted down by soldiers. Alcoholism and drug abuse became a problem in Indian communities for the first time in history. There were religious upheavals, such as the Ghost Dance

Northern Paiute shaman Wovoka (c. 1856–1932), the central figure of the Ghost Dance cult, leans against a post in this mid-day photograph, taken on a Nevada street corner. The watchful Wovoka, wearing his magic hat, stands between two worlds of light and shadow. In January 1889, he had a vision during an eclipse of the sun. In his own words, "When the sun died, I went to heaven and saw God and all the people who had died a long time ago. God told me to come back and tell my people they must be good and love one another, and not fight or steal, or lie. He gave me the dance to give to my people." This vision influenced tens of thousands of other American Indians. The Ghost Dance movement rapidly spread to the Great Plains, where the Sioux, Cheyenne, Comanche, Arapahoe, Shoshone, and other tribes held mass Ghost Dance ceremonies. The religious cult promised a new world featuring the return of the dead and the great bison herds. It died out following the tragic Battle of Wounded Knee at the Pine Ridge, South Dakota, Indian Reservation in 1890, when a Ghost Dance gathering turned into a pitched battle with soldiers.

Courtesy of University of Nevada Reno Library, Special Collections

First Graduating Class at the Stewart Indian School, Carson City, 1901. Dignified and well-dressed Indian scholars clutch their diplomas in this turn-of-the-century portrait. Washo Indian Richard E. Barrington (c. 1880–1967), later a prominent businessman of California and Nevada, occupies the central seat of honor.

Courtesy of Nevada Historical Society

Vocational Training for Girls at the Stewart Indian School, Carson City, about 1915. Less-than-ecstatic Indian maidens learn valuable modern cooking skills and master the intricacies of the sewing machine under the watchful eye of their teacher. There is little to soften this starkly institutional scene of stucco walls, hardwood floors, iron stoves, and hard work.

Courtesy of Nevada Historical Society

Two cultures stand side by side in this photograph of an Indian ranch on the Carson River near Dayton, about 1930. The dramatic shot illustrates the change of dwellings among Nevada Indians — the old traditional wickiup has been replaced by more modern frame buildings and a corral, while the Carson River flows by in the background as it has for countless centuries.
Courtesy of Nevada Historical Society

movements of 1870 and 1889, which were based upon a return to traditional folk-ways. The peyote cult, which reached Nevada about 1930, is a similar example of continued spiritual restlessness.

The reservation system received a severe set-back in 1887, when Congress passed the Indian Allotment or Dawes Act. This act provided for the allotment of reservation lands to individual tribal members to encourage them to give up wandering and cultivate their own, individually-held land. The act did not work out as planned. Of approximately 138 million acres in Indian possession in 1887, about two-thirds had passed to white ownership by 1934, when the Wheeler-Howard or Tribal Reorganization Act ended the policy of giving allotments.

When the wandering bands were brought together on the reservations, the leading men of the tribes agreed to strengthen Indian society by encouraging education and self-government. This policy, in effect now for more than three generations, has shaped modern life for Nevada's Indians.

The first step in this plan was the establishment of day schools on the reservations, beginning with Pyramid Lake in 1878, and Walker Lake in 1882. The Stewart Indian School, founded just south of Carson City in 1891, attracted Indians from all across the United States to study there. Many of the reservation day schools were vocational, that is, the boys were taught to use farm implements and equipment while the girls learned about cooking and sewing.

Centralized self-government came with the creation of the tribal police and, in 1886, a court of Indian Offenses. The three man court replaced prehistoric forms of justice such as blood feuds and witch-killings. Indians born within the United States became citizens in 1924, following an act of Congress recognizing and appreciating the service of Indians in the armed forces during World War I. In 1932, Indians were made subject to local laws, and most laws applying only to Indians were swept away.

The present form of government of Nevada's Indian tribes is based upon another act of Congress, the 1934 Indian Reorganization or Wheeler-Howard Act. This law provided for tribal self-government under Congressionally-approved constitutions, stopped the allotment system, and enabled the tribes to purchase additional land for their reservations and colonies. Within a few years, Nevada's Indians issued corporate charters or submitted constitutions recognized by Congress, which are the basis for tribal affairs today.

CHAPTER 2

Transportation

THE TRAIL BLAZERS

As we have seen in the first chapter, the earliest descriptions of the Great Basin people were written by members of trapping expeditions. The trappers, well-equipped with firearms, were hunting beaver or otter pelts to supply the market for fashionable hats in the United States and Europe. The trappers were called "mountain men," because they set their traps in the streams and rivers of the Rocky Mountain area. In addition to being trappers and businessmen, they were also explorers looking for a way across the Great Basin to the Pacific Coast. Geographers had long hoped and even believed that there was a river flowing through the Great Basin which led directly to the fertile valleys of California and the Pacific Ocean. On some early maps this river was actually drawn in and named "San Buenaventura".

During their explorations the trappers discovered the Humboldt River, Carson River, Carson Sink, Walker Lake, and many other terrain features of the Great Basin. These men blazed trails which are now transcontinental highways.

The Southern Route or Mormon Trail

Three main transcontinental routes cross Nevada—the northern, central, and southern. The southern route is the oldest. Exploration began in 1775–76, when Francisco Garces, a Spanish friar of the Franciscan Order, traveled in the area of the southern border of Nevada. He was searching for an overland route to link the cities of northwestern Mexico with the missions and harbors of southern California. Garces was the first white intruder to enter the geographical region of the Great Basin and the first to see Nevada.

Fifty years passed before another such roving explorer came into the area. In 1826, Jedediah Strong Smith, a member of the North American Fur Company, led a fur-trapping expedition west across the southern tip of Nevada. He traveled along the Colorado River into California, where he spent the winter hunting and trapping. In the spring of 1827, Smith and his men returned eastward over Ebbetts Pass, crossing the Great Basin from west to east.

During the winter of 1829–30, Antonio Armijo led a trading expedition from Santa Fe, New Mexico, to Los Angeles, California. He became the first man in history to find a trade route across the American southwest.

The very next year, during the winter of 1830–31, William Wolfskill led a pack train of mules, laden with fine wool blankets from Santa Fe, over the newly discovered road to southern California. Wolfskill, an old fur-trapper, arrived at Los Angeles in February, 1831. He traded the blankets for California mules and then sold the mules in New Mexico. Wolfskill made a considerable profit and opened up the Spanish Trail to regular commercial traffic.

The Spanish Trail to New Mexico was long, hazardous, and expensive. This made trade along the route difficult. When the Mormons emigrated to Utah in 1847, the

*Jedediah Strong Smith (1799–1831),
born in New York, was a fur-trapper and
trailblazer who led the first American party
to travel overland through the Southwest.
He discovered the southern route across Nevada
in 1826 and the central route in 1827.
Four years later, Smith was killed by Comanche
Indians on the Cimarron River in Kansas.*

Courtesy of Nevada Historical Society

*John D. Reese (1808–1888) was a merchant
from Salt Lake City when he built
Mormon Station, the first roofed house in
Nevada, during the summer of 1851.
In 1854, Reese and a squad of soldiers
discovered the central overland route,
later surveyed in 1859 by
U.S. Army Captain James H. Simpson.*

Courtesy of Nevada Historical Society

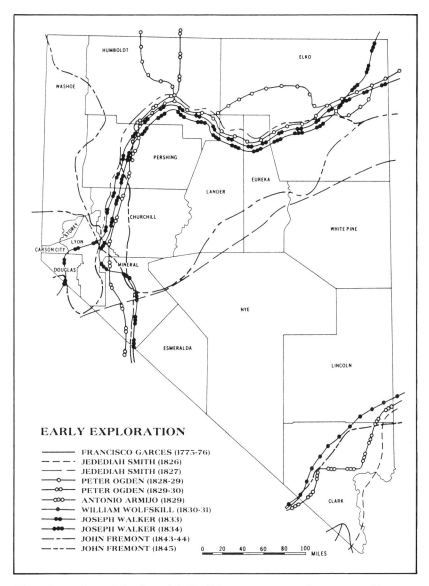

EARLY EXPLORATION

——————— FRANCISCO GARCES (1775-76)
— — — · JEDEDIAH SMITH (1826)
— — — — JEDEDIAH SMITH (1827)
——○——○— PETER OGDEN (1828-29)
——∞——∞— PETER OGDEN (1829-30)
——∞∞—— ANTONIO ARMIJO (1829)
——●——●— WILLIAM WOLFSKILL (1830-31)
——●●—— JOSEPH WALKER (1833)
——●●●—— JOSEPH WALKER (1834)
— — — — JOHN FREMONT (1843-44)
— — — — JOHN FREMONT (1845)

0   20   40   60   80   100
MILES

Nevada section of the Spanish Trail became a part of a new road between Salt Lake City and Los Angeles. This road was called the Mormon Trail. Congress encouraged the improvement of this route by awarding a contract to carry the mail between the two cities. Monthly service began in 1853. Today the Mormon Trail is a freeway, Interstate Highway 15. Tens of thousands of persons traveling between southern California and Utah pass over it every year.

The Central or Simpson Route

Jedediah Smith was the first person to use the central route. He found it during his fur-trapping expedition of 1827. The journey was so hard, however, that he lost his notes and maps and, in fact, barely survived. Smith described the crossing in a letter written July 17, 1827, to General William Clark of Lewis and Clark fame:

> After travelling twenty days from the East side of Mount Joseph [in the Sierra Nevada mountains of California], I struck the S.W. corner of the Great Salt Lake, travelling over a country completely barren and destitute of game. We frequently travelled without water sometimes for two days over sandy deserts where there was no sign of vegetation . . . When we arrived at the Salt Lake, we had but one horse and one mule remaining, which were so feeble & poor that

they could scarce carry the little camp equipage which I had along; the balance of my horses I was compelled to eat as they gave out.

In 1854, John Reese and four soldiers discovered a new and shorter route across Nevada between Salt Lake City and the Carson River. Unlike the California Trail, Reese's exploration did not follow any river. Until 1859, the new route was used mostly by cattlemen driving livestock between Carson Valley and Salt Lake City. In May and June of that year, U.S. Army Captain James Hervey Simpson surveyed a new wagon road along the route used by Reese which cut almost three hundred miles of travel from the California Trail across the Great Basin.

This Central Overland or Simpson Route was shorter than either the California Trail or the National Wagon Road designated by Congress in 1856. In 1860, the Pony Express carried mail using the Central Overland road. The transcontinental telegraph line, completed in 1861, followed the same route and mail-carrying overland stage coaches began using it in 1862. The Simpson road was a favorite of overland emigrants until the completion of the transcontinental railroad in 1869. It was one of the first routes on the nation's system of interstate highways. The road is now U.S. Highway 50; it was originally known as the Lincoln Highway.

The Northern Route or California Trail

This famous road is now a freeway, Interstate Highway 80, linking Chicago, Illinois, and San Francisco, California. The original route across Nevada was pioneered by Peter Skene Ogden, a member of the Hudson's Bay Company of Canada. In 1828, Ogden led a fur-trapping expedition into the Great Basin to search for beaver pelts. On November 9, he found the Humboldt River (later named after a German naturalist by John Fremont). Ogden wrote about his discovery in his *Snake Country Journal* entry:

> I had not advanced more than four miles when a fine large stream apparently well lined with willows was in sight. So glad was I to see it, that at the risk of my life over swamps, hills and rocks I made all speed to reach it, and the first thing that presented itself was a beaver house, apparently well stocked. A most pleasant sight to me and I hope it will repay us for all the trouble and anxiety it has caused me to reach it.

Peter Skene Ogden (1794–1854), was a Canadian-born fur-trapper for the Hudson's Bay Company who discovered the Humboldt River in 1828, pioneered much of what later became the California Trail, and made the first known north-south crossing of the Great Basin in 1829–30. He died a rich man in Oregon. The city of Ogden, Utah, is named after him.

Courtesy of Nevada Historical Society

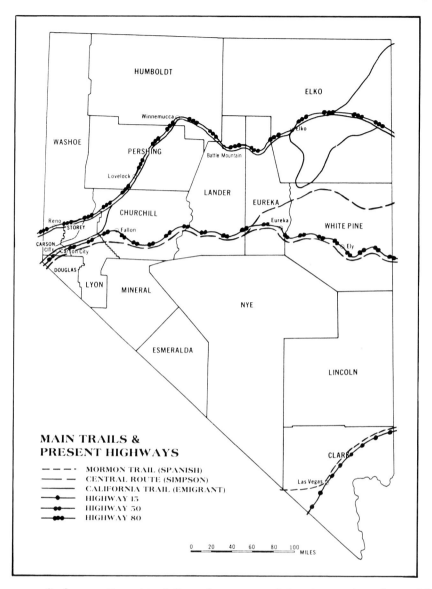

MAIN TRAILS &
PRESENT HIGHWAYS

- - - - MORMON TRAIL (SPANISH)
——— — CENTRAL ROUTE (SIMPSON)
——————— CALIFORNIA TRAIL (EMIGRANT)
—•—•— HIGHWAY 15
—••—••— HIGHWAY 50
—•••—•••— HIGHWAY 80

0   20   40   60   80   100
MILES

Ogden continued to follow the course of the river, where he and his men saw a number of Indians. In his *Journal* entry for November 19, 1828, the explorer wrote:

> The trappers now report the banks of the river are now lined with Indians. It appears on our arrival on this river they apprehended we were a war party, but they are now convinced we are come merely to wage war on the beaver, and this I trust we shall do most effectually, but they continue to annoy us having again stolen two traps and by following along the banks of the river make the beaver very wild.

In following the Humboldt, Ogden discovered two important facts. First, the river did not flow westward into the Pacific Ocean like the mythical San Buenaventura, but emptied into a lake or sink which had no outlet. Second, the Indians in the area already possessed guns and horses. These armed, mounted Indians — something never seen before in the Great Basin — had come hundreds of miles to Humboldt Sink from northern California where a number of Jedediah Smith's trappers were ambushed and murdered in the summer of 1828. Ogden's *Journal* entry for May 30, 1829, recorded this encounter:

> Early this morning one of the trappers started in the direction of the lake [Humboldt Sink], not only to taste the water but also to examine if it had an

outlet. Shortly after three of the trappers arrived and informed me they had four of the traps stolen, but had pursued the thieves by following their track and overtook them, and although they had the satisfaction of punishing them severely they had not the same in regard to their traps which they had but too well secreted.

We had scarcely received this information when the man who had gone towards the lake arrived and gave the alarm of enemies. By his account he had a most narrow escape, to the fleetness of his horse has his life been preserved.

He reports as follows. When rounding a point nearly within sight of the lake [Humboldt Sink], twenty men on horseback came in sight and on seeing him gave the war cry. He lost no time in retreating; one of the Indians had nearly overtaken him, and would had he not discharged his gun at him. He also informed us that the hills were covered with Indians.

Strongly suspecting from their conduct on the 26th instant, added to this day, I gave orders to secure the horses and having made all as secure as possible and the place would admit of, ten men, two thirds of my forces, started in advance to ascertain what the Indians were doing, and not to risk a battle with them as we are already too weak.

An hour after they arrived and reported the Indians, upwards of two hundred, were coming to the camp and were within a short distance and it was not their opinion they were well inclined towards us. Shortly after they arrived having selected a spot for them about five hundred yards from our camp I desired them to be seated, this order was obeyed.

I was soon convinced from their dress and being well loaded with arms and only one elderly man with them that it was a war party and no doubt had they not been discovered would have made an attack on us, and weak as we are in guns, having only twelve, they would have been but too successful. We have had a narrow escape. . . .

On examining these Indians we saw pieces of rifles, ammunition, arms and other articles. This I am of opinion must be some of the plunder of Smith's [Jedediah Smith] party of ten men who were murdered in the fall and from native to native has reached this. They would not inform me from whom they had received these articles from, this looks suspicious, on enquiring the cause of their visit the chief answered to make peace which was soon effected. I made him a present of a foot of tobacco, they had three land otters, but only one could I obtain from them; for the remaining two they demanded blankets for, which I would not comply with. More daring and bold Indians seldom or even have I seen, they requested to be allowed to come into the camp but this I refused.

Ogden led a second fur-trapping expedition across Nevada in 1829–30, this time traveling from north to south. He explored the Humboldt River more thoroughly and discovered a river and lake which were later named after Joseph Reddeford Walker.

Joseph Reddeford Walker (1798–1876) of Tennessee led a fur-trapping expedition into Nevada in 1833–34 and fought the first battle in the State between whites and Indians. He discovered Yosemite Valley, California, and later guided emigrant wagon trains and scouted for Lieutenant John C. Fremont. Walker River, Walker Lake, and Walker Pass bear his name.

Courtesy of Nevada Historical Society

In 1833, Walker led a fur-trapping expedition which traveled west down the Humboldt River. His band had trouble with the Indians, many of whom had never seen firearms. An eye-witness described one difficult moment which took place on September 4, 1833, in his diaries entitled *Narrative of the Adventures of Zenas Leonard:*

> A little before sun-set, on taking a view of the surrounding waste with a spy-glass, we discovered smoke issuing from the high grass in every direction. This was sufficient to convince us that we were in the midst of a large body of Indians; but as we could see no timber to go to, we concluded that it would be as well to remain in our present situation, and defend ourselves as well as we could.
>
> Before we had got everything completed, however, the Indians issued from their hiding places in the grass, to the number, as near as I could guess, of 8 or 900, and marched straight towards us, dancing and singing in the greatest glee. When within about 150 yards of us, they all sat down on the ground, and dispatched five of their chiefs to our camp to inquire whether their people might come in and smoke with us.
>
> This request Capt. Walker very prudently refused, as they evidently had no good intentions, but told them he was willing to meet them halfway between our breast work, and where their people were then sitting. This appeared to displease them very much, and they went back not the least bit pleased with the reception they had met with.
>
> After the five deputies related the result of their visit to their constituents, a part of them rose up and signed to us, (which was the only mode of communication with them) that they were coming to our camp. At this 10 or 12 of our men mounted the breast work and made signs to them that if they advanced a step further it was at the peril of their lives. They wanted to know in what way we would do it.
>
> Our guns were exhibited as the weapons of death. They seemed to discredit and only laughed at us. They then wanted to see what effect our guns would have on some ducks that were then swimming in the lake, not far from the shore. We then fired at the ducks — thinking by this means to strike terrour into the savages and drive them away. The ducks were killed, which astonished the Indians a good deal, though not so much as the noise of the guns — which caused them to fall flat to the ground. . . .
>
> This night we stationed a strong guard, but no Indians made their appearance, and were permitted to pass the night in pleasant dreams.

On October 4, 1833, at the Humboldt Sink, the trappers fought the first large scale battle between Indians and whites in Nevada. After defeating the Indians, Walker crossed the desert to Carson Sink, traveled up Walker River, and crossed the Sierra Nevada mountains. The party entered California in 1834, where they discovered

John Bidwell (1819–1900), born in New York, was a school teacher who helped lead the first party of overland emigrants to California in 1841. He became a prosperous rancher and was later elected to the U.S. House of Representatives. He died of a heart attack at the age of 80 while chopping down a tree.

Courtesy of Nevada Historical Society

The "Pyramid" as drawn by Fremont's artist.

Yosemite Valley and the Tuolumne or Merced grove of giant redwood trees. They returned that year over Walker Pass and recrossed Nevada by way of the Humboldt River.

In 1841, John Bidwell and John Bartleson formed an association of men and women to travel by wagon from Missouri to California (then a part of Mexico). The party, which included the first white woman and child to enter the Great Basin, traveled down the Humboldt River and found its way across the Forty-Mile Desert to Walker River. After many hardships and adventures, which included having to abandon their wagons and most of their equipment, the Bidwell-Bartleson party crossed the mountains over Sonora Pass and entered California. These thirty-four people were the first of many thousands of overland emigrants who, in the next few years, traveled west across the Great Basin.

Another expedition of emigrants, the Chiles-Walker party, crossed the Great Basin to California in 1843. Joseph Walker, the mountain man, guided them over the route he pioneered ten years earlier. Like the Bidwell-Bartleson party, the 38 emigrants of the Chiles-Walker party failed to get their wagons over the mountains and had to abandon them.

Army Exploring Expeditions

In 1843, Congress approved money for a U.S. Army exploring expedition into the far west to map out possible transcontinental wagon and railroad routes. Lieutenant John Charles Fremont, accompanied by Christopher "Kit" Carson, led the exploration of the Truckee and Carson River basins. On January 10, 1844, Fremont discovered Pyramid Lake, which he described in his *Narratives of Exploration and Adventure:*

> The hollow was several miles long, forming a good pass, the snow deepening to about a foot as we neared the summit. Beyond, a defile between the mountains descended rapidly about two thousand feet; and filling up the lower space was a sheet of green water, some twenty miles broad. It broke upon our eyes like the ocean.
>
> The neighboring peaks rose high above us, and we ascended one of them to obtain a better view. The waves were curling in the breeze, and their dark-green color showed it to be a body of deep water. For a long time we sat enjoying view, for we had become fatigued with mountains, and the free expanse of moving waves was very grateful. It was set like a gem in the mountains, which, from our position, seemed to enclose it almost entirely.

John Charles Fremont (1813–1890) of Georgia,
popularly known as "The Pathfinder,"
was a soldier and explorer who led U.S. Army
expeditions into Nevada in 1843–44
and 1845–46. Fremont was the presidential
candidate of the newly-formed Republican Party
in 1856; he later became a railroad promoter
and governor of Arizona Territory.

Courtesy of Nevada Historical Society

Christopher Houston "Kit" Carson (1809–1868),
a Kentucky-born mountain man, scout, soldier,
and Indian agent, passed through Nevada
for the first time with fur-trapper
Ewing Young in 1830, traveling over the
Spanish Trail. Carson was a guide for
Lieutenant John C. Fremont during the
U.S. Army exploring expeditions of 1843–44
and 1845–46. Carson River, Carson Sink,
Carson Pass, and Carson City
are all named after him.

Courtesy of Nevada Historical Society

Fremont then made the first winter crossing of the Sierra Nevada mountains in February, 1844, by way of Carson Pass. He was unable, however, to find a suitable crossing for wagons and had to abandon a small howitzer on the eastern slope of the mountains. Kit Carson was with Fremont during the epic winter crossing, which the scout recalled in his *Autobiography:*

> Our course was through a barren, desolate, and unexplored country until we reached the Sierra Nevadas, which we found covered with snow from one end to the other. We were nearly out of provisions but we had to cross the mountains, let the consequences be what they may. We went as far as we possibly could with our animals, when we were compelled to send them back. We then commenced making a road through the snow, beating it down with mallets. We made snowshoes and walked about over the snow to find out how far we would have to make a road. . . .
> . . . We returned to the place from which we had sent back our animals, and with nothing to eat but mule meat commenced the work of making the road. In fifteen days our task was accomplished, and we sent back for the animals. Driven by hunger, they had eaten one another's tails and the leather of the pack saddles, in fact, everything they could lay hold of.

WAGON ROADS WEST

In 1844, Truckee, a leader of the Northern Paiute Indians, showed mountain men Caleb Greenwood and Elisha Stevens how they could get their wagons into California over Emigrant Gap. The Stevens party, the first to cross the Sierra Nevada mountains by wagon, opened the Truckee River section of the California Trail. In that year, 53 persons traveled overland to California. In 1845, 260 persons took their wagons west over Emigrant Gap, and in 1846, the number of settlers migrating overland to California by wagon increased to 1,500.

Congress authorized Fremont to make a second expedition into the Great Basin to map the Humboldt, Carson, Truckee, and Walker River basins. In November and December of 1845, Fremont, with Truckee as his guide, crossed the Sierra Nevada into California by way of Donner Pass. One party of emigrants who followed the new route pioneered by Truckee and Fremont endured a tragic fate. The Donner Party, for whom the pass and lake were later named, attempted to cross the mountains late in the year. They ran into a heavy snowstorm which began October 28, 1846. The party was trapped near Donner Lake for almost four months. When the survivors were rescued on February 19, 1847, only 45 of the original 89 persons who left Fort Bridger, Utah, were still alive.

Roads to Gold

In May, 1846, while the Donner party and other emigrants were traveling westward to California, a war began between the United States and Mexico over disputed territory in southern Texas. The war ended February 2, 1848, with the Treaty of Guadalupe Hidalgo. Mexico gave up 1.2 million square miles of land, including Nevada and California, to the United States.

Neither the Mexican nor the United States Commissioners were aware when they signed the treaty that just nine days earlier — January 24, 1848 — workmen discovered gold in the American River at Sutter's Mill, California. This find turned out to be the first major gold strike in the United States, and a "rush" of prospectors, merchants, gamblers, and hangers-on began immediately.

The discovery had a dramatic effect on travel across Nevada. In 1847, 450 persons traveled overland to California; in 1848, the number dropped to 400. However, in 1849, an estimated 25,000 emigrants, called "49ers" from the year in which they migrated, traveled to California. They came on horseback, by wagon, buggy, and on foot. Most of them moved across Nevada. In the four years between 1849 and 1853, at least a quarter of a million people journeyed across the continent to the gold fields of California. This not only had a strong effect upon the Indians living in the path of the migration, but the movement of travelers worked great changes on the land, especially along the Humboldt River.

Returning soldiers of the Mexican-American War's "Mormon Battalion," starting from Sutter's Fort, built a wagon road over Carson Pass and Carson Canyon in 1848. This opened the Carson River section of the California Trail to overland emigrants traveling to the mines of central California.

Even then, travel was arduous. Some of the sufferings endured by the overland emigrants were described by black mountain man James Beckwourth, the discoverer of Beckwourth Pass, in his *Life and Adventures:*

> Much stock is lost in crossing the Plains, through their drinking the alkali water which flows from the Sierra Nevada. . . . There are also poisonous herbs springing up in the region of the mineral water, which the poor, famishing animals devour without stint. Those who survive until they reach the Valley are generally too far gone for recovery, and die while resting to recruit their strength.
>
> This general loss of cattle deprives many of the poor emigrants of the means of hauling their lightened wagons, which, by the time that they reach my ranch [near Beckwourth Pass, California], seldom contain any thing more than their family clothing and bedding. Frequently I have observed wagons pass my house with one starveling yoke of cattle to drag them, and the family straggling on foot behind. Numbers have put up at my ranch without a morsel of food, and without a dollar in the world to procure any. They never were refused what they

▲ *James Pierson Beckwourth (1800–1866), Virginia-born black mountain man, was the son of Sir Jennings Beckwith and a mulatto slave woman. He discovered Beckwourth Pass, which is named after him, and in 1851 formed a company which built a wagon trail from Bidwell's Bar, California, over the Sierra Nevada. He died on a hunting trip during a visit to the Crow Indians.*

Courtesy of Nevada Historical Society

◄ *Elisha Stevens (1804–1884), a blacksmith, was the leader of the first emigrant wagon train to successfully bring their wagons over the snowy Sierra Nevada range into California. He was a reclusive rancher near Bakersfield, California, until his death at the age of 80.*

Courtesy of Nevada Historical Society

asked for at my house; and, during the short space that I have spent in the Valley, I have furnished provisions and other necessaries to the numerous sufferers who have applied for them to a very serious amount.

One of the worst stretches of the California Trail was the Forty-Mile Desert, which had to be crossed by either the Truckee or Carson River sections of the route. There was no water on the desert; what the emigrants needed for themselves and their animals had to be carried. To avoid the scorching midsummer heat on their day-and-a-half-long trip across the shimmering sands, the wayfarers traveled by night. One 49er, Charles Tinker, almost died crossing the wasteland. He recalled:

> . . . when within 8 or 10 miles of the river I lay down several times to rest, it did not seam as though I could go any farther but it was death to stay their so I had to budge along as best I could thrugh the burning sand till I reached the water. water was all my wants I would have given all I possessed for a drink of cold water my tongue and lips was parched and fured over so it took one hour to soak it of.

After the gold rush began in 1849, merchants in California seeking to attract business and settlers to their towns financed new construction and improvement of roads connecting with the California Trail.

Mail Routes

The Congress had a policy of establishing a national road system, and so it encouraged the construction of overland and local roads by granting contracts to carry the mail for the U.S. Post Office. Just such a contract, made in 1851 between the United States and the firm of Woodward & Chorpenning, established the first transcontinental overland mail service.

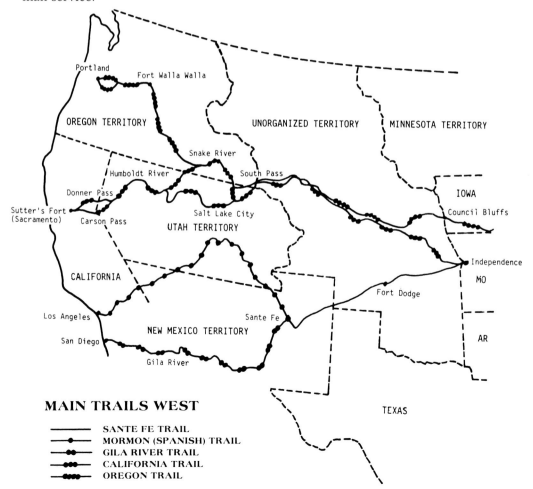

MAIN TRAILS WEST

——————— SANTE FE TRAIL
———•——— MORMON (SPANISH) TRAIL
———••——— GILA RIVER TRAIL
———•••——— CALIFORNIA TRAIL
———••••——— OREGON TRAIL

The Forty-Mile Desert. This Nevada wasteland was one of the most feared stretches of the California Trail. Overland emigrants had to make the crossing over a waterless track to reach the Carson or Truckee Rivers from Humboldt Sink. During the first years of the gold rush to California, hundreds of unprepared emigrants abandoned their wagons on the desert and died of thirst and exposure. Courtesy of Nevada Historical Society

The Overland Emigrants. Although Americans first began to migrate overland to California in 1841, large-scale travel did not begin until after 1848, when, within ten days, gold was discovered, and the U.S. took over control of the region. A rush to the gold diggings began immediately. In 1849 alone, an estimated 25,000 people emigrated overland to California, and most of them passed through Nevada. Culver Pictures

*Mormon Station. Built by John Reese and his merchant party from Salt Lake City
on land purchased from the local Indians during the summer of 1851, this log cabin trading post
was the first permanent settlement in Nevada. By 1855, a number of homes and stores stood
nearby, and the community took on the name of "Genoa" — Nevada's first town.*
Courtesy of Nevada Department of Transportation

The first deliveries were made once a month by pack trains of mules traveling between Sacramento, California, and Salt Lake City, Utah, by way of the California Trail through Carson Valley and Placerville. The first eastward-bound mail party left Sacramento on May 1, 1851, but Indian attacks on the pack trains began almost immediately. One of the contractors, Absalom Woodward, and his party were killed in an ambush on the Humboldt River later that year.

The Indian attacks and heavy winter snows made the first transcontinental postal service dangerous and uncertain. Early mail carriers, such as John "Snowshoe" Thompson, had to carry the winter mail over the mountains by snowshoe or ski. The mail station in Carson Valley on the eastern slope of the Sierra Nevada, called Mormon Station (1851) and renamed Genoa (1855), was the first permanent white settlement in Nevada.

Congress expanded overland mail service to southern California in 1852, when it authorized a route between Salt Lake City and Los Angeles by way of San Bernardino, California. The mail contractors established several way-stations along the Mormon Trail; one of these stations was at Las Vegas Springs in southern Nevada.

Congress entered into a new contract for the Sacramento-Salt Lake City mail route in 1853, providing that the monthly mail was to be carried by wagons with a four-mule team. That same year the U.S. Postmaster General designated Mormon Station (Genoa) as the first post office in Nevada.

Stagecoach Mail

Road building efforts during 1856–57 greatly improved the California Trail over the Sierra Nevada. This made it possible at last for stagecoaches to travel across the mountains. The first crossing took place in May, 1857, between Oroville, California, and Honey Lake Valley. Two more crossings followed within a few weeks. During June, 1857, a stagecoach traveled the Johnson's Cut-Off route between Placerville and Genoa by way of Echo Summit; then another stagecoach made the trip over the Big Trees Road from Calaveras County, California, to Genoa. Regular local stagecoach operations began that same year over the three routes.

These early staging activities encouraged Congress. It approved a transcontinental weekly overland stagecoach mail contract in 1858, between Salt Lake City and Sacramento by way of Genoa and Placerville. The first of the stagecoaches carrying mail to the east left Placerville on June 5, 1858, for Carson Valley and the plains. The experiment was quite successful; it followed the California Trail until 1862, when the overland stage began using the Simpson Route.

The U.S. Government ended transcontinental mail by stagecoach in Nevada after

John A. "Snowshoe" Thompson (1827–76). In the early years of settlement in Nevada, pioneer "Snowshoe" Thompson of Carson Valley brought the mail and light freight over the mountains by ski during the winter. Carrying sixty to eighty–pound packs, the Norwegian-born "mountain expressman" covered the ninety miles between Placerville and Genoa in three to five days. Thompson's skis, at first called snowshoes, were perhaps the first to cut fresh powder in the Sierra Nevada, and they were followed by tens of thousands of additional pairs of skis as the sport caught on. Captain James H. Simpson, the Army officer who surveyed the central overland route in 1859, described Thompson's cross-country and alpine ski techniques: "Mr. Thompson showed me how he walked on his snow-shoes last winter. They are smooth pieces of board from 6 to 8 feet long, 6 inches broad at forepart, 4 at middle, and less at ends, the forepart slightly turned up like a sleighrunner. A little in front of the middle portion a strap or thong is nailed across, in which he slips his toes, then there is a cleat nailed across, against which the heel of his shoe strikes or pushes. He then gently lifts the shoe, and at the same time pushing along with his foot, causes himself to slide first with one shoe and then with the other. He has at the same time a stick against which, as he goes down hill, he supports himself, and which he also uses as a brake. He says he has a standing bet with any one that, let him select his ground along a side-hill, he will travel a mile a minute; that he sometimes passes over precipices of 10 feet, and would land at a distance of 20 feet, and still stand upright. When a child in Norway he used, with other boys, to practice this kind of leap, and thus made himself an expert."

Courtesy of Nevada Historical Society

the completion of the transcontinental railroad in 1869, but stagecoaches kept operating on the branch roads until the early twentieth century.

Sam Clemens, better known as Mark Twain, traveled the California Trail route by stagecoach in the summer of 1861. Being a passenger wasn't at all easy. He described a crossing of the Forty-Mile Desert in his book *Roughing It:*

> On the nineteenth day we crossed the Great American Desert — forty memorable miles of bottomless sand, into which the coach wheels sunk from six inches to a foot. We worked our passage most of the way across. That is to say, we got out and walked. It was a dreary pull and a long and thirsty one, for we had no water.
>
> From one extremity of this desert to the other, the road was white with the bones of oxen and horses. It would hardly be an exaggeration to say that we could have walked the forty miles and set our feet on a bone at every step!
>
> The desert was one prodigious graveyard. And the log-chains, wagon tyres, and rotting wrecks of vehicles were almost as thick as the bones. I think we saw log-chains enough rusting there in the desert, to reach across any State in the Union. Do not these relics suggest something of an idea of the fearful suffering and privation the early emigrants to California endured?

Sometimes bandits would rob the stagecoaches and their passengers. There is a song about one such robbery of a stagecoach driven by veteran "whip" Baldy Green. Wells Drury recounted it in his book *An Editor On the Comstock Lode.* A part of the ballad goes:

> Now, as he was driving out one night,
>   As lively as a [rac]coon,
> He saw three men jump in the road
>   By the pale light of the moon;
> Two sprang for the leaders,
>   While one his shotgun cocks,
> Saying, "Baldy, we hate to trouble you,
>   But just pass us out the box."
>
> When Baldy heard them say these words
>   He opened wide his eyes;
> He didn't know what in the world to do,
>   For it took him by surprise.
> Then he reached into the boot,
>   Saying, "Take it, sirs, with pleasure,"
> So out into the middle of the road
>   Went Wells & Fargo's treasure.
>
> Now, when they got the treasure-box
>   They seemed quite satisfied,
> For the man who held the leaders
>   Then politely stepped aside,
> Saying, "Baldy, we've got what we want,
>   So drive along your team,"
> And he made the quickest time
>   To Silver City ever seen.
>
> Don't say greenbacks to Baldy now,
>   It makes him feel so sore;
> He's traveled the road many a time,
>   But was never stopped before.
> Oh, the chances they were three to one
>   And shotguns were the game,
> And if you'd a-been in Baldy's place
>   You'd a-shelled her out the same.

"Hands up!! Throw down that box!!!". A double stagecoach robbery on a remote stretch of a Nevada road in 1866, as reconstructed by an artist for the <u>Police Gazette</u>. The illustration shows the stage robbers unloading and breaking into bullion-bearing Wells Fargo strongboxes, while other bandits plunder the passengers.

Stagecoach from Golconda, 1887. Horse-drawn stagecoaches linked small mining camps with main transcontinental overland routes in Nevada for sixty years, before they were replaced by trucks, buses, and automobiles. The stagecoaches carried the mail, newspapers, bullion, and passengers and were one of the most important forms of transportation in the nineteenth–century West.

Courtesy of Huntingdon Library

*Henry M. "Hank" Monk (1829–1883).
This famous stagecoach driver handled
the Carson City-Lake Tahoe section of
the overland mail stage route in 1859,
when he took famous New York
newspaper editor Horace ("Go west,
young man") Greeley on a ride to be
remembered. Here is the way Mark
Twain retold the story in* Roughing It:
*"I can tell you a very laughable thing
indeed, if you would like to listen to it.
Horace Greeley went over this road
once. When he was leaving Carson City
he told the driver, Hank Monk, that he
had an engagement to lecture at
Placerville and was very anxious to get
through quick. Hank Monk cracked his
whip and started off at an awful pace.
The coach bounced up and down in
such a terrific way that it jolted the
buttons all off of Horace's coat, and
finally shot his head clean through the
roof of the stage, and then he yelled at
Hank Monk and begged him to go
easier — said he warn't in as much of a
hurry as he was a while ago. But Hank
Monk said, "Keep your seat, Horace,
and I'll get you there on time!" —
and you bet he did, too, what was
left of him!"*

*Monk drove stages in Nevada for more
than twenty years; when he died, his
obituary in the Virginia City* Enterprise
*stated, "In his prime he could turn
a six horse coach in a street with a team
at a full run with every line
apparently loose."*

*Stagecoach drivers had a certain
amount of prestige in the days before the
transcontinental railroad was completed.
Hubert Howe Bancroft, one of the most
prominent historians of the American
West, described it this way: "There
never was any stage service in the world
more complete than that between
Placerville and Virginia City.
A sprinkled road, over which dashed six
fine, sleek horses before an elegant
Concord coach, the lines in the hands of
a expert driver, whose light hat, linen
duster, and lemon-colored gloves
betokened a good salary and an exacting
company, and who timed his grooms
and his passengers by a heavy gold
chronometer watch, held carelessly, if
conspicuously, on the tips of his
fingers — these were some of
its features."*

Courtesy of Nevada Historical Society

The Pony Express and the Talking Wires, 1861. In 1860, the U.S. government contracted with the firm of Russell, Majors & Waddell to provide a transcontinental express mail service over the newly-surveyed Simpson route. But soon the Pony Express had a faster rival—the overland telegraph, which made the relay riders unprofitable and put the Pony Express out of business in October, 1861.

The Pony Express

The Pony Express, though short lived, has long been a famous subject in the history of the American West. It started in 1860, when the freighting company of Russell, Majors & Waddell began a transcontinental express service to carry important financial and government documents by fast mail between San Francisco and St. Joseph, Missouri — a distance of nearly 2,000 miles. They named the new enterprise "The Pony Express." It employed eighty riders and used the newly-mapped Simpson or Central Overland Route across Nevada. The first rider left Sacramento for Genoa, Carson City, and points east on April 4, 1860. The first rider from Salt Lake City arrived at Sacramento on April 13. Letters cost $5 an ounce to be carried by the Pony Express, and it took about 17 or 18 days for the riders to cover the San Francisco-St. Joseph road. The Pony Express stopped operations in October, 1861, when the transcontinental telegraph was completed.

Toll Roads to the Comstock

Branch roads, or routes leading from the overland trails into the interior of Nevada, were nearly all built for travel to various mining camps. The roads to the Comstock — the site of the Nevada's first big gold and silver discovery — are typical of these branch routes. During the spring and summer of 1850, emigrants discovered gold nuggets at the mouth of Gold Canyon on the Carson River section of the California Trail. At least one miner spent the winter of 1850–51 there, and from the summer of 1851, a colony of miners lived in Gold Canyon, digging and panning for gold. Supplying the colony with food and drink was profitable, and most of the supplies were packed into the camp from California by mule trains.

The discovery of silver in the blue mud which had frustrated and annoyed gold miners led to a "rush" on the Comstock Lode in 1859. As freighting increased, new roads were built to reach the new mining camps at Virginia City and Gold Hill, near the back of Gold Canyon. In September of 1859, construction started on the first of these roads to the Comstock. It was called the Devil's Gate toll road and it ran between Dayton on the Carson River and Gold Hill, by way of Gold Canyon.

Devil's Gate Toll Road, 1863. After the discovery of gold and silver on the Comstock Lode in 1859,
traffic to and from the new mines increased greatly. Businessmen built toll roads
and charged travelers a fee for using them. The Devil's Gate toll road, connecting Gold Hill with
the California Trail by way of Dayton and Silver City, was one of the main routes linking
the Comstock mines with the outside world.

Courtesy of Special Collections, University of Nevada Reno Library

William Wright, who wrote under the pen name of Dan DeQuille, described the road construction in his book, *The Big Bonanza:*

> Virginia City, being situated on a sort of sloping plateau, on the eastern face of Mount Davidson, at the height of over 6,000 feet above the level of the sea, was a place difficult of access. Wagons could be used in the surrounding valleys, but Virginia City could receive no freight except such as could be carried up the mountain on the backs of pack-mules. Soon after the discovery of silver, however, companies located routes for wagon-roads to the place and began the difficult work of building them, blasting out passageways in many places through solid rock along the sides of canyons, and it was not many months before they were completed, when lumber, timber, and many other much needed articles that could not be packed on the backs of mules poured into Virginia City, whose streets were soon crowded with huge "prairie schooners," as the great mountain wagons are called, drawn by long lines of mules or horses, all musical with bells.

A few months later, Kingsbury & McDonald, California road contractors, began work on the Kingsbury Grade, also called the Van Sickle Grade after one of the men who financed it. In the summer of 1868, the operation of this road was described as follows in the *American Journal of Mining:*

A GREAT WAGON ROAD

> The Placerville road is the best wagon road across the Sierra Nevada. It cost $585,000 and is now traveled from Shingle Springs to Van Syckles in Carson Valley, is 82 miles long. . . .
> In 1858, Sacramento and El Dorado each subscribed $25,000 to construct a wagon road across the mountain, but the road was not good enough for the

The Overland Telegraph. This illustration shows the lines and poles of the Overland Telegraph Company along a heavily trafficked portion of the road between Placerville, California, and Carson City. The "talking wires" share the steep grade with fast-moving stagecoaches, overland emigrants, freight wagons, carts, and travelers on foot. The Placerville & Humboldt Telegraph Company built a telegraph line between Placerville, California, and Genoa in 1858; they extended the service to Carson City in 1859 and to Virginia City in 1860. In 1858, the California Legislature passed laws offering financial incentives to provide companies to build a transcontinental telegraph system, and in 1860, the U.S. Congress passed the Pacific Telegraph Act. As a result, all the Pacific coast telegraph companies merged to form the Overland Telegraph Company and completed the transcontinental connection between Salt Lake and Carson City in 1861.

purpose, and in 1860, the present road was commenced by private enterprise and was finished in 1863. It was a vast service to the State and to Washoe during the silver excitement, and was for a time very profitable to the owners.

Although other routes have lower passes and easier grades, no other can compete with this for the ordinary purposes of wagon travel because this is the shortest route between Sacramento and Virginia City; is an excellent road, and is kept in fine condition.

The road is watered every evening along its whole length by water carts which are stationed at intervals of three miles. This is found to be the cheapest method of keeping the road in good condition, for if left dry, it would have deep dust which would obstruct the wheels and blow away, leaving deep ruts.

About one-fourth of the expense in keeping the road in order is required to keep the snow down. Last winter, snow lay for nine miles on the road, and ten span of horses were kept for the special purpose of breaking it down. It would be useless to shovel the snow from the road, which would immediately drift full.

The toll for a four-horse wagon from Shingle Springs to Van Sickles and back is $17.50, three-fourths being for the eastern trip. Most of the freight, however, has been carried in wagons drawn by more than four horses. The best teams have ten mules and two wagons, the second wagon being smaller and fastened immediately to the first. An ordinary load for such a team is 20,000 pounds. . . . The tolls on a round trip from Shingle Springs to Van Syckles are $26.26; and the total necessary outlay on a trip, $240. This is the most extensive toll road in the United States.

Also in 1860, contractors built the Ophir Grade toll road between Virginia City and the ore reduction mills on Washoe Lake. The last major route to the Comstock, completed in 1862, was the Geiger Grade toll route between the Truckee River section of the California Trail and Virginia City.

Similar road building activities took place all over Nevada. Wherever the ore finds were rich enough to be worked for several years, men built branch roads based on the promise of the commerce the route would sustain. Most of the principal branch roads built during nineteenth century Nevada — which includes much of the modern road system — were originally toll roads to mining communities, constructed by merchants and businessmen.

Toll Road Fortunes

The profit in toll road-building was in the volume of supplies and numbers of toll-paying travelers and freight wagons which passed over the road. In the early years of settlement Nevada's Legislature encouraged the construction of these branch roads by granting franchises or licenses for people to run them. Mark Twain, who worked as a newspaper reporter in Nevada during the 1860's, described the enthusiasm for toll roads in pioneer times:

> The Legislature sat sixty days, and passed private toll-road franchises all the time. When they adjourned it was estimated that every citizen owned about three franchises, and it was believed that unless Congress gave the Territory another degree of longitude there would not be room enough to accommodate the toll-roads. The ends of them were hanging over the boundary line everywhere like a fringe.
>
> The fact is, the freighting business had grown to such important proportions that there was nearly as much excitement over suddenly acquired toll-road fortunes as over the wonderful silver mines.

The Legislature fixed the rates that the toll-keepers could charge persons to use the road. In that way, the persons who used the road were also the persons who paid for it. Myron Angel's *History of Nevada* gives some sample rates:

> By an Act of the Territorial Legislature approved December 19, 1862, Ellen Redman and others were authorized to construct a toll-bridge across Carson Slough in Churchill County, and to charge toll as follows:
>
> For wagon drawn by six or eight animals $2.00
> For wagon drawn by four animals 1.50

For wagon drawn by two animals 1.00
For carriage and buggy, two horses 1.00
For carriage and buggy, one horse .... .75
For horsemen .... .25
For pack animals... 12½
For loose stock .... .10

The fine for crossing the bridge without paying toll was not less than ten dollars, nor more than $100. Any one maliciously injuring the bridge was liable to be fined from twenty-five dollars to $500. All fines to accrue to the Bridge Company. The rates of toll could be changed by the Governor and Legislature, and the Commissioners of Lyon and Churchill Counties could purchase the bridge in three years at its appraised cash value.

Of the total tolls collected, there was a 2% tax which went to the Territorial School Fund.

Sometimes people didn't want to pay the tolls, and there were violent confrontations. Some of the owners of heavily-traveled toll roads and bridges grew very wealthy. Since they were only granted for a limited period of time, during the 1870's and 1880's the licenses of most of the toll roads expired. The county governments then took the roads over and began to improve and maintain them at public expense.

Samuel Langhorne Clemens (1835–1910) of Missouri, better known by his pen-name "Mark Twain," was one of America's most popular writers. He began his literary career in Nevada, where he served in 1861 as secretary to his brother, the first Secretary of State of Nevada Territory. He soon quit that job, and after several unsuccessful prospecting expeditions, Clemens worked as a reporter for the Virginia City Territorial Enterprise. After two years of writing news stories under the name of "Mark Twain," he left the State to become a world-famous novelist and lecturer.

Courtesy of Nevada Historical Society

Pack Trains

During the earliest days of an old-time mining boom, most of the supplies were carried into the mining camps by mule. Mules were sturdy but also stubborn! Packing by mule train over steep and rocky trails could be an exciting and exasperating experience. Prospectors also used mules and burros to get around in the desert and to carry supplies. They were very popular in the nineteenth and early twentieth centuries as a means of transportation, as this 1881 article from the Dayton *Lyon County Times* shows:

PHILOSOPHER JACK. A.S. Dildine, Deputy County Surveyor of Churchill county, owns a trained mule which has a well of mule wisdom in its head. He is known to all the inhabitants of Mason Valley and Churchill county as "Philosopher Jack," and in addition to various useful items of knowledge is possessed of several small accomplishments which verge closely upon art. He has been trained to wag his tail at his master like a dog, and bleat like a lamb. When Jack is unharnessed he needs no tying, as he follows his master around faithfully, and if not fed promptly will back up and kick at him affectionately, to remind him of the delay, and Mr. Dildine generally acknowledges the barley.

While Mr. Dildine is at work Jack usually accompanies him, and where it is necessary to run a line over a place too steep for mule climbing his doleful brays, alternating with lamb-like bleatings are kept up until a path can be found by which he can make his way into comfortable proximity with his master. Jack bids fair to live a long life; the whip has no terrors for him; he has never felt it, neither does a heavy load worry him; he stops and rests whenever so inclined; he is an excellent judge of a good place at which to stop and brace at either an up or down grade. He is particularly in love with soft muddy spots as halting places, and load or no load will stop and rest, much to the annoyance of his master. Knowing himself to be a pet he calmly wags his muddy tail after being helped out of the mire, turns away wrath by a gentle bleat, and turning an extensive but indifferent ear to the remonstrances of his human companions, moves off quietly with his load, confident that he is not for sale at any price.

Teamsters and Freight Wagons

Once the roads to the mining camps were improved, freighting — the business of hauling goods to market — increased substantially. People going to and from the camps traveled by stagecoach, while goods hauled to the camps were carried by large freight wagons drawn by teams of mules or oxen. The men who drove the wagons were called freighters or teamsters.

The early freighters with their wagons were an impressive sight. This description was written in the summer of 1865 by a reporter for the *Reese River Reveille,* Austin's principal newspaper:

FREIGHT. – Large quantities of freight, embracing general merchandise, lumber, and machinery, have arrived in town today, and our streets have been rendered musical by the jingling bells of a dozen splendid mule teams, and ever and anon the air has been resonant, and the very hills have reverberated the tremendous objurgations and naughty ejaculations of the drivers of bull teams as they dragged their slow length along. Ye Gods! with what originality and emphasis these fellows do swear.

*"The Grade." J. Ross Browne's drawing shows a pack train descending the Sierra Nevada
mountains between Placerville and Genoa in the spring of 1860. These mules are packing a cargo
of wet goods—whiskey, gin, and brandy—for sale to the miners of the Comstock Lode.
In the foreground, several horsemen are bogged down in a muddy quagmire, while the sure-footed
pack mules step nimbly around them. In July, 1854, William H. "Uncle Billy" Rogers
started the first regular mule train service into Nevada; it ran every week between Placerville
and Carson Valley, and the fare for passengers was $12 per trip.*

Courtesy of Special Collections, University of Nevada Reno Library

Freighting Wagons at Cave Rock. In this late afternoon Lake Tahoe scene, mule-drawn Conestoga wagons stop on the road for the photographer. Freighting wagons supplied outlying Nevada communities for two generations before they were replaced by trucks and tractor-trailers.

Courtesy of Special Collections, University of Nevada Reno Library

Camels in Nevada. The U.S. Army imported camels into the U.S. in the 1850's to test their usefulness in packing supplies across the deserts of the Southwest. Although they were practical, not everyone liked them. Horses and mules, in particular, were terrified of camels.
The Army ended its camel experiments before the beginning of the Civil War, but freighters used them to pack salt and cargo between Virginia City, Austin, and Eureka. Alfred Chartz, in a deposition taken for the Alpine case, remembered an experience he had as a young man, involving the beasts: "It was a cold, dry winter, the year 1870. I know I drove up to Virginia City every day up to January 1st on a wagon, and had no difficulty at all from snow. We used to meet a camel train there every week or so packing salt to the mills. They traveled at night, by Virginia City ordinance, because they scared animals so bad, and I traveled at night and I generally met them. I had more trouble than any man you ever saw to escape with my life with those camels, they split my wagon one time; I had a calf in it and it never hurt the calf but skinned me up pretty bad, but the calf was all right." Camels eventually went out of commercial use in Nevada and were turned out into the deserts, where they had to fend for themselves. Never very numerous, the camels were thought to have died out after 1910.

Freighting was not all hard work and profits. It could be dangerous, too, according to this 1893 article from the Dayton *Lyon County Times:*

> RUNAWAY. – Last Tuesday afternoon Pete Quilici's four horse team hitched to a hay wagon ran away from the upper end of Main street. When the team reached the Odd Fellow's building one of the horses fell down. The other horses turned at this point and started to run across the creek, dragging the horse that was down. In crossing the creek the entire team went down and became so tangled that they were caught before they could go further. Strange to say, none of the animals was seriously injured, the horse that was dragged only having a little skin taken off his side.

RAILROADS IN NEVADA

Railroads were frequently built under the same or similar circumstances as wagon roads. The pioneer railroad in Nevada was the Central Pacific, part of the first transcontinental railroad system. Two other transcontinental rail lines cross Nevada; they were built by the Union Pacific and Western Pacific railroad companies. With the exception of the logging railways, all of Nevada's branch railroads were built to connect remote communities with one of the transcontinental lines, and the railroads prospered or failed with the communities they served.

Transcontinental Railroads

The Central Pacific (C.P.R.R.) system, now owned by the Southern Pacific, began when the company was formally incorporated during the summer of 1861. Surveyors began work immediately and laid out a route by the end of August, roughly along the California Trail's Truckee River route. In Congress, a bill providing financial subsidies and incentives for a transcontinental railroad, the Pacific Railroad Bill, was passed and

"Two Ways of Going West." This illustration from an 1877 copy of Frank Leslie's Illustrated Weekly *magazine shows the effect of the transcontinental railroad on overland travel. The original caption to this picture read: "An emigrant train is by no means a rare sight, even in these days of steam and Pullman hotel coaches. We have passed several of them along our route, yet it is always a source of interest to watch the slow-moving caravan crossing the great, illimitable waste. There is the great wagon packed with bedding, household stuff, ancient trunks, ironmongery, and crockery, with a calico gown and a sunbonnet or two perched in front, and a guard of stalwart male emigrants on foot and in the saddle, each carrying his gun and pack — a sturdy, resolute and possibly dangerous customer. There they go toiling beside us for one second and then left far behind, the children waving to us with ragged straw hats and little flapping aprons, and the women turning to look half-wistfully after our flying train."*

The First Transcontinental Railroad. This woodcut from <u>Frank Leslie's Illustrated Weekly</u> shows Chinese workmen in the Sierra Nevada stacking wood, delivered down steep flumes to fuel the steam locomotives of the Central Pacific Railroad. The pioneer transcontinental rail line through California and Nevada was built with the help of hundreds of Chinese laborers between 1863 and 1869.

then signed into law by President Abraham Lincoln on July 1, 1862. Construction began on the shops and engine houses in Sacramento, California in January, 1863, but the first tracks were not laid until that October. The Central Pacific Company employed large crews of Chinese workmen to grade the railroad right-of-way over the Sierra Nevada.

The C.P.R.R.'s financial backers first built the Dutch Flat Wagon Road in 1864, over the Sierra Nevada range at Donner Pass. The tracks of the Central Pacific were then built over the roadway, but progress through the mountains was very slow. Many people predicted that it couldn't be done. The rail line finally reached the summit of the Sierra Nevada range in November of 1867. The next month, the first railroad locomotive entered Nevada at Crystal Peak, near present-day Verdi, only 23 years after the Indian leader Truckee had first shown the Stevens party how to get wagons over the Sierra Nevada mountains.

As workmen built the tracks across the State, towns appeared where the railroad builders decided to locate mainline stations. Railroad promoters and local businessmen established Reno in April and May of 1868. The tracks reached Wadsworth on July 22 of that year and crossed the Forty-Mile Desert to Lovelock in August. The first trains arrived at Winnemucca on September 16, 1868. They were at Carlin by January 25, 1869, and in Elko on February 8th. The railroad was completed with great fanfare at Promontory Point, Utah, on May 10, 1869. The Central Pacific's tracks were joined by a golden spike with the tracks of the Union Pacific railroad, forming the first transcontinental rail system. In 1899, the Southern Pacific bought the Central Pacific and operates the railroad to this day.

Nevada's second transcontinental railroad took even longer to build. In 1890, the Union Pacific's directors decided to construct a rival route across Nevada to connect Salt Lake City with Los Angeles. The route that they surveyed was approximately that of the Salt Lake-San Bernardino mail route of 1853, which followed the Spanish Trail through

Central Pacific Railroad Shops at Carlin, 1869. Nine engines appear in this photograph
of C.P.R.R. shops and enginehouse on the Humboldt River. These facilities made Carlin a leading
shipping point for northeastern Nevada.
Courtesy of Nevada Historical Society

the southern part of our State. Although work started at once, the Legislature did not give the Union Pacific Railroad (U.P.R.R.) a charter to cross Nevada until 1901. The tracks reached Caliente in 1903 and Las Vegas in 1904. On January 30, 1905, U.P.R.R. workmen completed the rail connection through to Los Angeles.

By contrast, the third and last transcontinental railroad across the State was built between 1907 and 1909 — not quite three years. The Western Pacific Railroad (W.P.R.R.) Company was incorporated in 1903, to build a track linking Oakland, California with Salt Lake City along a route more or less following the National Wagon Road of 1856. Completed in 1909, the W.P.R.R. crossed the Black Rock and Smoke Creek Deserts to Honey Lake and then spanned the mountains at Beckwourth Pass.

Freight charges on the railroads were often a source of controversy. Politicians, ranchers, and townspeople complained that the rates for hauling were too high, resulting in higher prices for goods. Many people also believed that the railroads controlled the Nevada State Legislature and local officeholders. In 1880, Nevada's Congressman, Rollin M. Daggett, made some strong accusations in a stirring speech, but he was defeated for re-election. The subject of railroad regulation was a stormy political issue until the Legislature created the Railroad Commission in 1907 to set freight rates.

Branch Railroad Lines

Branch lines in Nevada can generally be divided into two types based on the freight most often carried: mining railroads and logging railroads. There were also two types of the mining railroads. The eight major mining railroads linked mining communities with one of the three transcontinental railroads, while the minor lines joined producing

Reno-bound, this Western Pacific Railroad train was moving a mile a minute when this 1911 photograph was taken in Sierra Valley, near Loyalton, California. Courtesy of Nevada Historical Society

V.&T.R.R. Engine House at Carson City. No less than ten sets of tracks converge on the turntable of the Virginia & Truckee Railroad facilities in Carson City. The V.&T.R.R., built to connect the mines of the Comstock Lode with the transcontinental railroad at Reno, was constructed between 1869 and 1872. Courtesy of Special Collections, University of Nevada Reno Library

Steaming into Reno. A brightly-polished locomotive pulls into Reno across the V.&.T.R.R. iron bridge over the Truckee River. Sometimes called "the crookedest railroad in the world" because of its many turns, the V.&.T.R.R. soon monopolized all transportation to and from the Comstock Lode mines. After the State of Nevada built a modern road system and trucks and buses began to compete with the V.&.T.R.R., the company's profits fell, and the railroad went out of business in 1950. Courtesy of Nevada State Railroad Museum, Carson City

Eureka Mill Narrow Gauge Mining Railroad. Built to connect the Eureka reduction mill on Carson River with the V.&.T.R.R., this line is typical of a number of small railway systems across the State designed to carry ore. These small branch lines were dependent upon the mines for their revenue, and when the mines gave out, so did the railways. Courtesy of Nevada Historical Society

Snowplow Engines Clearing Heavy Snow. This photograph, taken during the Winter of 1916,
shows the effect of heavy snowstorms on railroading operations. During very bad storms
the rail lines could be closed, resulting in a "snow blockade" which sometimes lasted for weeks.
Courtesy of Nevada Historical Society

mines with ore reduction mills. The logging railroads of Nevada were small. They joined logging camps and sawmills or linked the mills with a larger railroad so that the lumber could be transported to market.

The Virginia & Truckee Railroad (V.&T.R.R.) was the first and most famous of the major mining railroads. William Sharon and other businessmen representing the Bank of California built the V.&T.R.R., which eventually linked the mines of the Comstock Lode with the transcontinental railroad at Reno. Because the Bank controlled many mines, its directors wanted to reduce freight rates charged by the teamsters who hauled goods by wagon.

Construction began in February, 1869, on the first stretch of the rail line to connect Virginia City and Gold Hill with Carson City. The tracks were completed that November, and trains were running between Carson City and the Comstock in December. In 1871, the Virginia & Truckee Railroad's workmen started work to extend the railroad north to Reno. They completed the project in August, 1872.

In 1906, the V.&T.R.R. management built a spur line south to Minden. However, after 1924 the railroad became unprofitable. The tracks between Carson City and the Comstock were abandoned in 1939 and pulled up in 1941. In 1950, the railroad went out of business. Some of its old engines, cars, and equipment may be seen in the State Railroad Museum at Carson City. At Virginia City there is a short "sight-seeing" ride still operating on the old V.&T.R.R. line.

The other major mining railroads were the Eureka & Palisade Railroad (E.&P.R.R.), Nevada Central Railroad (N.C.R.R.), Carson & Colorado Railroad (C.&.C.R.R.), Tonopah & Goldfield Railroad (T.&G.R.R.), Las Vegas & Tonopah Railroad (L.V.&T.R.R.), Tonopah & Tidewater Railroad (T.&T.R.R.), and Nevada Northern Railroad (N.N.R.R.). There were also a number of minor lines which joined mines and mills or provided short access to a larger railroad.

General Freight Lines

There were two large railroads that hauled general loads of freight for long-distance shipment and were not primarily dependent upon mining communities. These were the

Streetcars over the Truckee. A Reno municipal railroad car makes its way across the Virginia Street bridge over the Truckee River. The old Riverside Hotel and the Washoe County Courthouse are in the background.

Courtesy of Nevada Historical Society

Oregon Short Line and the Nevada, California & Oregon Railroads.

The Nevada, California & Oregon Railroad (N.C.&O.R.R.) linked the ranching communities of southern Oregon and northeastern California with the transcontinental railroad at Reno. Although construction began in 1881 from Reno, progress was very slow, and the railroad did not reach its northern terminus at Lakeview, Oregon, until 1912. A portion of the line was sold to the Western Pacific Railroad, and in 1926, the Southern Pacific bought the remainder. Both companies still operate trains over sections of the old N.C.&O.R.R. line.

The Oregon Short Line, also known as the Idaho Central Railroad, was the last major railroad to be built in Nevada. The Oregon Short Line was a subsidiary company of the Union Pacific Railroad. It connected southern Idaho's ranching communities with the transcontinental railroad at Wells, Nevada. Construction began in 1907, but work stopped in 1910, before the tracks got out of Idaho. In 1924, the Union Pacific resumed track-laying activities and reached Wells at the beginning of 1926.

Municipal Railroads

The cities of Austin and Reno also had their own railroads, or municipal streetcar lines, but these became unprofitable and went out of business. Austin's system operated between 1880 and 1889 and Reno's system between 1904 and 1927.

TRANSPORTATION COMMUNITIES

Many of Nevada's communities began as way stations on the old overland roads. These include Genoa, Nevada's first settlement, and Carson City, which were both founded in 1851. Among other stations, Las Vegas and Dayton started in 1852. Fallon began as nearby Ragtown in 1854, and Elko was established that same year. Lovelock dates from 1855 and 1861 stations near the Humboldt Sink. Winnemucca began as a station in 1861, as did Battle Mountain after 1866. Other towns which got their start as road wayside stations on well-traveled routes are Wellington (1861), Glenbrook (1861), Yerington (1869), and Gardnerville (1878).

Many other towns began or grew as railroad stations. The Central Pacific and the Carson & Colorado Railroads were especially active in founding new communities. The

C.P.R.R. started the towns of Reno, Wadsworth, and Carlin (1868), and Verdi, Elko, and Wells (1869). The C.P.R.R. set up another of its stations at Palisade in 1870, and the railroad company also established the City of Sparks in 1904. The C.&C.R.R. founded Luning, Hawthorne and Wabuska in 1881, while the Virginia & Truckee Railroad was responsible for putting Mound House (1869) and Minden (1906) on the map.

All of these transportation communities have interesting stories behind them. Only a few may be discussed here, unfortunately, and many informative tales about Nevada's towns remain to be told.

Battle Mountain

Battle Mountain got its name from a fight which took place during the summer of 1857, between Indians and a band of overland emigrants under the leadership of a man named Pierson. The town, located just off the California Trail near Copper Basin Spring, began as a mining camp in 1866. After the Central Pacific Railroad was built along the Humboldt River in 1868, Battle Mountain became a station. The town became a shipping point for supplies to Austin and later to Tuscarora.

The freighting traffic to Austin was so lively that in 1880–81, the Nevada Central Railroad was constructed to link that mining town with Battle Mountain. The branch railroad's round house and machine shops were located in Battle Mountain, which increased the area's prosperity. By 1881, the shipping from Battle Mountain was considerable. Myron Angel, in the *History of Nevada,* gave a description of the town at that time:

> For forty miles each way, north and south, the country is supplied from Battle Mountain, creating a trade of about $10,000 per month. The business of the town is represented by the following establishments: Two general merchandise stores, one clothing store, a livery stable, brewery, five saloons, three hotels, one tin shop, one blacksmith shop and wagon repair shop, salt works, one harness and shoe shop, two newspapers, post-office, express office, a school house, the railroad depot and sixty dwellings make up the remainder of the place.

Battle Mountain was also a shipping point for the cattle ranches in the area. Its position as a shipping point was strengthened by the construction of the transcon-

Mixed Train from Battle Mountain, 1884. A narrow-gauge locomotive of the Nevada Central Railroad is shown pulling out of town for Austin, past cattle, mail, and flat cars. The N.C.R.R. connected the Austin mines with the transcontinental railroad at Battle Mountain, where the N.C.R.R. had its shops and enginehouse. The railroad, completed in 1880, operated until 1938.

tinental Western Pacific Railroad through North Battle Mountain in 1907, and also by construction of the Victory motor highway, which later became U.S. Interstate 80.

Today the area is a center for ranching and tourism, as well as a transportation community. It has been the center of government since 1980, when the officials of Lander County moved the county seat there from Austin.

Elko

The City of Elko was originally planned by officials of the Central Pacific Railroad to serve as a station for freight and passengers moving through northeastern Nevada. The lots were laid out in December, 1868, even before the tracks were built through to the site. The location was selected by businessmen looking for a convenient terminus for a toll road which they intended to build to the mines of Hamilton in White Pine County.

The C.P.R.R. put the first lots up for sale on January 15, 1869, and a little settlement quickly grew up around the railroad station. That March, the State Legislature created Elko County and made Elko the seat of the County's government. By July, the town had a vigilance committee to maintain order in the streets, as the Elko *Independent's* local correspondent noted:

> It has been quite fashionable of late for gentlemen of the blow-the-top-of-your-head-off order who carry concealed weapons to draw their pistols on the slightest provocation thereby endangering the lives of peaceable citizens. Several shots have been fired recently in the town, all accidental of course, by parties hastily drawing their pistols to resent imaginary insult fortunately without resulting in serious injury to life or property. It appears some of our citizens are determined to put a stop to this shooting business. The following notices, copies of which are wirtten in red ink, are posted conspicuously about the town.
>
> NOTICE: Shooting has ceased to be a virtue and certain men are marked. They are requested to behave themselves or leave town; otherwise abide the consequences.
>
> Signed Citizens Committee.

Elko got an opera house and a church in the first year of its existence. The town prospered, chiefly because of the freighting business located there. Wagons hauled supplies from the railroad freight depots north to the mines of southern Idaho and the Cope Mining District, southwest to the Railroad or Bullion Mining District, and south to the mining towns of White Pine County. The University of Nevada, located at Elko between 1874 and 1885, added to the cultural life of the community.

Although the mines went out of production by the end of the nineteenth century, Elko survived as a town because it was the principal shipping point for the County's very sizeable livestock industry. The construction of the Western Pacific Railroad started an economic revival at Elko in 1907. That year the town formed a Chamber of Commerce

"The Town of Elko, Nevada, on the Humboldt Desert." This 1877 view from the Central Pacific Railroad station was made by an artist for Frank Leslie's Illustrated Weekly *magazine.*

to encourage business and prosperity in northeastern Nevada. Considerable improvements followed. Electricity came to Elko in 1913, and the town got a public municipal water system in 1917.

Elko also benefitted from the road improvements of the Nevada Department of Highways, aided by the U. S. government. The town was situated on Nevada Route #1 — the State's first auto road, designated in 1913 — which was later improved as the Victory Highway, and then U. S. Highway 40. It is now called U. S. Interstate 80. Still on the main transcontinental route today, Elko's prosperity is due to transportation, with its revenues from trucking, tourism, and railroad shipping.

Winnemucca

In 1858, Alex Chauvin built a station for the newly-started transcontinental stagecoach mail service between Sacramento and Salt Lake City. He located the station at a ford on the big bend of the Humboldt River on the California Trail. By 1861, the ford was owned by Joseph Ginaca, who established a ferry there during the floods of 1862.

The discovery of silver at Humboldt City, Unionville, and Star City resulted in an increase in freighting traffic to the mines along the overland road. When one of Ginaca's competitors built a toll bridge over the Humboldt River in 1863, Ginaca responded by building one of his own in 1865. Freighting became even more lively with the discovery of rich silver ore in southern Idaho. What was at first a pack route for mule trains to Boise, Idaho, was improved into a wagon road in 1866. The Unionville *Humboldt Register*'s editor had a talk with Frank Baud, one of the toll bridge owners, in November of 1867 and published an article on the town:

> Frank Baud was in town last Wednesday, and reports business flourishing at Winnemucca. New and substantial buildings are going up, and all branches of business are rapidly increasing. On the mines work is progressing, with most excellent prospects ahead.

Winnemucca, 1868. The Humboldt County seat as it looked in the early years of settlement, before the railroad came to town.

Courtesy of Nevada Historical Society

> This town has superior advantages, being centrally located on the Humboldt river, in the vicinity of rich mines, as well as in a fine surrounding agricultural country. The French Company's new mill will soon be ready to run. Blossom & Wise are erecting buildings for an extensive livery business. . . .
>
> Before many months the locomotive will sound its shrill whistle in Winnemucca, when passengers will leave the cars and take coaches for the Gold Run mines in one direction, to Paradise Valley and through to Idaho in another. Mr. Baud informs us that the travel has been large during the past few months. He is now beginning to realize the spirit of his former dreams of wealth, and is happy.

The newspaper article was correct in anticipating the arrival of the railroad. When the tracks of the Central Pacific reached Winnemucca in September of 1868, the community increased substantially in size. Freighting from the town also increased, with wagons hauling goods as far as Idaho, Reese River, Unionville, and Star City. The location of the C.P.R.R.'s machine shops and railroad yards at Winnemucca also added to the local economy.

Although the freighting business dwindled towards the end of the nineteenth century, as the outlying mines ceased production, the town maintained its importance as a shipping point for cattle raised in Paradise Valley and elsewhere. Freighting revived after the discovery of silver at Tonopah in 1900. Soon afterwards, other mines were discovered all over the State. A number of them were in Humboldt County or nearby, and for the next twenty years, hauling cargo to the newly discovered mines was a profitable activity.

Like Elko, Winnemucca also prospered from its location on one of the main transcontinental routes. It too was on the C.P.R.R. and Nevada Route #1, later the Victory Highway, U. S. Highway 40, and U. S. Interstate 80. Freighting by truck is still a large part of Winnemucca's economy, as is tourism and railroad shipping. All of this comes from Winnemucca's being situated at a heavily traveled crossroads.

Las Vegas

The City of Las Vegas owes its existence and success to transportation. The place was originally a stopping point on the Spanish Trail called Las Vegas Springs, where men, horses, mules, and oxen could rest and find water. Travelers liked to stop at Las Vegas because it was at the edge of a fifty-five mile wide desert that had to be crossed to reach Los Angeles to the southwest, Salt Lake City to the northeast, and Santa Fe to the southeast. This desert stretch of the road between Las Vegas Springs and the Muddy River was called *jornada de muerto* or the "journey of death." In December, 1852, a station was built near Las Vegas Springs. It was part of the winter transcontinental mail route between Salt Lake City and Los Angeles known as the Mormon Trail. In April, 1854, this service was increased to a permanent monthly mail delivery to San Diego, by way of San Bernardino, California, over the same road.

Then, in April of 1855, Brigham Young, the Territorial Governor of Utah and head of the LDS or Mormon Church, announced that Las Vegas Valley would be settled by an agricultural colony. The first settlers arrived in the summer and immediately planted corn and other produce around Las Vegas Springs. The colonists established a fort and a post office, called Bringhurst, in January of 1856. Three months later they discovered large deposits of lead at Potosi, some twenty-seven miles southwest of the spring, and began mining there. However, for reasons covered in Chapter 4, the mission or colony was told to withdraw in February of 1857. By the end of the summer of 1858, the last settlers had left the valley.

Las Vegas remained a station on the Mormon Trail after the settlers withdrew. Freighting wagons were constantly moving along the road between Los Angeles and Salt Lake City. Only a few people lived in the area for the next forty-five years.

In 1904, the Union Pacific Railroad built its tracks south from Caliente across the *jornada de muerto* desert and reached Las Vegas on October 20. A considerable hauling business started immediately from the U.P.R.R. station at Las Vegas to the mines of Bullfrog and Rhyolite, where as many as fifty freighting wagons a day moved on the newly-constructed road.

By 1905, Las Vegas was on the main railroad line between Salt Lake City and Los

Angeles. The site was divided into lots and sold at auction on May 15 by U.P.R.R. officials. The city got electric power the next year. The U.P.R.R. aided the local economy by establishing its engine yards and machine shops at Las Vegas, and when the State Legislature created Clark County in 1909, Las Vegas became the center of that County's government. The town was incorporated in 1911.

The town also benefitted from the Arrowhead Highway, built roughly along the route of the Mormon Trail between 1914 and 1924. It linked Salt Lake City and Los Angeles and opened up Las Vegas to tourism.

The construction of Boulder Dam on the Colorado River also contributed to Las Vegas' economic prosperity. Authorized by Congress in 1928, the dam was built between 1931 and 1934 by the businessmen of Six Companies, Inc. It was a massive project that required immense amounts of material to complete, most of it hauled by truck from Las Vegas.

Immediately after World War II, large hotel-casinos began to open in Las Vegas, drawing tourists travelling by automobile and bus over the improved roads from southern California. The inexpensive electrical power provided by the hydroelectric generators of Boulder Dam allowed these hotel-casinos to make extensive use of air conditioning systems to cool the hot, dry climate of Las Vegas. It also provided the energy to light the desert night with the neon signs which made the city famous. For the first time, Las Vegas became a place to visit and not just a place people passed through to get somewhere else.

As a result, Las Vegas boomed and today is the largest and richest city in Nevada. It owes it all to transportation.

The Old Mormon Fort at Las Vegas Springs. This old fort, dating from 1855, was the first permanent building ever constructed in the place that was to grow into Las Vegas. The site became the Octavius D. Gass ranch, later owned by Archibald Stewart. Stewart sold eighteen hundred acres to Union Pacific Railroad interests, and the U.P.R.R. proceeded to build a transcontinental rail line through the property. Almost in passing, they founded Nevada's largest city.

*Las Vegas Townsite Auction. On the morning of May 15, 1905, U.P.R.R. attorney
C.O. Whittemore (with white suspenders) and auctioneer Ben E. Rhoades (standing, looking over
his shoulder at cameraman from platform) stood on a wooden stand under a canvas awning
to sell lots on the new townsite of Las Vegas to a crowd of businessmen and spectators. Most of the
lots were sold within the first two days.*

Courtesy of Doris V. Hancock Collection, University of Nevada Las Vegas Library

Reno

Reno, "the Biggest Little City in the World," was built between three way stations at the
intersection of the Truckee River section of the California Trail and the freighting roads
south to the Comstock Lode mines. H. H. Jameson is credited with having set up a
temporary station on the Truckee Meadows to trade with the overland emigrants in
1852. Another temporary trading post was established in 1854, and in 1857, a third
trading post began operating at a ford of the Truckee River where the California Trail
crossed the road to Honey Lake Valley. This station, later called Glendale, was the first
permanent building on the Truckee River. In 1860, the station keepers built a free
bridge over the river, and a little ranching settlement formed around the spot.

The second of the three way stations which became Reno was settled by Granville
Huffaker in 1858, as a cattle ranch. When the rush to the Comstock Lode began in the
summer of 1859, the freighting wagons coming over Donner Pass and from Honey Lake
Valley had to go past Huffaker's place, which soon became a stopping place for
travelers.

C. W. Fuller settled the last of the three stations when the rush to Virginia City and
Gold Hill began in 1859. The site he chose was a ford over the Truckee River, a little to
the north of the California Trail. This was an easier and shorter route between Honey
Lake Valley and the mines of the Comstock than the road which ran through Glendale.
Fuller built a bridge at the crossing in 1860 and sold it the next year to Myron Lake. The
State Legislature granted Lake a toll road and bridge franchise at the end of 1862. Lake's
toll road extended from the Truckee Meadows to the California State line, roughly along
the route of U. S. Highway 395.

All of these stations profited from the freighting activity through the area, but the
boom really started when the Central Pacific Railroad came into the valley in 1868. The
C.P.R.R. bought 160 acres from Lake for use as a townsite and auctioned off lots on May

*Lake's Crossing of the Truckee. Alongside Northern Paiute chief Winnemucca, Myron C. Lake
stands proudly in front of his hotel and toll bridge in June of 1862. The crossing,
shown in this painting by Nevada artist C. B. McClellan, was originally settled by C. W. Fuller
in 1859; it turned into a city nine years later, when Lake donated a townsite to the
C.P.R.R. which later became Reno.*

Courtesy of Special Collections, University of Nevada Reno Library

9, 1868. The city immediately became a center of teaming operations, especially south
to the Comstock. The nearness of the railroad to the mines at Virginia City and Gold Hill
redirected nearly all the freight going there through Reno. The more expensive wagon
route through Placerville and Genoa became much less heavily traveled as the goods
moved south from the railroad station on the Truckee Meadows to Virginia City, by way
of the Geiger Grade.

The substantial trade and high freight rates encouraged the construction of the
Virginia & Truckee Railroad through to Reno, linking the Comstock with the transcontinental railroad. The town prospered, and in 1871, the Washoe County seat moved
from Washoe City to Reno. The warehouses along Commercial Row were full of goods
destined for reshipment from Reno, and ranchers used the town as a shipping point for
livestock to San Francisco and Chicago.

In 1885, the Legislature moved the University of Nevada from Elko to Reno. This

*A late afternoon panoramic view of Commercial Row, Reno, about the turn of the century.
Passengers are crowded around the Southern Pacific Railroad depot, as the Overland Limited,
pulled by two coal-burning steam locomotives, prepares to travel west into the Sierra Nevada
for a scenic sunset ride. At one time four railroad lines operated to and from Reno,
which for some seventy years was the biggest city in Nevada.*

Courtesy of Nevada Historical Society

enhanced the cultural life of the town. For years Reno led the State in innovations — the first gas street lighting, the first electric street lighting, the first municipal telephone system, the first radio and television broadcasts — often because Reno was one of the first communities in Nevada to get to see and hear about the new ideas that traveled along with the freight shipments.

When automobile roads were being built, the first State highway ran through Reno, and the town profited from the construction. The freighting wagons, stagecoaches, and the V.&T.R.R. were replaced by motor cars and buses, but the people and supplies still moved through Reno. The city became a center of tourism during the 1920's and grew with the gaming industry after World War II. Its strategic location as a distribution center on the transportation net makes Reno the largest city in northern Nevada.

HIGHWAYS AND AIRWAYS

In 1903, the first transcontinental crossing of the United States by automobile took place, by way of Nevada, over old roads and wagon trails. As more and more people began to own automobiles, however, they began insisting on better roads. In 1913, ten years after the first transcontinental crossing, the Legislature enacted a motor vehicle licensing law requiring owners of automobiles to license them. The fees were set aside to help pay for roadbuilding and upkeep. At the same time, the State began to designate routes which were the most heavily traveled so that these could be improved first. In 1917, the Legislature created the State Department of Highways to perform this job, and in 1923, the State added to highway funds by enacting a gasoline tax, with the revenue to be used for roadbuilding and maintenance.

As the state improved its roads, automobiles, trucks, and buses began to replace buggies, wagons, and stagecoaches. The early automobile stages were large taxis,

Dining on the desert in Nye County, about 1910. These happy motorists munch refreshments in the open air near their capacious touring car, a White "steamer." Ten years earlier, this quartet would have trotted out to the same site in an even more dusty, horse-drawn buckboard wagon.

Courtesy of Nevada Historical Society

Auto Stage for Buckhorn, 1913. By the time this photograph was taken, auto stages had replaced the stagecoach in most parts of the State. Passengers for the Buckhorn diggings got off the train at Palisade and then spent two hours in an open touring car, having forty miles of bad roads, heat, dust, and wind to reach their destination. The one-way fare was $10.

Courtesy of Nevada Historical Society

Bicyclists at Cherry Creek. Men, women and children lined up to be photographed with their bicycles on the wooden sidewalks of the White Pine County mining camp of Cherry Creek, about 1908. Bicycles were first brought to Nevada in 1869, and were originally called velocipedes, while the people who rode the bicycles were known as wheelmen. Riders formed social clubs to take weekend trips through the countryside for fun and relaxation, just as they do today.

Courtesy of Nevada Historical Society

capable of traveling much faster than the stagecoaches. They were colorful, too, as this 1907 advertisement from the *Death Valley Chuck Walla* indicates:

> Go Automobiling in Death Valley with Alkali Bill. The Death Valley Chug Line. Runs cars daily from the Front on Borax Smith's railroad to Greenwater. Alkali Bill himself meets every train and whizzes you over the desert 45 miles by way of Death Valley and the famous Amargosa Canyon, past the borax tanks of 20 Mule Team fame to Greenwater in less than three hours. Better write ahead or wire your reservations if you have the time. Alkali Bill's Death Valley Chug Line, Greenwater, Inyo County, California.

The federal government contributed heavily to Nevada's roadbuilding after 1916, when Congress passed the Federal Aid Road Act (Bankhead-Shackleford Act). That act was amended in 1919 to aid states building rural roads. In 1921, Congress passed the Federal Highway or Phipps-Townsend Act, which provided financial assistance to states working toward the completion of a system of interstate highways.

More assistance came in 1928, when Congress passed the Oddie-Colton Highway Act. This provided for a sliding-scale increase in federal aid to states building interstate roads over the public domain. Tasker Oddie, ex-Governor and U.S. Senator from Nevada, helped sponsor that bill. The Oddie-Colton Forest Highway Act and the Public Domain Highway Act were also passed by Congress in 1930. All provided further federal assistance to state road building projects over the public lands.

By the 1920's, buses and trucks had become competitive with railroad lines, and within twenty years, most of the branch railroads went out of business. The locomotives were sold, and the rail lines abandoned or torn up for scrap. Travel by horse, mule, or ox team became almost unheard of as Nevada entered its modern period of transportation. Then Congress established the present interstate road system beginning in 1956, when it passed the National Defense Highway Act.

The most modern form of transportation is travel by air. The first aviation event in Nevada was an ascent by balloon from the Magnolia Saloon in Carson City during 1868,

Steamboats on the Colorado River. The steamer <u>Mohave</u>, shown here pulling away from the Southwestern Company mill in Eldorado Canyon, was one of many ships which carried supplies, cargo, and bullion on the Colorado River. Steamboats plied the water as far upriver as Callville, bearing freight which was then taken by wagon into Arizona. Later, the steamers served the mining camps of southern Nevada.

Courtesy of Nevada Historical Society

First Air Mail to Reno, September 11, 1926. Pilot J.P. Woodward and a proud reception committee hold the mail from Salt Lake City in this mid-day photograph, while two mechanics prepare the airplane's engine for take-off.
Courtesy of Nevada Historical Society

but the first airplane flight into the State didn't occur until 1910. It also took place near Carson City, where pilot Ivey Baldwin made a short summer flight at the old Raycraft ranch. The next year, between September 17 and November 5, 1911, C. P. Rogers made the first transcontinental airplane flight — actually a series of short flights from New York to Pasadena, California. The airplane pilots at first faced the same problem as did the pioneers: how to get over the mountains. This problem was solved on March 22, 1918, when the first flight over the Sierra Nevada arrived at Reno from Sacramento.

In the last few years, the National Championship Air Races have attracted many fliers and enthusiasts to Reno each fall. There are many private pilots in the State, and in at least one area, the Moorman Ranch near Ely, the owner uses his private plane to round up cattle on his immense acreage.

The federal government helped encourage commercial aviation by granting contracts for limited air mail service. The first flight to stop at Reno, piloted by Bert Acosta and World War I ace Captain Eddie Rickenbacker, arrived in 1920. Regular transcontinental air mail service began in 1926; an airplane flown by Leon Cuddeback for Varney (later United) Air Lines and carrying 64 pounds of mail made the first regular flight into Nevada, landing at Elko. That same year, Congress passed the Air Commerce Act, providing federal aid for commercial airlines and airports. Today, almost every aspect of aviation is controlled by the Federal Aviation Act and its administrative agencies. Air travel is very important for Nevada and opens up the State to tourists and goods brought in by air freight. Both Las Vegas and Reno have runways large enough to serve the largest airliners of the major airline companies.

CHAPTER 3

Mining

Mining is one of Nevada's most important industries. It is older than the recorded history of the State. Prehistoric Indians in southern Nevada mined salt, while in northern and western Nevada they mined flint and scinter for projectile points. In historic times, mining has been of even greater importance — it was one of the main reasons for people from all parts of the world to come into the State to live.

LORE OF THE MINES

Mining is a special world to itself, with its own language, challenges, and concepts. People are interested in it because it produces so much money and gives jobs to hundreds of thousands of persons all over the world. Valuable metals are found by prospecting — wandering the countryside looking for indications of rich ore. The people who look for the minerals or metallic ore are called prospectors. An assay is a chemical test which tells the value of the ore.

When prospectors "struck it rich," they were able to sell their claims, sometimes for large sums of money. More often, however, they discovered little or nothing in the way

Prospectors' Outfit, about 1905. Everything's ready to go as two shaggy "desert canaries" prepare to serve as beasts of burden, while determined prospectors survey the scene. The little cart carries their food, shelter, clothes, and tools, and in the background, the tents of Goldfield adorn the surrounding plain.

of profitable ore. In 1885, the editor of the Pioche *Record* wrote about prospecting and the people who looked for precious metals:

> A number of men keep running over the hill searching for the hidden treasure, and there is hardly a day that some one of them does not come into Pioche, with his samples of a "new find," and his hopes worked up to the highest pitch; but the returns from the assayer generally knocks all the great expectations of the poor prospector asunder, his wealth vanishes, the castles he erected in the air are blown away, and his aspirations to represent Nevada in the United States Senate is set aside till the near future, when he is bound to strike it big, and he leaves town disappointed, though his courage has not failed him.

Prospecting expeditions made most of the important ore discoveries in Nevada, but sometimes gold could be found by accident. Sam Davis, a newspaper editor and author of the *History of Nevada*, told the story of one such find from 1891 in a ballad:

'Twas a dreary day at Pine Nut, and gloom was everywhere.
There was sadness in the little camp and sorrow in the air.
A more doleful set of faces one would not care to see.
The day the boys laid out the corpse of poor old Bill Magee.

'Twas pneumonia or whiskey — they couldn't quite decide
That sent the fleeting soul of Bill across the Great Divide;
But with very little wrangling over life's extinguished lamp,
They arranged a mighty funeral to advertise the camp.

I know of places where a man who shuffles off his coil
Is pitched face down with boots-on in scarce a foot of soil;
But now the boys of Pine Nut said such things had had their day,
And they'd bury Bill with socks on, in a decent Christian way.

So they hired a Carson preacher, of noted funeral skill,
And agreed on forty dollars for some extra words for Bill.
There are some parsons in the land that'd go a little higher,
But this man was no grafter, but my own illustrious sire.

At two o'clock the coffin passed through Bill's cabin door,
With Otto Schulz and Joe Raycraft and Jackson at the fore,
Tony Kramer, with his goggles, helped to hold the coffin up,
Then followed tall Miles Johnson and his little brindle pup.

Pratt, with a Heitman flour sack sewed firmly on his pants;
Bill Peckham, Baldy Adams, Lew Stevenson, Old Nance;
And loomin' up ahead of all, the big long-bearded Zern,
All headin' toward the bourn from which none can return.

They finally reached the yawning grave beneath a spreading tree,
The parson told how pure had been the life of Bill Magee;
And as they heard the kindly things the clergyman had said,
They almost thought that angel's wings was sproutin' from the dead.

They let the coffin down with hands as steady as a clock's,
And then began to shovel in the gravel on the box,
When suddenly they stopped the work. Somebody hollered "'Whew!'"
And then a golden nugget came a-flashin' into view.

Joe Raycraft, straddlin' o'er the grave called out, "'I locate here;'"
And then Lew Stevenson gave Joe a swat upon the ear;
Next Johnson jumped aboard of Lew in a most decided way,
And then the savage brindle pup plunged headlong in the fray.

Then Baldy Adams pulled his gun, and Billy Peckham his,
And in 'bout a half a second the lead began to whiz.
For several humming minutes it was a fearful fray,
With all upon the ground before the smoke had cleared away.

The parson, when he heard the shots, whipped up his old gray mare,
To find the coroner and send that functionary there.
When that official reached the spot, immediately did he
Tack a location notice on the headstone of Magee;

Remarkin' to the wounded: "'I regret you can't agree.
I'll record these placer diggin's and consider it my fee.'"
And so before the sun was down the records were complete,
All in accordance with the law at Douglas county-seat.

And now the thrifty coroner, as many are aware,
Is livin' off that placer claim, a multi-millionaire,
While the parson oft has mentioned, confidentially to me,
From that eventful day to this he never got his fee.

Once the ore is located, the prospector must stake his claim by measuring the area he wants to mine and then record the measurement or survey with the local government. This protects him from other people stealing his discovery or "jumping his claim." The ore must then be mined. There are three types of mining operations: placer mining, strip or open pit mining, and tunnel mining. All three may be found in Nevada. Each is described in this chapter.

After the ore has been dug out of the ground, the commercially valuable part must be separated from the worthless rock. This procedure is called milling or refining and is performed in a reduction mill, smelter, or refinery. The first mills in Nevada originally received their power from water wheels or steam engines, but modern mills and refineries are powered by electricity and reduce the ores by chemical processes.

Because mining requires skilled workers and expensive equipment, it costs a great deal to run a mine. Most mines are operated by corporations in which many people buy stock to finance the enterprise.

Basic Magnesium, Inc. facilities at Henderson. This aerial view shows just a part of the sprawling plant which created a populous Clark County community in 1941. A large supply of ore from Nye County and inexpensive electrical power from Boulder Dam made the City's success possible.

Courtesy of Special Collections, University of Nevada Las Vegas Library

"He Came, He Saw, He Stuck." The Wonder Boosters—a group of local businessmen—made their point about reality and myth in the mining camps of the early twentieth century in this cartoon postcard. The Churchill County settlement flourished between 1906 and 1919.

Boom and Bust at Rhyolite. These pictures graphically illustrate the difference between bonanza and borrasca in a mining town. When the mines stopped producing, the inhabitants departed, leaving a ghost town, as in these Nye County photographs. Rhyolite began in 1905; by 1920 it was abandoned, leaving only ruins. Around the decay, the lone and level sands stretch far away.

Courtesy of Nevada Historical Society

The most important metals and minerals mined in Nevada are gold, silver, copper, lead, and rare earths. So much silver was discovered in Nevada that it was nicknamed "the Silver State." Of the various metals, gold, silver, and copper were originally used to make coins for the United States government, although no gold or silver and very little copper are used by our government today. The government stopped minting gold coins in 1933, discontinued making silver coins in 1970, and reduced the copper content of the penny in 1983. These metals are currently used for jewelry and in manufacturing. Lead and the rare earths also have industrial uses, like strengthening steel used in building jet aircraft.

Where gold and silver were involved, most mining operations had a similar history. After the first rich discovery, there was a "rush" of people to get to the mines. Then there usually was a period of turbulence in the new camp, with housing shortages, fights, claim-jumping, and lawsuits. If the mines were extensive, the workmen in the mines would try to fix their wages with threats to the mining companies of strikes and labor disorder. As the ore bodies of the mines began to give out, people would desert the communities, leaving "ghost towns."

THE COMSTOCK LODE

The tale of the discovery of the Comstock Lode in Storey County shows many different aspects of mining. Between the time of its discovery in 1859 and its decline beginning in 1879, the mines of the Comstock Lode were internationally famous for their richness and for the advances in mining technology which they produced. During that period more than $500,000,000 in gold and silver were taken from the Lode. But this was not the first find of gold and silver in Nevada, nor was it the last.

Gold Canyon

The overland emigrants were the first people to discover gold and silver in Nevada. The earliest known finds date from 1849. In 1850, a number of emigrants found gold nuggets where the California Trail along the Carson River passed by a canyon — Gold Canyon. John Orr, who gave the canyon its name, was one of the lucky ones. During the summer of 1850, he was camped along the Carson River with his partner Nick Kelly. Thirty years

Elements of Placer Mining. The miner in the left foreground is panning gravel and sand from the stream. Behind him, in the right foreground, workmen are "fielding" or dumping ore-bearing gravel into a "long Tom." In the center, two burly miners are winching up rich ore from a shallow shaft or "coyote hole." In the background, the man on the left is washing ore in a "cradle," while miners tunnel into a hill. Other workmen are operating a flume and sluice in the distance.

later, Orr described his experiences to a newspaper reporter writing for the San Francisco *Alta California:*

> Kelly and Orr went up the canyon until a little fork was reached, when work was begun. The party had few tools, and Orr had nothing but a butcher knife.
> While Kelly was working, Orr noticed a very narrow place at the fork, where the water barely covered a slab of slate rock. Idly he examined it, and noticing a small crevice near the edge, drove the butcher-knife into it, breaking out a piece. The water running over it washed away the underlying dirt, and in a few seconds Orr discovered a golden nugget where the rock had covered. It was quickly removed and found to weigh $8.25. Prospecting was continued, and though gold dust was found in several places throughout the canyon, Orr's was the only nugget found. The party lacked tools and provisions, and being bent on reaching California, abandoned the canyon and arrived at Leek Springs July 4th, 1850.

At least one man spent the winter of 1850–51 at the diggings. John Reese saw this man mining in June, 1851, when he arrived with his company of traders at Mormon Station: "Not a single white man was there [in Carson Valley] then. The nearest white man was a man in Gold Canyon who had a trading post there before and he wintered in a kind of small dug-out. . . . His tent was on the side of the hill, half underground, covered over with rags or any old stuff."

Over 100 men worked the gravel of Gold Canyon during the autumn of 1851. A colony of prospectors spent the winter of 1851–52 there, joining the solitary miner of the year before. Among these was one of Reese's employees, a teamster named "Old Virginia" Fennimore. In the spring of 1852, two men named Loomis and Haskell started a trading post at the mouth of Gold Canyon for local miners and overland emigrants on the Carson River section of the California Trail. The place later became the town of Dayton.

On December 31, 1853, the camp of miners celebrated by holding the first social dance in Nevada at the little station. At that time, there were only four white women in the State, and all of them attended the party.

The miners of Gold Canyon used the placer mining method rather than digging tunnels. The gravel and sand bars in the canyon contained coarse lumps of gold. When miners caught the gravel in small pans and washed the dirt with water, the heavier gold stayed in the pan while the lighter sand and rock spilled out. The miners carefully collected the small coarse bits of gold ounce by ounce. Soon the miners began working the gravel on a larger scale, sifting hundreds of pounds of dirt through screens or "rockers" to remove the larger rocks. It was then washed with water through a long narrow box called a "long tom." The box had small ridges along the bottom to catch the heavier particles of gold moving with the water through the wooden contraption.

These new, improved methods of mining produced much more gold than the old time-consuming process of panning. Miners formed work gangs or mining companies to extract the ore. The "long toms" or sluices needed water to operate in the dry canyon, which meant that water ditches had to be dug.

A need for laborers in the Gold Canyon placer diggings brought the first Chinese to Nevada. They came in large numbers during the summer of 1856, to build a water ditch for Jacob Rose, after whom Mount Rose is named. The Chinese workers lived in a camp of their own near Dayton.

Eliot Lord, in his book *Comstock Mining and Miners,* described life in the first mining settlement at Gold Canyon:

> Few occupations are more monotonous and colorless than the work of a scattered colony of placer miners along the line of a creek. The Gold Canyon miners toiled in the usual way with long toms and rockers, washing the sand from the various bars, and when the richest placers were exhausted, carrying sacks and buckets of earth from the neighboring ravines to the nearest spring or to the creek itself. At nightfall they would return to their huts, cook their simple suppers of bacon and potatoes, with bread and tea, smoke a pipe or two, and then wrap themselves up in their blankets to sleep until daybreak. In summer most of the huts were merely heaps of brush, rather inferior to the Pah-Ute lodges. The winter cabins were usually of rough stones, plastered with mud and covered with canvas, boards, or sticks, overlaid with earth. Sometimes holes

Gold Canyon Placer Mining. Sluice boxes and gravel bars adorn the foreground of this photograph from the 1880's, while onlooking placer miners consider the prospects of getting rich by working the place. Placer mining was hard work, but if the ore was rich, miners could make quite a bit of money.

Courtesy of Nevada Historical Society

were made in the walls for ventilation, but generally the cracks and open doorways were sufficient. Glass windows were an unthought-of luxury.

In January, 1858, the miners formed their own government to regulate mining claims and maintain order in the area around Gold Canyon. The area ruled by the miners was called the Columbia Mining District – the first quartz mining district ever formed in the Great Basin.

At this time, the miners were experiencing hard times. The placer bars of Gold Canyon were starting to give out — less and less gold was being found. Prospectors continued to search for the precious metal further up the Canyon, but the gold there was mixed with a heavy clay and was difficult to work.

One of the miners wandering up toward Mount Davidson was "Old Virginia" Fennimore. On January 28, 1859, Fennimore, Henry T. P. Comstock, and several other miners discovered a rich vein of gold and silver-bearing quartz at the head of Gold Canyon. John Bishop, who was with the prospecting party, described the discovery in Dan DeQuille's *The Big Bonanza:*

> Where Gold Hill now stands, I had noticed indications of a ledge and had got a little color. I spoke to "Old Virginia" about it, and he remembered the locality, for he said he had often seen the place when hunting deer and antelope. He also said that he had seen any quantity of quartz there. So he joined our party and Comstock also followed along. When we got to the ground, I took a pan and filled it with dirt, with my foot, for I had no shovel or spade. The others did the same thing, though I believe that some of them had shovels. I noticed some willows growing on the hillside and I started for them with my pan. The place looked like an Indian spring, which it proved to be.
>
> I began washing my pan. When I had finished, I found that I had in it about fifteen cents worth of gold. None of the others had less than eight cents, and none more than fifteen. It was very fine gold; just as fine as flour. Old Virginia decided that it was a good place to locate and work.

The next difficulty was to obtain water. We followed the canyon along for some distance and found what appeared to be the same formation all the way along. Presently Old Virginia and another man who had been rambling away, came back and said they had found any amount of water which could be brought right there to the ground. . . .

After we had measured the ground we had a consultation as to what name was to be given the place. It was decidedly not Gold Canyon, for it was a little hill; so we concluded to call it Gold Hill. That is how the place came by its present name.

About six months later, in June of 1859, Peter O'Riley and Pat McLaughlin were digging a hole not far from Fennimore's claim, to store water from a stream they were using to wash their ore. About four feet into the pit the two men struck a bed of blackish-colored sand different from the yellow clay and gravel they had been digging. Eliot Lord described what happened next:

Simply as an experiment they concluded to wash a little of the sand in their rocker, though they had slight hope that it would yield any return. From the trench sand they had been getting only a few specks of gold dust, but when the new earth had been shaken in the rocker and the muddy water had drained away they saw the bottom of the cradle covered with glittering dust. Overjoyed at their good fortune they began to wash hastily the precious earth, and again and again swept up a golden layer. The dust was of a pale yellow color, and the miners supposed that it was alloyed with some base metal, but it was unmistakeably gold, and even with their rude cradle they were fast making a fortune.

H. T. P. Comstock, who was with "Old Virginia" Fennimore when Gold Hill was discovered, also claimed the ground where O'Riley and McLaughlin were mining. To avoid trouble, they gave Comstock and his partner Emanuel Penrod a share in the mine, which they named the Ophir. The lode which O'Riley and McLaughlin discovered was

"Be It Ever So Humble." During 1903-4, dugouts like these were home to many Goldfield residents. Housing problems were characteristic of Nevada boom towns.

Courtesy of Nevada Historical Society

Discovery of the Comstock Lode, June, 1859. This sedate painting by James Harrington, showing H.T.P. Comstock at left, does little to convey the dramatic excitement which gripped the Pacific Coast after Patrick McLaughlin and Peter O'Riley's find of fabulously rich silver and gold deposits in what is now Storey County.

Henry Thomas Paige Comstock, the man for whom the Comstock Lode was undeservedly named. He sold out early, drifted through Idaho and Montana looking for another Comstock Lode, and died a suicide.

From *The Big Bonanza* by Dan DeQuille

named after Comstock, in much the same way that America was named for Amerigo Vespucci rather than Christopher Columbus.

Camps of miners quickly appeared at Gold Hill and at Virginia City, the site of the Ophir mine. In a letter to the St. Louis *Republican,* Comstock himself described how the Storey County seat was named:

> Virginia City was first called Silver City. I named it at the time I gave the Ophir claim its name. Old Virginia and the other boys got on a drunk one night there, and old Virginia fell down and broke his bottle, and when he got up he said he baptized that ground Virginia — hence Virginia City — and that is the way it got its name. At that time there were a few tents, a few little huts, and a grog-shop; that was all there was. I was camped under a cedar-tree at that time — I and my party.

Rush to Washoe

The discovery of the new gold deposits revived interest in the Gold Canyon area, but the miners on the slopes of Mount Davidson did not know the true value of their find. All this changed within a few weeks, when the "Rush to Washoe" began. Dan DeQuille, who was a local newspaper reporter that year, recalled the excitement in *The Big Bonanza:*

> About the 1st of July 1859 Augustus Harrison, a ranchman living on the Truckee Meadows, visited the new diggings about which so much was then said. . . . He took a piece of the ore to Grass Valley, Nevada County. . . . The ore was assayed and yielded at the rate of several thousand dollars per ton, in gold and silver.
>
> All were astonished and not a little excited when it was ascertained that the black-looking rock which the miners over in Washoe — as the region about the Comstock lode was called — considered worthless and were throwing away was almost a solid mass of silver. The excitement by no means abated when they were informed by Mr. Harrison that there were tons and tons of the same stuff in sight in the opening that the Ophir Company had already made in the lead. It was agreed among the few who knew the result of the assay that the matter should, for the time being, be kept a profound secret; meantime they would arrange to cross the Sierras and secure as much ground as possible on the line of the newly discovered silver lode.

BOUND FOR WASHOE   D—N WASHOE

"Bound for Washoe" and "D--n Washoe." These 1876 illustrations from Dan DeQuille's
<u>The Big Bonanza</u> *show that many were called but few were chosen to make large sums of money in a mining boom — even the boom that opened Nevada to settlement.*

But each man had intimate friends in whom he had the utmost confidence in every respect, and these bosom friends soon knew that a silver mine of wonderful richness had been discovered over in the Washoe country. These again had their friends, and, although the result of the assay made by Mr. Atwood was not ascertained until late at night, by nine o'clock the next morning half the town of Grass Valley knew the wonderful news.

Judge Walsh and Joe Woodworth packed a mule with provisions and, mounting horses, were off for the eastern slope of the Sierras at a very early hour in the morning. This was soon known, and the news of the discovery and their departure ran like wildfire through Nevada County. In a few days hundreds of miners had left their diggings in California and were flocking over the mountains on horseback, on foot, with teams, and in any way that offered. Many men packed donkeys with tools and provisions and, going on foot themselves, trudged over the Sierras at the best speed they were able to make.

The new mines yielded the first silver ever discovered in the United States. They produced hundreds of millions of dollars worth of ore. None of the discoverers got rich, however. Comstock sold his interest in the Ophir mine for $10,000, which he used to buy stores in Carson City and Silver City. He went broke, became a prospector in Idaho and Montana, and then committed suicide in September, 1870, near Bozeman, Montana. McLaughlin sold his interest in the claim for $3,500, which he soon lost. Within a few years, he was working as a cook for a gang of men for $40 a month. He died a pauper and was buried at public expense. Penrod parted with his section of the mine for $8,500 and soon spent all the money. He was more fortunate than the rest. He later became a prospector in Elko County and served as an Assemblyman in the State Legislature. "Old Virginia" Fennimore sold his share for an old horse, a pair of blankets, and a bottle of whiskey. He died at Dayton in 1861 when, after getting drunk, he tried to ride a bucking mustang. The horse threw and dragged Fennimore, killing him. O'Riley held his interest long enough to sell it for $50,000, which he then lost on the stock market. He went back

"The Gold Diggings of 1859." Busy miners and new structures crowd this illustration of activity on the Comstock Lode. Flumes, rockers, and pans abound in this scene of hard work during a beautiful day, in the first year of the "Rush to Washoe."

From The Big Bonanza by Dan DeQuille

"Song of the Honest Miner." This sad story of discovery, dissipation, and death happened often enough to provide any number of stories and ballads about the evil effects of alcohol and cards.

From *The Big Bonanza* by Dan DeQuille

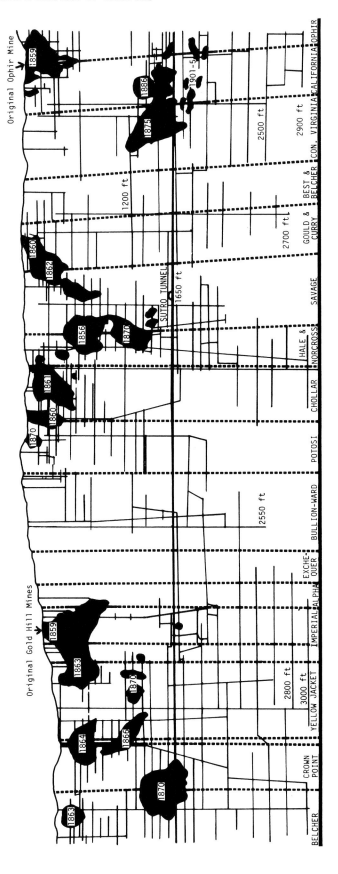

"Vertical Section of the Comstock Lode." The solid black areas show the deposits of rich ore, with the year in which they were discovered. The solid lines show major shafts and tunnels, while the vertical dotted lines indicate mine boundaries. Note how many of the mines never struck a rich ore body at all.

to prospecting again, almost died in a cave-in, and went insane. He never recovered, and later passed away in a mental hospital in California.

Once the rush was on, miners immediately began to dig all around the Comstock Lode, locating thousands of claims in the area. There were violent fights and lawsuits over who owned the rich claims.

Many of the lawsuits were caused by the poor recordkeeping of the miners, as Dan DeQuille described:

> V. A. Houseworth, the "village blacksmith," was the first recorder at Gold Hill, and the book of records was kept at a saloon, where it lay upon a shelf behind the bar.
>
> The 'boys' were in the habit of taking it from behind the bar whenever they desired to consult it, and if they thought a location made by them was not advantageously bounded, they altered the course of their lines and fixed the whole thing up in good shape, in accordance with the latest developments.
>
> When the book was not wanted for this use, those lounging about the saloon were in the habit of snatching it up and batting each other over the head with it.

The search for valuable ore is difficult, even on the surface of the earth where the prospector can see and test an outcropping to find out whether mining it would pay. The job of discovering valuable ore underground is often even more tricky. On the Comstock Lode, for example, many companies dug mines which produced nothing, while other companies extracted fabulous sums of gold and silver. The reason for this was the geology of the Comstock Lode, explained by DeQuille:

> Some have compared the vein-matter of the lode to a great pudding into which has been stirred raisins, currants and plums; sometimes you find a currant, sometimes a raisin, and sometimes a plum, while again you are blessed with nothing better than the matter of which the mass of the pudding is composed.

This is clearly shown in a vertical section of the Comstock Lode, which illustrates the principal mines and ore bodies.

Hazards of Underground Mining

The miners at Gold Hill and on the Ophir claim at Virginia City began to have difficulty getting their ore out of the ground because the gold and silver vein was very wide and deep. When the minerals were dug out, great caverns were left under the ground. Cave-ins, which killed and injured the workmen, were caused by the collapse of wooden timbers supporting the earth over the tunnels. No one knew what to do about it until Philipp Deidesheimer, the superintendent of the Ophir, invented a system of "square-set timbering" in 1860, which allowed underground mining on a scale much greater than ever before. The mining companies then hired more and more miners to dig tunnels and shafts following the veins. In turn, this made mining much more profitable, as well as much more expensive. Soon, large corporations were formed to finance the mining operations. At San Francisco, brokers sold shares of stock in the mining corporations to the public to raise the money to dig the mines, with the shareholders expecting to share in the profits.

If the miners who worked for the mining corporation struck a rich pocket of gold or silver ore, called a bonanza, the value of the corporation's stock went up. If the mine was unsuccessful or uneconomical, a condition known as a borrasca, the shares of the corporation would go down in value, and the company might even have to go out of business. Many fortunes were made and lost on the Pacific Coast by people who speculated or gambled on the value of these mining stocks. As Dan DeQuille noted in *The Big Bonanza:* "Among miners, 'borrasca' is suggestive of long faces, sad hearts, and empty pockets, while 'bonanza' shows us faces wreathed in smiles, hearts that are merry, and purses that are plethoric."

As the mines were dug deeper in search of the elusive pockets of gold and silver, the miners faced another challenge: the heat. The temperature of the rock at twenty-two hundred feet beneath the surface was 120 degrees fahrenheit, and the mines eventually were dug to a depth of more than three thousand feet. At times the air was as hot as 140

"Cave-in of the Mexican." This 1863 J. Ross Browne drawing shows the kind of hair-raising incident that was common in the Comstock mines until the invention of square-set timbering.

From *A Peep at Washoe and Washoe Revisited* by J. Ross Browne

"Mining on the Comstock." This 1876 illustration provides an education in nineteenth-century mining technology. The square-set method of timbering, the size of the bonanza ore bodies, the system of shafts and tunnels, with elevators and ventilation shafts, as well as the tools of the miner are all clearly shown.

Digging the Tunnel. In this view of the miners digging in a stope, the square-set method of timbering protects the crew. While workmen drive their picks into the ore, others sort the rocks and operate a hoist.

Phillip Diedesheimer, the mining engineer whose invention of square-set timbering in 1860 made it possible to mine the extraordinary ore deposits of the Comstock Lode.

The Silver Miners. Stripped to the waist, these brawny workingmen of the nineteenth century are going on shift in the intense heat of the lower levels of the mines of the Comstock Lode.

Courtesy of Nevada Historical Society

"The 'Man at the Wheel' Operating the Shaft Elevator." This 1877 drawing by an artist for Frank Leslie's expedition shows the huge machinery necessary to mine the Comstock Lode.

From *Out West on the Overland Train* by Richard Reinhardt

"New York Speculators." This 1863 sketch by J. Ross Browne shows a scene common to most mining ventures, ancient and modern. The excited but impoverished miners are showing speculators—men with money to risk or speculate—just how wealthy they can become by investing in the *Great Excelsior Silver Mining Co.* From *Adventures in the Apache Country* by J. Ross Browne

A Little Difficulty with Disappointed Speculators [about 1875]. A San Francisco stock broker faces the wrath and revolvers of shareholders unhappy with their disastrous loss based on his advice. Many fortunes were won or lost in mining stock investments on the San Francisco Stock Exchange.

*Adolph Heinrich Sutro (1830-1898)
of Prussia, builder of the Sutro Tunnel,
came to Nevada with the original "Rush
to Washoe" and made a fantastic profit on his
world-famous tunnel. This publicity shot
shows the hard-working Sutro in shirtsleeves,
swinging a pick and encouraging investors to get
his tunnel project started.*

Courtesy of Nevada Historical Society

*The Sutro Tunnel, about 1889. This Lyon County structure was one of the most spectacular
engineering achievements of its day.*

Courtesy of Special Collections, University of Nevada Reno Library

degrees, and occasionally super-heated water leaked into the tunnels, emitting dense clouds of steam and gas. Huge blowers ventilated the mines, and in the hellish depths the miners ate ice — ninety-five pounds a man per day in 1878 — to keep cool. The work shifts were cut to just one-half hour and then to fifteen minutes. Only the introduction of power rock drills allowed the mining to go forward.

Water was another serious problem for the Comstock miners. Subterranean pools of water flooded the mines, delaying production and costing hundreds of thousands of dollars to drain. On January 18, 1863, a miner in the Ophir tunnel carelessly drove his pick through a clay seam 313 feet beneath the surface. A stream of water broke through the wall and turned into a torrent, forcing the miners to drop their equipment and flee for their lives. Within two days, a lake twenty-one feet deep, thirty feet wide, and one hundred feet long formed in the mineshaft. The miners used all their available pumps to drain the mine, but these could only keep the lake in check and not reduce its size. Five months later the stream of water was still flowing into the tunnel.

When the Ophir Company finished draining that underground reservoir, they began digging again but soon ran into another flooding problem. On Christmas Day, 1864, another water-pocket was tapped in a shaft. The water rushed in with such force that the miners narrowly escaped drowning. The next day, water filled the shaft 160 feet deep.

The Sutro Tunnel

Pumping these flooded tunnels and shafts was extremely expensive, even using the latest and most efficient machinery. This created a problem, and Dan DeQuille described the solution in his *History of the Comstock Silver Lode and Mines:*

> In order to overcome these water troubles, Adolph Sutro early conceived the idea of running an immense drain tunnel under the Comstock Lode from the lowest possible point. A survey was made by Mr. H. Schussler, and work was commenced on the great drain tunnel (since known as the Sutro Tunnel) October 19, 1869. It starts at the edge of the valley of the Carson River, at a point nearly east of Virginia City, and has a length of 20,145 feet — nearly 4 miles. It taps the central parts of the Comstock Lode at a depth of about 1,650 feet. The tunnel is 16 feet wide and 12 feet high. Drain flumes are sunk in the floor and over these are two tracks for horse-cars. It required nearly eight years to construct the tunnel, and the total cost was about $4,500,000. Although the leading mines had their shafts down nearly 3,000 feet before the tunnel was finished, yet it was of great use, as it saved 1,600 feet of pumping.
>
> From the main tunnel branches were run north and south along the east side of the vein for a distance of over two miles, with which the several companies connected by drain drifts from their mines. The flow of water through the tunnel has at times been over 10,000,000 gallons in twenty-four hours.

The Sutro Tunnel was finally finished in July, 1878, and was regarded as one of the engineering marvels of the age. Sutro himself made a fortune, and for twenty years he was one of the most powerful landowners in San Francisco. He served that town as its mayor in 1894–96.

The Virginia City and Gold Hill Water System

Although there seemed to be plenty of water below the surface, there was little in the arid hills around Virginia City and Gold Hill. The water in the area around the Comstock Lode, including that in the mines, was barely fit for human consumption. Sometimes it was actually poisonous. J. Ross Browne had a few words to say in *A Peep at Washoe* about the drinking water of Virginia City when he visited there in 1860:

> The water was certainly the worst ever used by man. Filtered through the Comstock Lead, it carried with it much of the plumbago, arsenic, copperas, and other poisonous minerals alleged to exist in that vein. The citizens of Virginia had discovered what they conceived to be an infallible way of "correcting it;" that is to say, it was their practice to mix a spoonful of water in half a tumbler of whiskey, and then drink it. . . . With hot saleratus bread, beans fried in grease, and such drink as this, it was no wonder that scores were taken down sick daily.

The water supply situation did not improve when thousands of people came to live in Virginia City and Gold Hill. To supply them, the Virginia City & Gold Hill Water Company built 21 miles of pipe and 45 miles of flumes across Washoe Valley to bring water from Marlette Lake. Henry Schussler, the surveyor for the Sutro Tunnel, designed a siphon to convey the water down from the lake, over Washoe Valley, and then up nearly 2000 feet to the Comstock Lode towns. Construction began in June, 1873, and was completed by August 1st of that year. Enlarged in 1875 and 1887, the water system was considered one of the major engineering achievements of that time. In 1975, it was designated a national landmark by the American Society of Civil Engineers.

Milling

Another problem for the miners was getting the gold and silver out of the ore, once it was dug out of the ground. During the first months of mining, the rocks were packed by mule to San Francisco for refining. Some companies sent their ore as far away as Great Britain to be reduced to gold and silver bars. This was of course very expensive, even though the ore was quite rich.

Mining engineers then invented the "Washoe Pan Process" for separating the gold and silver from the other minerals. The large rocks first had to be broken up into smaller pieces. This was done by smashing the ore with larger, harder rocks in an arrastra, or by crushing them with power machinery called "stamps." The ore was then ground in iron pans until it was a fine powder, to which the mill-men added quicksilver (mercury), salt, and copper sulphate. This mixture was roasted and stirred, then poured into an elaborate system of settling basins which separated most of the previous ore from the base rock, called tailings.

Mining and milling affect the environment, sometimes for the worst. Pollution has been a problem in Nevada since at least the time of the Civil War, with ore reduction mills and sawmills getting most of the blame. The reduction mills of western Nevada processed Comstock Lode tailings with cyanide, a deadly poison, to extract the small amounts of remaining rich ore. During the summer of 1898, the editor of the Dayton

Boom at Belleville. The nineteenth-century smokestacks of the Upper Mill belch steam and smoke, as well-dressed businessmen deal at arm's length. On a nearby trestle, a Carson & Colorado Railroad engine is prepared to take out the ore that the plant is processing.

Courtesy of Special Collections, University of Nevada Reno Library

"Melting and Molding the Bullion in the Assay Office." The molten silver, heated in brick furnaces, is poured into bars, while spare tongs for handling it hang on the walls in the background.

From *Frank Leslie's Illustrated Weekly*, 1877

Lyon County Times complained about the chemicals leaking into the water of Carson River:

> DEADLY CYANIDE. — The cyanide which escapes into the Carson river from the plant at the Eureka mill has been fatal to a number of animals about Dayton. Many chickens have died from drinking the water; several dogs and cats have keeled over after quenching their thirst with river water, and several horses have been made quite sick by drinking from the river. Again THE TIMES would caution the residents of this place to drink none but well water during the low stage of water in the river.

Toxic wastes are still with us today, as legislators and citizens face the challenges of balancing community prosperity and the public health. More and more rules and regulations are proposed to solve what is certainly a national problem, but the result of the legislation remains to be seen.

Logging

The mills which worked the ore and reduced it to rubble and ingots were powered by steam. The fires which produced the steam were fed by pine trees, firs, and cedars from the surrounding forests. The mills needed plenty of cordwood to operate, and the millmen weren't the only people who required a steady supply of timber. The miners used tens of thousands of trees to shore up their tunnels and shafts. The railroads used tens of thousands more to power their steam-driven locomotives and for ties to maintain the tracks. Also, the townsfolk of Nevada needed wood to stoke their stoves for cooking and heating.

Small-scale logging began with the appearance of the first settlers and increased tremendously with the opening of deep tunnel mines after 1860. The trees were felled by ax and saw, stripped of their limbs, and cut into sections for sale at the sawmill. As the demand for wood increased, especially on the Comstock, the forests on the eastern slope of the Sierra Nevada began to disappear. Dan DeQuille, writing in his 1876 work *The Big Bonanza*, mentioned the effects of logging companies:

> The Comstock lode may truthfully be said to be the tomb of the forests of the Sierras. Millions on millions of feet of lumber are annually buried in the mines,

> nevermore to be resurrected. When once it is planted in the lower levels it never again sees the light of day.
>
> The pine forests of the Sierra Nevada Mountains are drawn upon for everything in the shape of wood or lumber, and have been thus drawn upon for many years. For a distance of fifty or sixty miles all the hills of the eastern slope of the Sierras have been to a great extent denuded of trees of every kind — those suitable only for wood as well as those fit for the manufacture of lumber for use in the mines.

Transporting the wood was a problem with many solutions. Wood cut in the mountains around Carson Valley was floated down to the quartz mills on the Carson River. By 1875, woodcutters were floating 100,000 cords of timber downriver to Empire, where the wood was collected and shipped by wagon.

Flumes were another development to transport timber from the mountain sawmills to railroad depots along the line of the V.&T.R.R. A flume is a chute built of wood, through which just enough water flows to float and move the cut timber. These were especially useful where the mountains were too steep to move the lumber by wagon. A number of major flumes were built in the 1870's, to supply the wood needed to rebuild Virginia City after the fire of 1875 and to excavate and process the "Big Bonanza" and other rich ore bodies. By 1880, there were ten flumes operating in western Nevada, totalling over 80 miles in length. The largest was over twenty miles long and cost $250,000 to build.

In some areas bordering Lake Tahoe, lumbermen moved the cut trees by steam locomotive over narrow-gauge logging railways. Steamboats towed floating logs across the lake to sawmills, where the wood was cut and shipped to market.

The supply and demand for timber dwindled through the 1880's as many of Nevada's mines went out of production. Most major logging operations ceased in the 1890's.

Seizing Control of the Comstock

Because mining on the Comstock both required and produced large sums of money, it attracted the interest of very capable people. Much of the financial history of Nevada in

Deforestation at Summit Camp in the Sierra Nevada. Logging locomotives brought the lumber from the sawmills of Lake Tahoe to Summit Camp. From there flumes carried the wood to Carson City.

Courtesy of Nevada Historical Society

Where Incline Got Its Name. The Incline tramway was an ingenious component in a system which provided lumber and cordwood for the Comstock. Trees felled in the woods around Lake Tahoe's south shore were trimmed into logs, roped into huge rafts, and towed north across the lake by steamboats to Sand Harbor. From there, the logs were hauled by a short rail line to the Sierra Nevada Wood and Lumber Company sawmill at Mill Creek, where they were sawed into lumber and cordwood. From the sawmill, the wood was then carried up the Incline in six cars on rails, connected to a continous cable driven by a steam engine. At the top of the Incline, the wood was dumped automatically into a flume which whisked it away to Lakeview at the south end of Washoe Valley, where the wood was picked up by the Virginia & Truckee Railroad and taken to Virginia City.

Well-stocked lumberyard's wood piles tower over a V.&T.R.R. engine and its crew south of Carson City. Planks and beams stretch north to the horizon, all cut at the Glenbrook mills of Lake Tahoe. From there, the lumber was hauled to Spooner Summit and then sent down a flume, shown here. Its lateral branches (two of three are visible) made unloading and storage easier for the lumbermen.

The Verdi Lumber Company sawmills on the Truckee River. Cutting all those trees generated a lot of sawdust, and this created a problem—pollution. Although lawsuits to stop sawdust pollution of Nevada waterways began as early as 1863, court action was largely ineffective throughout the nineteenth and early twentieth centuries. The sawdust blocked rivers, preventing trout and salmon spawning runs and killing the fish. The Truckee River had to be repeatedly re-stocked with fish after the 1870's.

"Everlasting Oblivion Lay Directly Ahead." A thrilling ride on the Sierra Nevada Wood & Lumber Company flume was just the thing to banish boredom in the nineteenth-century woodcutting camps.
Courtesy of Nevada Historical Society

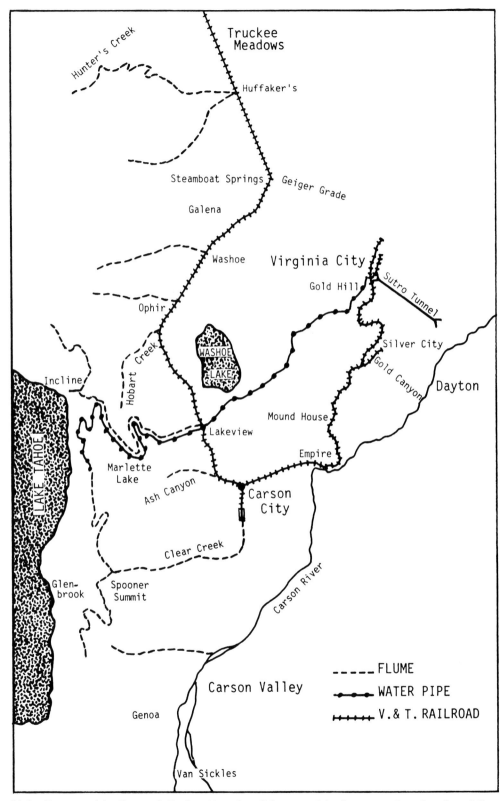

Major Features of the Comstock Region. Note that all but one of the flumes terminated at the rail line of the V.&T.R.R., on which the lumber was moved to market. The Virginia City & Gold Hill Water Co. system crosses the center of the map.

the nineteeth century is the story of these people who amassed great fortunes from the blessings of nature and the work of tens of thousands of people.

When it became clear that the Comstock Lode would not be readily exhausted, three very capable men succeeded in getting control of much of the wealth the mines produced. Two of them were W. C. Ralston and Darius Ogden Mills of California. With William Sharon assisting them, they nearly took over the Comstock and much of western Nevada. In 1864, Ralston and Mills founded the Bank of California at San Francisco. That autumn, Mills and Ralston sent Sharon as their agent to establish a branch bank in Nevada. Sharon arrived at a time of temporary borrasca. With the substantial resources of the Bank of California behind him, Sharon loaned money to many of the reduction or refining mill companies of the region. These companies were suffering hard times, waiting for the mines to find another rich pocket of ore.

During 1865, Sharon demanded that the loans be repaid. Most of the mills couldn't do it. The properties were then sold at mortgage. The Bank of California bought the mills, along with a number of mines, sawmills, timber companies, and other businesses. The bank also tried to gain control of other mines by buying up shares of stock. Hundreds of people gained and lost fortunes as stock in the Hale & Norcross mine went from under $300 a share in January, 1868, to almost $3000 in February, and up to $10,000 a share in March. By September of that year, the stock was selling for $41.50 a share.

The Bank of California organized its properties as the Union Mill & Mining Company and, before long, had control of most of the Comstock. William Sharon, later U.S. Senator from Nevada, supervised the operations. In 1875, a financial panic caused the Bank of California to temporarily suspend operations. Its head, W. C. Ralston, died mysteriously, and Sharon took over a considerable part of the holdings.

The Bank of California had rivals. The most influential of these was the Central Pacific Railroad group, run by Leland Stanford, Mark Hopkins, Charles Crocker and Collis P. Huntington. This group was sometimes called the "The Big Four."

Another group, known as the "Silver Kings," consisted of James G. Fair, John W. Mackay, James C. Flood, and William S. O'Brien. The Silver Kings got control of the Hale & Norcross mine from William Sharon and shortly afterwards struck a lucrative pocket of gold and silver ore on the Comstock Lode. The group then took over another mine in 1872, which most people thought worthless — the Consolidated Virginia. After eight months of tunnelling, the Silver Kings struck an incredibly rich section of rock called the "Big Bonanza." The Virginia City *Enterprise* published Dan DeQuille's news report on the discovery under sensational headlines:

HEART OF THE COMSTOCK!

A Mass of Sulphuret and Cloride Ores!!

Crystalized Ores That Are Almost Pure Silver!!!

Shining Like a Casket of Black Diamonds

Historian Eliot Lord, in his 1883 work *Comstock Mining and Miners,* described the find in similar terms:

> No discovery which matches it has ever been made on this earth from the day when the first miner struck a ledge with this rude pick until the present. The plain facts are as marvelous as a Persian tale, for the young Aladdin did not see in the glittering case of the genii such fabulous riches as were lying in that dark womb of rock. The miner's pick and drill are more potent than the magician's wand. Under their resistless touch the bars of the treasure-house were broken through and its hoard revealed to the dazzled eyes of the invaders. The wonder grew as its depths were searched out foot by foot.... When, finally, the 1,500-foot level was reached and ore richer than any before met with was disclosed, the fancy of the coolest brains ran wild.

Mackay and Fair used all their resources in extracting the glittering riches. The workmen broke all previous records in sending out ore, as Eliot Lord related:

> The scene within this imperial treasure-chamber was a stirring sight. Cribs of timber were piled in successive stages from basement to dome four hundred feet above, and everywhere men were at work in changing shifts, descending

*William Sharon (1818-1885), United States
Senator from Nevada between 1875 and 1881.
He dominated Nevada's economic life for
almost twenty years.*

*James Graham Fair (1831-1894), born
in Ireland, was eighteen years old when he
joined the gold rush to California, and by the
age of thirty he owned a quartz mill. In 1873,
Comstock Lode miners supervised by Fair
discovered the "Big Bonanza," which made
him and his partners — John Mackay,
James C. Flood, and William S. O'Brien
— rich men. He became United States
Senator from Nevada between 1881 and 1887.*

and ascending in the crowded cages, clambering up to their assigned stopes with
swinging lanterns or flickering candles, picking and drilling the crumbling ore,
or pushing lines of loaded cars to the stations at the shaft. Flashes of exploding
powder were blazing from the rent faces of the stopes; blasts of gas and smoke
filled the connecting drifts; muffled roars echoed along the dark galleries, and at
all hours a hail of rock fragments might be heard rattling on the floor of a level.
. . . Half-naked men could be seen rushing back through the hanging smoke to
the stopes to examine the result of the blast and to shovel the fallen mass into
cars or wheelbarrows. While some were shoveling ore and pushing cars, others,
standing in the slippery piles, were guiding the power-drills which churned
holes in the ore with incessant thumps, or cleaving the softer sulpherets with
steel picks swung lightly by muscular arms.

The Big Bonanza was the last major discovery of rich ore on the Comstock. It was
largely exhausted by 1879, and the value of the Comstock's ore production went into
decline. The costs of recovering the precious metals increased as the mines became
deeper. As mining became less profitable, many mining companies went out of business. The mines shut down, and miners were put out of work. They left the Comstock
for other mining booms in other towns and other states.

John W. Mackay (1831-1902), of Ireland, worked his way up from hard rock miner to millionaire and mining magnate in partnership with Fair, Flood, and O'Brien. He parlayed his Comstock fortune into even greater riches in the development of transoceanic submarine telegraph systems. His son Clarence and his wife left millions of dollars to the University of Nevada, donated in John W. Mackay's name.

Virginia City continued to be home to many, however. Some mines continued to operate, although not on the scale of the bonanza period. The Virginia & Truckee Railroad continued to haul goods to and from the Comstock, and the affairs of Storey County were still settled in the courthouse at Virginia City. Piper's Opera House, a historic site in the old gold and silver camp, showed motion pictures in the great hall where some of the finest actors and artists of the late nineteenth century had performed. After most of the remaining mines closed in the 1920's, Virginia City became a tourist attraction with historic ruins, museums, and legends. As colorful a ghost town as ever lived, Virginia City still thrives today, but with only a small and intermittent mining industry.

NEVADA'S MINING COMMUNITIES

Nevada still has a number of mining communities. They are fascinating places, full of history and memories. Some are still sizable towns and cities, while others are just spots on the map — desolate places where not one stone stands on another. A few of Nevada's most important mining communities are described here, but they are not the only places in the State which have an exciting past.

Austin

On May 2, 1862, William M. Talcott discovered silver ore while hauling wood over a cut-off of the Simpson route. Talcott, a former Pony Express rider, kept the stagecoach station for the overland mail in Reese River valley. He sent some samples of the quartz rock he had gathered in Pony Canyon, the site of his discovery, away to Virginia City to be assayed. When the ore proved to be rich, there was a rush of people to the location. State Senator M. J. Farrell gave a classic account of the rush in a lecture for the Reese River Pioneers, later reprinted in Angel's *History of Nevada*:

> When I arrived in Austin in April, 1863, there was but one house, unfinished, and a few brush tents. . . . I made a trip to California, in September of that year, and the emigration was then at its zenith. . . . In fact, the road was literally crowded with people in wagons, stages, carriages and carts, on horseback, on donkeys, with saddles and without saddles, with hand-carts, wheelbarrows, on foot, and in every other conceivable mode of traveling, all rushing wildy to Reese River, the land of promise, the poor man's paradise, the Mecca of fortune's devotees. They seemed to have but one idea, with which they were perfectly saturated, and that was to get to Austin *quick*. It was impossible not to get excited when brought in contact with this eager crowd of people; and those who smiled

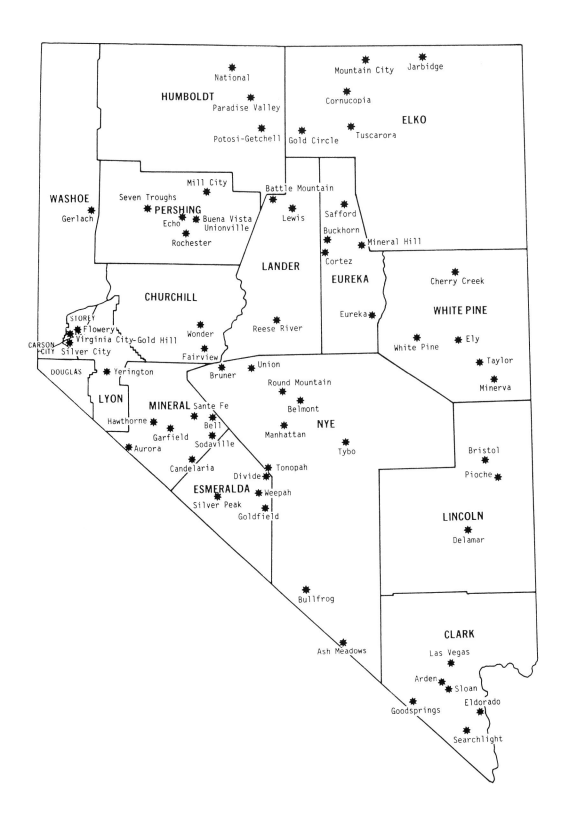

The Million Dollar Mines of Nevada. These mining districts produced a total yield of $1,000,000 or more from 1859 to 1940.

at the recital when at a distance, in California or at the East, were the wildest of the wild when they reached here. Houses were built, tents erected, and brush shanties thrown together, and in an incredibly short space of time a town had sprung up as if by the touch of an enchanter's wand. Water was scarce, and an enterprising firm that retailed it in carts cleared from $1,000 to $1,200 per week. The dust became unbearable, by reason of the immense amount of teaming and travel, and an Austin bath was described as composed of two inches of cold water in a big tub, a piece of brown soap, a napkin, and a dollar and a half.

In 1863, the town became the county seat of Lander County. The mines continued to produce rich profits, and in 1864, Austin was incorporated as a city. Thousands of people were traveling to and from Austin at that time, and it was very difficult for them to find a place to stay — a typical situation in the earliest days of a mining rush. In his article "Washoe Revisited," published in the popular magazine *Harper's Illustrated Weekly,* J. Ross Browne told the story of a friend who wandered through Austin in search of a bed in the summer of 1864:

> Unable to secure lodgings elsewhere, he undertook to find accommodations in a vacant sheep corral. The proprietor happening to come home about midnight, found him spread out under the lee of the fence. "Look-a-here, stranger!" said he, gruffly, "that's all well enough, but I gen'rally collect in advance. Just fork over four bits or mizzle!" My friend indignantly mizzled. Cursing the progressive spirit of the age, he walked some distance out of town, and was about to finish the night under the lee of a big quartz boulder, when a fierce-looking speculator, with a six-shooter in his hand, suddenly appeared from a cavity in the rock, saying, "No yer don't! Take a fool's advice now, and git!" . . . In vain my friend attempted to explain. The rising wrath of the squatter was not to be appeased by soft words, and the click of the trigger, as he raised his pistol and drew a bead, warned the treasspasser that it was time to be off. He found lodgings that night on the public highway to Virginia City and San Francisco.

The Manhattan Silver Mining Company gained control of the mines around Austin between 1865 and 1871. At that time, Austin was the second-largest city in Nevada. During the winter of 1879–80, the 93–mile–long Nevada Central Railroad was built to connect the Austin mines with the transcontinental railroad at Battle Mountain. The Manhattan mines produced over $19 million in silver by 1887, but they ceased production in 1890. The mines operated only intermittently after that. The Lander County seat has since been moved to Battle Mountain. The railroad was scrapped in 1938. Today, Austin is a quiet town on U. S. Highway 50. It is a supply point for outlying communities and is no longer dependent upon mining.

Eureka

On September 19, 1864, a five-man prospecting party from Austin discovered an unusual rock cropping in a place later named New York Canyon, not far from the Simpson Overland Road. The metallic ore turned out to be a mixture of silver and lead — the first important find of this type ever made in the United States. The miners immediately faced a problem, however. Their ore could not be separated into silver and lead by any of the local reduction mills.

In late 1869, two businessmen, D. E. Buel and G. C. Robbins, bought up substantial interests in several of the mines around Eureka. By the end of the year both discovered that the ore could be reduced into silver, lead, and other metals by a smelting process. They immediately began building large furnaces. Not much time passed before the two businessmen were replaced by two corporations, the Eureka Consolidated and the Richmond, locked in mortal combat for control of the mines.

The newly profitable mines and mills started a boom in Eureka. People rushed in from outside to settle the town. In 1875, a railroad was built to connect the mines at Eureka and nearby Ruby Hill with the transcontinental railroad at Palisade. This made Eureka the central shipping point for most of the mining camps in eastern Nevada. Mining production in Eureka peaked in 1878, when the ore output was valued at over $5 million.

The Story of Eureka. This nineteenth-century view shows many aspects of life in the mining camps of the American frontier — the importance of transportation, the heavily armed inhabitants, their diversions and social affairs, and the absence of many women.

Eureka. The Eureka County seat had about 9,000 people living there during the height of the mining boom in 1878. They came from places as far away as Italy, England, and Mexico to earn a living here. The town had four churches, two militia units, an opera house, five fire companies, and nine cemetaries in its heyday.

Courtesy of Nevada Historical Society

Charcoal Furnaces South of Ward. These nineteenth-century structures in White Pine County furnished the charcoal needed to superheat the ore smelters which refined silver and lead from the refractory rock.

Courtesy of Special Collections, University of Nevada Reno Library

MAP
OF
EUREKA DISTRICT
NEVADA.

SCALE.

JANUARY 1900

The smelters which reduced the ores could process 750 tons of rock per day. It took 25 to 35 bushels of charcoal to smelt each ton. This fact led to labor disturbances in 1879. That August, the mining companies decided to reduce the price they were paying charcoal-burners for coal from 30¢/bushel to 27½¢/bushel. The Charcoal Burners' Association, numbering several thousand members, refused to accept the cut in price. They prevented any charcoal from being delivered to the smelters and took over the town of Eureka on August 11. Governor John H. Kinkead called out the State militia to deal with the disturbance, but the trouble was over before troops arrived. On August 18, 1879, a Eureka County Sheriff's posse of nine men attacked a group of about one hundred striking charcoal-burners at Fish Creek, killing five of them. Another six strikers were seriously injured. This gun battle ended the charcoal-burners' war, and the Association accepted the lower prices offered by the mining companies.

It wasn't long before the mining companies ran into trouble. In 1881, the miners struck water, which began to flood the tunnels and shafts of the main mines. The companies kept the mines open with pumps, but this made operations much more expensive. The last bonanza ore body was exhausted by 1885, and no new treasure-troves of silver were found. In the early 1890's, the main smelters closed, and mining operations continued on a small scale with intermittent success. Today, Eureka is a beautiful place to visit. The courthouse still handles the business of the County, and there are historic churches, homes, and cemeteries to see.

Ely

Although the Comstock is the most famous of our mining districts, the copper mines around Ely have produced more wealth than those of any other mining region in Nevada. This little-known fact alone makes the area of great importance in the history of the State and shows the scale and richness of the twentieth century copper "booms."

The original discoveries were made in 1867, when an Indian guide took a party of prospectors from Egan Canyon to the present site of Ely. The location was just off the Simpson overland route, which made the gold and silver find accessible. The copper ore in the vicinity was then considered not worth digging up, for copper was not then much in demand. Later, when electricity came into practical use, it moved over electrical wires made almost entirely of copper. This caused the demand for copper to rise. When the price of copper rose as well, businessmen began looking for more copper to mine.

The town was named for the president of a local smelting company, Smith Ely. The gold and silver mines were never very extensive, and the settlement was little more than a stagecoach station and post office through the 1870's. In 1886, White Pine County moved its governmental operations from Hamilton to Ely, resulting in some local prosperity.

Two miners from Shasta County, California, arrived in Ely during the summer of 1900 and recognized the area's potential copper wealth. The two young men, David Bartley and Edwin F. Gray, got a lease to work several claims not far from town at a place called Ruth. Along with the lease, they had an option to buy the mine, but the two had no money. Fortunately for them, they found a friend, W. B. Graham, who ran the Ely general store. Graham advanced them mining supplies and food — a "grubstake" — for two years. Bartley and Gray were able to find rich rock, but freighting the copper ore 150 miles to the nearest railroad station was very expensive.

In 1902, a mysterious stranger visited Bartley and Gray. He was an old miner from the Comstock Lode who called himself Williams. This man came and went over a period of several weeks, sharing his food, swapping yarns, and occasionally doing a little digging. Not long afterwards, Mark Requa, a businessman from Virginia City, visited the two Californians. He got right to the point. After he introduced himself, he asked Bartley and Gray how much they wanted for their mine. They replied, "$150,000." Requa said, "All right, let's go down to Ely and fix up the papers." The stranger, it seemed, had been hired by Requa to scout out mines to buy.

Requa immediately began to develop the property and bought additional properties in the neighborhood. In 1905, he and others financed the construction of the

The Liberty Pit at Ruth, from the lower levels. In this White Pine County scene, an immense self-propelled mechanical shovel dumps tons of copper-bearing rock into the ore car. A well-stoked steam engine stands ready to ascend the spiral grade to the surface and deliver the ore to waiting smelters. The workingmen, dwarfed by the machinery, show the huge scale of twentieth-century strip mining.

Courtesy of Nevada Historical Society

First train to Ely. This 1906 photograph shows the arrival of the initial Nevada Northern Railway train ever to steam into the White Pine County seat, while crowds of people watch.

Courtesy of Nevada Historical Society

An aerial view of the Liberty open pit Kennecott Copper Corporation mine at Ruth during the late 1950's in White Pine County. These deposits provided ore for over 60 years, during which time the town of Ruth had to be relocated on several occasions to allow room for continued mining activity.

Courtesy of Nevada Historical Society

Nevada Northern Railroad, which linked Ely one year later with the transcontinental rail line at Cobre in Elko County. There was quite a rush to the copper mines, and in 1907, the voters incorporated the town of Ely, so they could form a government to deal with the usual problems that new mining communities have.

That same year, the mining companies started strip mining operations at Ruth. This was the most economical means of excavating the ore there. Strip mining is the wholesale removal of the ore, the topsoil, and the underlying rock — a process which can level mountains or leave an immense pit. Production at Ruth and at nearby mines increased dramatically after the huge smelter at McGill was built in 1908. The mines continued to operate until the early 1980's. The peak year of production was in 1942. The area, under the control of the Kennecott Copper Corporation, had already yielded more than a billion dollars in copper, gold, and silver by 1958.

Ely's mines have gone out of production, but the mining community continues to be a center for ranching and tourism. Ely is also a supply and distribution point for eastern Nevada.

Pioche

The winter of 1863–64 was a hard one in Lincoln County, and the Indians who lived there suffered from cold and hunger. One Indian went to a Mormon missionary named William Hamblin at Meadow Valley and offered to show him an outcropping of valuable metallic ore, in return for some food and supplies. Hamblin took him up on the deal and discovered the famous Panaca Ledge. He located his claim in March of 1864.

Not all the local Indians were as friendly as the man who showed Hamblin the ledge. Warlike Shosone tribesmen discouraged mining in the area until after 1866. Local miners also had trouble separating the silver from the rest of the rock. An attempt to build a smelter failed, and in 1869, the discouraged miners sold their claims to San Francisco businessman F. L. A. Pioche, after whom the town was later named.

Pioche's early efforts to reduce the silver were also unsuccessful, but in the first months of 1870, miners tried a new technique from the Comstock mines which allowed them to profitably refine the metal from Meadow Valley ore. By the middle of that year, a town appeared near the new reduction mill, and a "rush" began. Franklin Buck, looking for someplace to settle after leaving the mines of White Pine County, was an early arrival in the camp. On February 20, 1870, he described the new settlement in a letter to his relatives in the East:

> The town at the mines where we have located is the pleasantest place I have seen. . . . The mines, the most extensive and richest I have ever seen. . . . Of course, somebody had laid out a town and taken up the land but Mr. Bush the proprietor gave me a lot and Jennie one and we selected our spot and have a house nearly finished. Last week came a rush of people and such a staking off of lots you never saw. You could not buy one now for 100 dollars. Some 1,000 houses have been built and started and from present appearances we shall soon have a population of three or four hundred people.

In fact, within five months, Pioche's population was well over one thousand and growing. In 1871, it replaced Hiko as the county seat of Lincoln County. Like most of the mining camps, Pioche attracted mostly men, about half of whom were foreign-born. At the time of the United States decennial census in 1870, only 83 women lived in Pioche.

In its early years, Pioche had a reputation of being a tough town. The mines were rich, so people wanted to take over the claims from the owners. They did this by means of lawsuits and violence. The rival mining companies hired bullies and gunmen called "roughs" (after their manners) to "jump" the claims of others or protect their own claims. In an 1872 official report, the U.S. Commissioner of Mining made these remarks:

> Two classes of persons reap a rich harvest, lawyers and "roughs." The former are paid to maintain the titles, and the latter to hold the ground. Pioche has been a bloody camp; but it is to be hoped that the days of violence are passing away. The lawyers, however, still have a strong hold, and the complexity of suits and cross-suits is such that no stranger can hope to unravel or comprehend.

Within just a few years after it was founded, Pioche had a population of five or six thousand people. The goods to supply the town were sent by the transcontinental railroad to Toano or Elko. From there, teamsters hauled the supplies by freight wagon south to Pioche. Between 1872 and 1873, local businessmen, trying to cut freighting costs, built a railroad, the Pioche & Bullionville, to serve the mines; it was completed in 1873, amid great celebration.

Ore production at Pioche reached its peak in 1872. After that, the large and rich deposits near the surface were mined out. No new bonanzas were discovered. In 1874, the lower shafts and tunnels in the mines began to flood. The extra expense of pumping and the cost of continuing lawsuits made the mines less profitable. By 1878, the town was nearly deserted. Local ranchers, who had supplied the miners and townspeople with produce, started to experience hard times. In 1880, the mines closed. Local mining companies eked out a barely profitable existence by reprocessing the tailings or waste rock from the original rich discoveries. With nothing to carry, the Pioche & Bullionville Railroad was abandoned and scrapped after 1881.

The mines reopened in 1888. During 1890–1892, there was a brief revival of mining activity in the area. Not long afterwards, however, the mines stopped producing on a regular basis. Pioche survived, however, and remained the county seat. The town began to recover with the construction of the second transcontinental railroad after 1907. A spur (branch) rail line was built connecting Pioche with the Union Pacific's main route between Salt Lake City and Los Angeles.

The town began a new era when Boulder Dam was built in 1935. The relatively inexpensive electric power provided by the dam made it economical to smelt the lead and zinc ore around Pioche. As a result, the years between 1935 and 1959 were a bonanza period for the town. During that time, the mines produced about $80 million

"The Smooths." Conflicts over claims to rich ore often led to lawsuits, such as the one shown here in this 1863 sketch by J. Ross Browne. Miners were not the only people to rush to new mining regions; lengthy litigation over rich claims brought wealth and fame to many attorneys.

From *A Peep at Washoe and Washoe Revisited* by J. Ross Browne

"The Roughs." Many mining companies employed hired gunmen to protect or establish their claims. This 1863 drawing by J. Ross Browne shows a group of heavily-armed Comstock Lode ruffians waiting for the moment when workmen from two rival companies meet and fight in the subterranean gloom.

From *A Peep at Washoe and Washoe Revisited* by J. Ross Browne

Pioche in 1881. 1870-1873 was the heyday of this picturesque mining community. The rich ore deposits here were the basis for many years of prosperity for the Lincoln County seat. Today the town's mines intermittently produce manganese, tungsten, zinc, and lead.

Courtesy of Nevada Historical Society

worth of lead and zinc — more than during the earlier nineteenth century silver boom.

Today, Pioche is a quiet town with many spots of scenic and historic interest. Visitors can see local mines and ruins, the Masonic temple, the "million dollar" courthouse, and the modern county offices.

Tonopah

Just because large and rich outcroppings of ore were near well-traveled routes did not necessarily mean that they would be immediately discovered. The area around Tonopah is an excellent example of how unexpected a find of gold or silver can be. T. A. Rickard, a reporter for the *Mining and Scientific Press,* told his readers in 1908 how the region had been crossed by prospectors for twenty-five years before anyone noticed that hundreds of millions of dollars worth of precious ore were poking up from the ground:

> The country had been abandoned by the prospector. It was one of the has-beens of history. The old trails still left faint lines across the sagebrush desert, and over the bare rocky ridges, and spoke of a period of strenuous search for gold and silver. Some of these abandoned paths of exploration went close to the places where rich mines have been discovered.
>
> . . . Like navigators that pass a treasure island in a fog and hear the muffled roar of the breakers only as a warning of danger, so these old prospectors went past the hungry-looking outcrop of selecified rock, never dreaming that they crossed the wealth they were seeking with such invincible restlessness.

James Butler was the man who actually made the first discovery of rich silver ore. Although others had camped right under the ledge, they didn't see it. In May, 1900, Butler was looking for one of his burros that had strayed away. He found the animal sheltering itself from the wind under a rock cliff that later became known as the Mizpah vein. Butler broke off thirty or forty pounds of the dark ore to have it assayed. When he took it to the assay office, the assayer threw some of the samples away, saying that he wouldn't give a dollar for a thousand tons of the stuff.

The story didn't end there, of course, as T. A. Rickard explained:

> On his way out, Butler got some more of the black mineral and took it to Belmont. T. L. Oddie, an attorney who happened to be there in connection with the operation of a quicksilver mine, then sent the samples to Walter C. Gayhart, an assayer at Austin. [Note: Gayhart was also the principal of the Austin School.] Butler had promised Oddie a quarter interest, and Oddie promised Gayhart a half of his quarter for the making of an assay. Money was scarce; they were all of them "busted." Gayhart's assays showed that the selected specimens ran from $300 to $400 per ton. Oddie thereupon sent an Indian runner to Butler's ranch, which was 45 miles from Belmont, to tell him of the strike, but Butler remained inactive.
>
> He was reported to be the laziest . . . man in the world.

After nearly a month, Butler and his wife Belle went out and located a number of claims. In the middle of November, 1900, the Butlers and Oddie began work after taking a photograph of their discovery.

The discoverers had some trouble protecting their diggings. Oddie, who later became Governor and U.S. Senator from Nevada, described one of his early experiences to a friend, Marjorie Moore Brown, for her book *Lady in Boomtown:*

> Some ruffians moved in from Salt Lake and tried to jump the Mizpah, the original claim. Ralph Wardle and I went up on the hill to put them off and found three men down the fifteen foot shaft. Wardle and I climbed down the ladder, and before we knew it, we were in a hand-to-hand scrap, three of them against two of us. People down in town got wind of trouble on the hill, so the sheriff rounded up some men to go up there with him. He poked his head over the edge of the shaft, looking to me like the angel Gabriel, and yelled, Hey! *you* fellas got no business on this property. Quit fightin' and get outta that hole!
>
> One of them let go of me long enough to yell back, 'You can't stop us, Sheriff. You gotta have a warrant to stop us, and you can't get it. The Court House is seventy miles away in Belmont.'
>
> The Sheriff yelled back, 'You come outta there and we'll talk about it.' By this time half the town was up on the hill. We all scrambled up the ladder.
>
> Then the Sheriff said, 'Now I'll show you coots whether I can do something about this or not. All you fellas who are in favor of the Tonopah Mining Company's claim come over here.' About fifty men came over and stood by me.
>
> 'Now all you other rattlers who think these men are not thieves join up with them over there. Now, Oddie, I'll arrest anyone that comes over here from over there. You hire a man to ride to Belmont and get out a warrant for malicious mischief, and we'll file that suit. And while you're at it, Oddie, hire enough men to keep these coyotes outta that hole. I'll stay here until you get back.'

Later, Oddie hired Wyatt Earp, the famous Kansas and Arizona lawman, and paid him and about twenty other men to keep jumpers off the Mizpah claim.

Butler, Oddie, and their partners didn't have enough money to develop the new mines, but they didn't want to end up like "Old Virginia" Fennimore, H. T. P. Comstock, and the rest. Instead of selling their claims, the discoverers leased them to miners who paid back a portion of the ore they produced. This system proved quite popular, and by the spring of 1901, more than one hundred different leases of claims were recorded. Another feature of this system was extremely unusual — almost unheard of. The leases were all made on verbal promises. Despite the fact that they weren't in writing, almost no lawsuits resulted from any disagreement over the terms of the leases.

The needs of the miners digging out the silver ore at Tonopah stimulated a substantial freighting business between the new mines and the southerly depot of the Carson & Colorado Railroad at Sodaville. After the completion of the Union Pacific's transcontinental railroad to Las Vegas in 1905, merchants opened a second route to the city of Tonopah, by way of Goldfield and Bullfrog.

In 1902 and 1903, miners discovered additional deposits of silver ore so rich that the town continued to prosper for years. This in turn brought more extensive mining activities and more miners. Many of the new arrivals came from lesser or declining mining camps throughout the West. Construction on new hotels, dance halls, theaters,

Pioneers of Tonapah. This Nye County photograph shows (from left to right) the first tent in town, the ore discovery that built the town (arrow) and its discoverers: Tasker Oddie, Wils Brougher, Mrs. Belle Butler, and James Butler.

Courtesy of Nevada Historical Society

Tonopah, September 7, 1905. A light dusting of snow, brought in by the famous "Tonopah Low," covers Mount Butler and the adjacent hills. The mixed collection of buildings in Nye County's capital are scattered over the landscape in this early photograph of the silver boom at Tonopah.

casinos, churches, hospitals, stores, and homes began almost immediately.

Marjorie Moore Brown went to Tonopah with her husband Hugh, a lawyer, in the earliest days of the boom. One of the few women in the city at that time, she described what it was like:

> When my thoughts return to the women of Tonopah, I recall how my sympathy went out to the brides. As soon as a young man made a stake, he invariably went back for the girl he left behind. Many were entirely unfitted for the life of a mining camp. The older women, wives of engineers, mine officials, and tradesmen, seemed adequate, but you could almost tell by looking at the brides whether they would be able to stick it out.
>
> The problems of housekeeping on the desert were very real. During the bitter cold winters the wind moaned and whistled through the cracks in the board-and-batten houses. In the terrific summer heat, you had to cook over a wood stove with one eye always watchful for insects. Have you ever inadvertently crushed a stick bug and lived with that stench for days? Have you ever turned suddenly to look at your baby on the floor and found a scorpion on his arm? Have you ever found a bedbug on your pillow and faced the task of getting rid of the pests? The women used to say that it was no disgrace to get bedbugs, but it was certainly a disgrace to keep them.
>
> We were successors to that wonderful race of pioneer women who have been scattered over the West since the western trek began, women who brought their babies into the world in lonely places, women who cooked for their sick neighbors. These were women who washed the dead and laid them out, and rode horseback for miles to help a beleaguered home.

Conveniences of civilization like electric power and running water weren't long in coming to Tonopah. A power plant was built and placed in operation at the end of 1902, and a water supply shortly followed. The mills needed water to reduce the ore, and the townsfolk needed it for cooking and cleaning. Because the fast-growing camp was several miles away from Tonopah Springs, water was brought in from outside. This first system, built in 1903, was improved and extended over the years so that the city had the benefits of modern plumbing. This made a lot of difference in living conditions, as Mrs. Brown noted:

> A glorious item in the new house was inside plumbing, which meant hot water! The water hole named Tonombe, fourteen miles to the north, proved to be an underground stream. This water was pumped to the surface and piped into town. Two high-pressure tanks on the hill behind our house furnished all Tonopah with running water. After two years we had no more use for the outhouse. What a relief! And now I no longer had to send my laundry on the three-week journey to Reno. . . . Out of my own experience, I know hot running water is one of the most effective agencies of civilization.

In 1903, businessmen began construction on the Tonopah (later the Tonopah & Goldfield) Railroad which connected the mining camp with the transcontinental railroad at Reno, by way of the Carson & Colorado and Virginia & Truckee Railroads. All of Tonopah celebrated on "Railroad Day," when the tracks into town were finished. There were speeches, decorations, outdoor and indoor bands, contests, and dancing.

Tonopah became a prominent distribution and supply point for west-central Nevada communities. It was also the outfitting point for many prospecting expeditions exploring the surrounding waste lands. Prospectors working out of Tonopah then discovered a number of other sites of rich gold and silver ore — Goldfield, Bullfrog, Rawhide, Rhyolite, and other camps.

As Tonopah grew in importance, its transportation links to other communities were greatly improved. The Tonopah Railroad was extended to Goldfield in 1905, to handle freighting to and from that new mining camp. Two other branch lines linked Tonopah to the transcontinental railroad between Salt Lake City and Los Angeles. One of these — the Las Vegas & Tonopah Railroad (abandoned in 1918) — became part of U.S. Highway 95 between Reno and Las Vegas.

The silver mines of Tonopah reached their peak production in the period from 1910–1914. The ore production then began to decline. The mines went out of business in

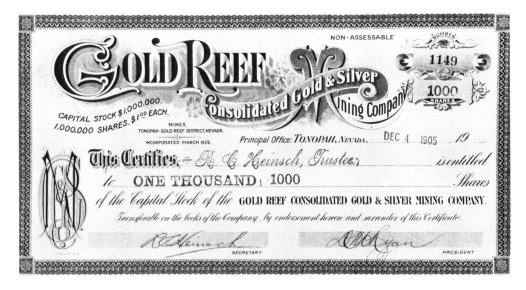

about 1940. Not long afterwards, the two remaining railroads serving the town also ceased operations.

Tonopah became the Nye County seat in 1905, replacing Belmont. This, and the fact that the town was a natural supply point for central Nevada, kept the town alive during the hard years which followed the mine closings. It is particularly well-located, because the town is at the crossroads of two major routes across the continent — U.S. Highway 95 and U.S. Highway 6 between Salt Lake and Los Angeles, via Ely, Nevada, and Bishop, California.

Goldfield

On December 4, 1902, Harry Stimler and William Marsh were camped at a place called Rabbit Springs, about thirty miles south of Tonopah. While prospecting on nearby Columbia Mountain, they found some black-looking quartz. When they examined the quartz they discovered that it was exceedingly rich in gold. Although a heavy wind came up which filled the air with blowing sand, the two men traced the quartz to a ledge about twenty feet wide. Stimler and Marsh located several claims there, which they later sold to George Wingfield and George Nixon.

Other prospectors came and also found rich deposits of gold in the area. One lucky lessee (a person who paid the mineowner for the right to dig) was able to scrape up $8,800 worth of ore from the loose ground left after the sagebrush had been removed from the topsoil. Miners at the Jumbo claim took out $100,000 in gold-bearing quartz from the first 47 feet that they dug. In October, 1903, promoters laid out a town site and began selling lots. The first building was a saloon. Within a month, 150 people lived in the camp. Then the rush began. As described by "Fitz-Mac," a reporter for the Goldfield *News* in 1906:

> . . . [W]hen the news of the strikes reached Tonopah, the excitement became so hot that the camp was menaced with spontaneous combustion. Hundreds of men who had joined in the first rush in May and staked claims by the score, but failed to do the location work within the 90-day period required by law, were thrown with foaming paroxysms at the thought of the riches that had slipped through their hands. . . .
>
> The first consideration with all delinquents who retained their senses, was to get to Goldfield and protect their titles. Men rushed for the livery stables. Wives sprang to the duty of hustling grub and water — water above all things for the run across the scorching desert that separated the two camps by 25 miles. Bottles were filled to go in the pockets, canteens filled to sling over the shoulder, kegs and cleaned vehicle cans were filled to store in the vehicles. . . .
>
> All Tonopah stampeding for Goldfield — the road lined with hurrying, scurrying caravans of wagons and drays and carriages, and men ahorseback and

men afoot and men pushing their outfit on wheelbarrows, for be sure such insanity is not limited to those able to pay for a ride. . . .

A motley caravan, struggling helter-skelter, in a long line of sweltering dust across the desert to the southward. . . .

Within two years of Stimler's and Marsh's discovery, six or seven thousand people were living in Goldfield. As with Tonopah, modern conveniences were not far behind. Electric power came to the town in early 1905, and workmen finished the Tonopah & Goldfield Railroad that same year. In 1907, Esmeralda County moved the county seat from Hawthorne to Goldfield, making the mining camp a county seat.

Through careful investment buying, George Wingfield and George Nixon were able to gain control of most of the productive mines in Goldfield by 1907. Although Goldfield did not have the kind of serious law-and-order problems of most of the nineteenth century frontier mining camps, it had turbulence of a different kind — strikes and labor violence.

The International Workers of the World (I.W.W.), also known as the "Wobblies," participated in several strikes against the mine owners of Goldfield in 1907. One of the biggest issues was "high-grading." The ore that was mined at Goldfield was very rich or "high-grade." Even small chunks of rock in some mines were quite valuable. Some pieces may have been nearly solid gold. Some of the miners would take these very rich, small pieces of rock and steal them. This was called "high-grading", and it cost the mining companies many thousands of dollars each year. The companies' officials tried to stop the high-grading by making the men take off their work clothes in one room and then move to another room to change into their fresh clothes before they left work. The I.W.W. objected and called for the workers to strike against the mining companies. Many workers did strike and left their jobs. Tension was high during the strike, as Joseph McDonald, then a local newsboy and later a newspaper executive, recalled:

> . . . [T]he reason they had the strike more than anything else was Goldfield was a high grade camp. And these fellows went in there, they made so much money stealing ore, high grading, that they used to even forget to go after their paycheck. And so finally, the mining company put in change rooms. And some of the guys in the miners' union thought that was wrong, that they cut off their source of supply. . . .
>
> So the strike became quite an affair. And the mines published a little news-

Goldfield's Beginnings, November, 1903. This early view shows the future Esmeralda County seat as a collection of sheds and tents set out in the sagebrush.

George Wingfield (1876-1959), born in Arkansas, was a vaquero and gambler when he met Winnemucca banker George S. Nixon around the turn of the century. The two formed a team which dominated Nevada political and economic affairs after 1907, financed by their Goldfield Consolidated Mines Co. Almost wiped out in the Great Depression, Wingfield made a financial comeback through other mining ventures and remained influential until his death.

Courtesy of Nevada Historical Society

George S. Nixon (1860-1912) of California. Nixon was a worker in a box factory, a telegrapher, and bank clerk who later became a state legislator and then U.S. Senator from Nevada in 1905-1912. In partnership with George Wingfield, Nixon prospered with the rise of Goldfield and died a wealthy man.

Courtesy of Nevada Historical Society

Goldfield in 1907. The town was already of imposing size in this photograph taken in its most troubled year. Labor strikes and violence gripped the town during a struggle for control of the region between the I.W.W. and the Goldfield Consolidated interests of Nixon and Wingfield.

Courtesy of Nevada Historical Society

> paper. I forget now what they called it, a little newspaper. And it sold like hotcakes, those things did. . . . (I)t was just a rabid, red hot sheet. But it sure did sell. I used to sell those.

The threats of violence caused Governor John Sparks to send a telegram to President Theodore Roosevelt, asking for federal troops to protect Goldfield. The soldiers arrived, but were withdrawn shortly afterwards. The Legislature then met in a special session called by Governor Sparks and voted to create the Nevada State Police. These actions and the resistance of the mining companies broke up the I.W.W. influence in Goldfield. The strike failed and the troublemakers scattered.

It is hard to imagine terrain as rich as that found around Goldfield. Almost all of the town's ore production, amounting to nearly $90 million, came from a zone less than a mile long and only a few hundred feet wide. One lease produced $4,600,000 in gold ore from a claim just a little over two acres.

These bonanzas couldn't last forever. 1910 was the peak year of production for Goldfield, and the area's fortunes began to decline after that. In 1918, after the major bodies of ore were exhausted, Wingfield and Nixon's Goldfield Consolidated closed its mill. The mines of the town continued to operate for twenty more years or so. The mills still processed the tailings from the bonanza mines, but the industry was dying. Production became sporadic by the late 1940's. Many people left town, but it is still the Esmeralda County capitol. It is on U.S. Highway 95, which brings tourists into Goldfield to see its ruins and appreciate its historic greatness. As J. W. Scott once wrote of the place:

> *Splendid, magnificent, Queen of the Camps,*
> *Mistress of countless Aladdin's lamps*
> *Diety worshipped by kings and tramps,*
> *The lure she is of the West.*

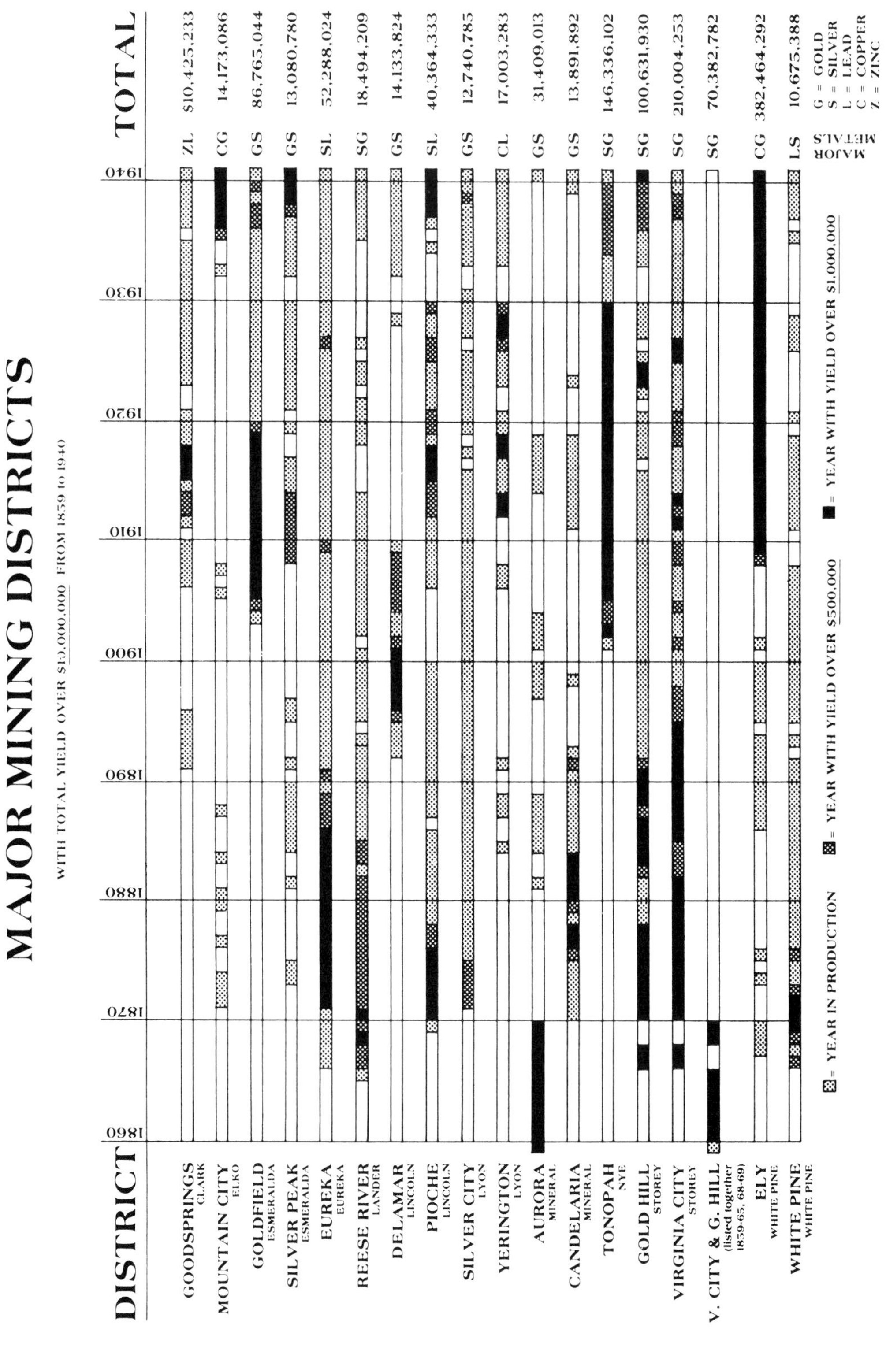

MAJOR MINING DISTRICTS

WITH TOTAL YIELD OVER $13,000,000 FROM 1859 to 1940

DISTRICT		MAJOR METALS	TOTAL
GOODSPRINGS	CLARK	ZL	$10,425,233
MOUNTAIN CITY	ELKO	CG	14,173,086
GOLDFIELD	ESMERALDA	GS	86,765,044
SILVER PEAK	ESMERALDA	GS	13,080,780
EUREKA	EUREKA	SL	52,288,024
REESE RIVER	LANDER	SG	18,494,209
DELAMAR	LINCOLN	GS	14,133,824
PIOCHE	LINCOLN	SL	40,364,333
SILVER CITY	LYON	GS	12,740,785
YERINGTON	LYON	CL	17,003,283
AURORA	MINERAL	GS	31,409,013
CANDELARIA	MINERAL	GS	13,891,892
TONOPAH	NYE	SG	146,336,102
GOLD HILL	STOREY	SG	100,631,930
VIRGINIA CITY	STOREY	SG	210,004,253
V. CITY & G. HILL (listed together 1859-65, 68-69)		SG	70,382,782
ELY	WHITE PINE	CG	382,464,292
WHITE PINE	WHITE PINE	LS	10,675,388

G = GOLD
S = SILVER
L = LEAD
C = COPPER
Z = ZINC

■ = YEAR WITH YIELD OVER $1,000,000

▨ = YEAR WITH YIELD OVER $500,000

▨ = YEAR IN PRODUCTION

Years axis: 1860, 1870, 1880, 1890, 1900, 1910, 1920, 1930, 1940

CHAPTER 4

Ranching

Before the appearance of white intruders in Nevada, prehistoric Indians grew crops of beans, squash, and other vegetables in the valleys of southeastern Nevada. Northern Paiute Indians along Walker River knew about irrigation and harvesting before the State was settled by people from outside, and the ancient Anasazi were masters of the art of farming. The herds of cattle and sheep that came in with the settlers, however, were a new and substantial intrusion on the Indian way of life. The need for lush green grass and precious water placed whites and Indians in competition for the scarce spots of fertile land.

THE LAND

Ranges of mountains running from north to south divide Nevada into a series of valleys. Some of these valleys are fertile, while many more are desolate. Where water ran free along the Carson, Colorado, Humboldt, Truckee, and Walker Rivers, farmers could raise crops. Other valleys contained scrub brush and bunch grass on which livestock could graze.

Success in ranching depends to a great extent on the weather and the land—whether there's enough water and whether the climate and the soil are good. The story of water and how it is used is especially important since Nevada is the most arid state in the Union.

THE WATER

Water in Nevada is often measured by extremes of drought and flood. Of the two, floods are the more spectacular. Again and again in Nevada history, a combination of unusually heavy snows followed by warm rains have resulted in heavy flooding on the Carson, Humboldt, Truckee, and Walker Rivers.

William M. Stewart (U.S. Senator from Nevada in 1864–1875 and 1886–1904) was an early businessman on the Comstock Lode who had first-hand experience of this sort of catastrophe. With the help of two partners he acquired a valuable mine at Gold Hill and built two quartz mills on the Carson River during the spring and summer of 1861. As Stewart tells it in his Reminiscences:

> If the winter had been as usual I would have had the foundation of a fortune of a million; in fact, in November, 1861, I had an offer for my interest in the two properties of $500,000. But about the middle of December there came the most terrific snowstorm ever known in Nevada. When the snow was five or six feet deep in Virginia City, where it seldom falls a foot deep, and when the valley about Carson was also covered several feet with snow, a warm rain set in, and the flood was terrible. It filled the mine with water and carried away both mills; while the hay, the grain, and the ore at the mill were all swept away; nothing was left on the bar where the mill was built, which before the flood was covered

Flood of the Carson River at Empire, 1907. This photograph shows just how bad it can get in Nevada when there's too much water, while the cameraman standing on a pile of flotsam records the scene for posterity.

Courtesy of Nevada Historical Society, Davis Collection

with a heavy growth of cottonwoods from one to three feet in diameter, and it became a mass of boulders and nothing else. I lost $500,000 in a night.

Carson River has cut new channels several times over the past hundred and thirty years. Within the recent past, Las Vegas on Las Vegas Wash and Reno on the Truckee River have also suffered from costly floods. They have caused great loss of property, death and suffering. The risk of this type of disaster has been reduced, at least on the Truckee River, by construction of flood control and storage dams.

On other occasions during the past, there have been very heavy winter storms bringing snow which did not quickly melt off. A storm like this doomed the Donner Party in 1846. As recently as 1952, storms blocked transcontinental railroad operations over Donner Pass. In some neighborhoods roofs have collapsed under the weight of the snow, and communities have been cut off from the outside world for weeks. These storms have a particularly severe effect on ranching. In the deep snow cattle cannot move around on the range to look for food, and they freeze to death or starve. In a few very bad winters the weather has threatened most of the livestock in the State.

One such winter occurred in 1889–90. Called "the Winter of the White Death," it killed an estimated 134,000 cattle and 129,000 sheep in northern Nevada. The storms came at the end of a three-year drought in the area, which began in 1886. In Elko County, the biggest of these storms raged for three weeks without a break. The snow lay three feet deep on the level, while howling winds piled up snowdrifts twenty feet high. In Elko, the temperature dropped to sixty degrees below zero in early January, and it stayed at about forty degrees below zero through February. The situation was almost as bad elsewhere in Nevada. Only about half of the cattle in the State survived, and many ranchers went bankrupt.

Drought

Because water is a scarce and valuable resource, people quarrel over who will get to use it and how it will be used. In Nevada, battles over water have taken three forms: private feuds, lawsuits, and government regulation.

The private feud is a confrontation between ranchers and other water users involving threatened or actual violence. It usually took the form of angry words or physical interference with someone's irrigation system. In August, 1887, the *Lyon County Times* of Dayton printed an article on how tempers ran high over the low water that year:

> WATER TROUBLE. – For about a week, up to last Saturday, the Cardelli Bros., Italian ranchers on the Carson river had men with shotguns parading up and down the big Italian ditch owned by Johnny Ghiglieri and others, to prevent the water from being turned onto the Ghiglieri ranch. Mr. Ghiglieri stood the pressure as long as he could, but last Saturday after seeing that his crops were drying up, he came up to the gate and turned the water onto his ranch in spite of shotguns, guards and dogs. As soon as Cardelli heard of this he came immediately to town and it was supposed from all the talk that was done that there would be a regular Italian war in no time. Matters were settled up, however, without bloodshed.

Private controversies often turned into lawsuits where judges settled ranchers' grievances in court rather than by violence. Another story from the Dayton *Lyon County Times*, dating from late July, 1892, shows the transition:

> WAR IN GOLD CANYON. – For the past two weeks there has been a turbulent state of affairs in Gold Canyon over a water right. The King brothers, who recently bought some mining property and a water right in the canyon have been bothered by having their water taken by J. Ferretti, who owns a little ranch in Dana Canyon, and who has built a small ditch to take the water onto his ranch from Gold Canyon. The Kings told him he must stop using the water, but he claimed it, and put a couple of shot gun men on the ground and got out an injunction on the 19th. The Kings had the injunction raised this week and the boys are now at work using the water that belongs to them for sluicing, but it is hard to tell when trouble will be had again.

Although many of the lawsuits were small, some were very important in Nevada's history because the judges who decided the cases also decided who was going to get the water and how they could use it. There is a well-defined correlation or correspondence

Bone-dry soil on a desolate waste could be made to bloom with water and hard work, but without the water this ranching family couldn't even raise a herd of horned toads. In this twentieth-century photograph the couple tend their garden, while the haystack in the corral attests to their industry or wealth. The life-bringing irrigation ditch appears in the foreground.

between years of drought and the onset of these water rights cases in court, a fact noted by Grace Dangberg in *Conflict on the Carson.*

The first of the major lawsuits was an attempt by the Bank of California to gain control of the waters of Carson Valley so its subsidiary, the Union Mill & Mining Company, could operate its water-powered reduction mills on Comstock Lode ore year-round. The Bank was successful in this first lawsuit, which began in 1864, and in a second lawsuit, *Union Mill & Mining Co. v. H. F. Dangberg, et al.,* brought in 1871. In a third water rights lawsuit with the same name, which started in 1889, the Carson Valley ranchers were successful in protecting their water rights. The 1897 decision which settled this case in their favor committed Nevada to the legal doctrines of "prior appropriation" (first in time, first in right) and "beneficial use" of water in resolving the competing claims.

Other lawsuits, just as important but not so dramatic, settled water rights in State courts for the other major crop-producing river valleys. On the Truckee River, a solution to its problems of water use and allocation began in 1889 with *Reno Mill v. Stevenson,* while water rights on the Walker River were decided between 1902 and 1919 in *Miller & Lux v. Rickey.* In 1937, the Supreme Court of Nevada determined which lands had a right to the Humboldt River system.

Government Regulations

The State government has regulations which are supposed to provide fair evaluation and decision of different claims to the right to use water. In 1899, the Legislature passed a law providing that continuous and beneficial use of water created a vested right to use that water. The idea of a vested right protected people who had been properly using the water from new-comers, when there wasn't enough water to go around. In 1903, the Legislature set up the office of State Engineer. The State Engineer was placed in charge of a permit system in 1907. The permit system, which is still in use for surface and underground water, applies to everyone in Nevada who wants to appropriate or use water for new irrigation. These people must apply for a permit from the State to use the water, but the permit will not be issued if there's not enough water.

TALES OF THE PIONEERS

The United States Congress encouraged people to move into Nevada and other western states and make the land productive. In 1862, the famous Homestead Act became law. It allowed persons who settled up to 160 acres of surveyed public land to buy it for a very low price if they built a house on the property and lived there. The Desert Land Act of 1877 continued the policy of settling the federal lands by providing easy terms for sale of land to settlers who improved it by irrigation.

One of the very first settlers was John Reese, the explorer and businessman who built Nevada's first permanent house at Genoa during the summer of 1851. This is how he described his first year in the State's pioneer settlement:

> I had some 17 men with me and all in my employ. A good many of them worked for me quite a while, in chopping timber and building log houses, &c. I paid them about $75.00 a month, and they worked well. We got pine there that would make good shingles. That year I fenced a field of some 30 acres and plowed it up ready for the next year. I put in Wheat, Barley, Corn and Water Melons in one side, and mixed things all round.

The first ranchers harvested the natural wild grasses that grew in the river bottoms and lowlands. In Carson Valley the blue joint grass grew as high as a man's head in the early days — six or seven feet high. The old timers used to say that when a man went to see his friends, he would have to guide himself by the sound that his neighbor made when sharpening his scythe. The scythe — a long blade mounted on a pole — was used to cut the grass in the years before reaping and threshing machines. The farmers toiled from sunup to sundown, but even an expert scytheman could only cut about two acres of grass each day.

The ranchers sold the dried grasses or hay to passing emigrants and teamsters to

feed their animals. This was often quite profitable, and many of the early ranches began as stations for travelers who were looking for a place to graze their livestock and spend the night — like an agricultural gas station and motel operation. Sarah Allen and her husband Lem, of Churchill County, used to have a station in the years before Lem Allen became Lieutenant Governor of Nevada and the Speaker of the State Assembly. In 1926, she described the place in a deposition for the *U.S. v. Alpine Land & Reservoir Company* *(Alpine)* water rights case:

> We ran a station and the post office and we had that for twenty years. Yes, anybody that came along and wanted a hotel we took them in, and big teams were on the road, freight teams, if they came to our place they stopped and if they didn't they went to Mr. Magee's about a mile and half beyond.
> The store was not much it was what they called a Paiute store. Of course [it had] prints and shoes and things like that — just a country store.

Andrew J. Newman, who gave a deposition in the same case, lived on the Carson River below Dayton. His family also operated a station during the 1860's and 1870's for travelers along the Simpson or central overland route. Newman, who was just a boy when his parents set up the station, remembered it clearly:

> Most of them in those days had their own blankets; we accommodated them with beds. It was a story and a half high house, and we had a large upstairs there with single beds; then the balance of the house was used for the families to live in; and there was a great deal of our customers that had their beds with them, and slept in the wagons, and outside, and teamsters, you know.

Indian workmen were very important to the early ranchers, as Lyon County pioneer Timothy B. Smith acknowledged in his *Recollections of the Early History of Smith Valley:*

> In justice to the Paiute Indians it must be said that during the first years we were among them, though we would gladly have seen them leave the country because of the anxiety and annoyance they caused us, yet a few years later I do not see how we could have managed without their assistance in the harvesting of our large crops of hay as well as in some other lines of work. What they did was generally pretty well done. As hay stackers and in the use of the horse fork they excelled.

Mormon Colonies

The Church of Jesus Christ of Latter Day Saints, usually called the Mormon Church, was very active in starting ranching communities in Nevada during the nineteenth century. It sent Church members to settle the fertile valleys of the State on three separate occasions, each about ten years apart. In 1855, the Church sent a number of families to Las Vegas in southern Nevada and to Carson, Eagle, and Washoe Valleys in western Nevada. The settlements in western Nevada were especially extensive and involved hundreds of people taking up the axe and plow. In a letter published in the San

*Lemuel Allen and his wife Sarah Ann, 1881. The Allens were among the earliest settlers
in Lahontan Valley when they stopped to live along the lower Carson River in 1862.
Allen, a rancher and attorney, served Churchill County as its District Attorney, then as its
Assemblyman, and finally as State Senator. He was three times elected Speaker of the Assembly,
and twice elected President of the State Senate. Of his ranch, Allen wrote: "In February, 1867,
we rented a place which nowadays is four miles southwest of Fallon so we could sell our hay,
it being on the main teamsters' road. In the fall of 1868, we bought that place and lived on it
for forty-four years."*

From Angel's *History of Nevada*

Francisco *Western Standard* in March, 1856, Orson Hyde, the leader of the Mormon
settlement effort on the eastern slope of the Sierra Nevada, called for volunteers:

> Bring with you all useful kinds of seeds adapted to the growth of the climate;
> especially the seeds of righteousness, life and salvation. The latter have not been
> very extensively tested in this soil; yet with proper care and cultivation, we
> think they may take root and produce a plentiful harvest.

By that August, a correspondent of the Stockton *Argus* wrote that "Two hundred
Mormon families have settled in Carson Valley, and about 350 in the Washoe Valley the
present year." Just one year later, in 1857, the Church recalled these and the Las Vegas
settlers to Salt Lake City, fearing at that time that the United States government would
invade Utah Territory and destroy their religion.

In 1864, the Church sent a mission to colonize the Muddy River Valley in the
southeastern part of the State. They founded Panaca, the first town in southern Nevada,
and built the port of Callville on the Colorado River. Frederick Dellenbaugh, an artist
and topographer for John Wesley Powell's U.S. exploring expedition to the Colorado
River, visited St. Thomas in 1871 and was impressed by the Church's Muddy River
colony. He spoke his mind in his reminiscences of the expedition, *A Canyon Voyage:*

> As pioneers, the Mormons were superior to any class I have ever come in
> contact with, their idea being home-making and not skimming the cream off the
> country with six-shooter and whiskey bottle. . . .
> In all Mormon settlements, the domestic animals were incorporated at once
> and they received special care; butter, milk, and cheese were consequentially

*Brigham Young of Vermont (1801–1877),
prophet and revelator of the Church of
Jesus Christ of the Latter Day Saints, led the
Mormon people westward to Utah across the
mountains and prairies in 1846–47. The first
governor of Utah Territory, Young sent
exploring and colonizing missions to southern,
eastern, and western Nevada, hastening
settlement of these remote regions.
The photograph was taken in 1853.*

Courtesy of Nevada Historical Society

*William Bringhurst, President of the
LDS mission to Las Vegas, was responsible for
setting up a ranching community there in
1855–1858. The town's first post office
bore his name.*

Courtesy of Nevada Historical Society

abundant; but in a "Gentile" frontier town all milk, if procurable at all, was drawn from a sealed tin. The same was true of vegetables.

However, these ranching communities were abandoned in the same year Dellenbaugh saw them, when they were discovered to be inside the Nevada boundary line and thus subject to Nevada laws and taxes.

In 1877, the Mormons founded Bunkerville in the Virgin River Valley in southern Nevada. This town was more enduring than the others and still exists today as the center of a ranching community.

Irrigation

When the number of travelers moving across Nevada increased, so did the market for hay. The ranchers then found that the wild grass they cut along the river bottoms wasn't enough to supply the passers-by, who were willing to pay large sums of money for more. The ranchers in Nevada met this challenge by irrigation, which allowed them to grow grass over larger areas. The first step was to dig ditches to carry the water and divert it to low-lying ground with fertile soil.

The pioneer irrigating ditch in Western Nevada was built by ranchers on Carson River in 1854. Benjamin Palmer, Nevada's first black settler, came into Carson Valley in 1853 and had his own ranch there for over forty years. In 1894, he described this ditch while testifying in the *Union Mill & Mining Company v. H. F. Dangberg, et al.* water rights case as "a cut four feet wide and 16 or 18 feet long, to let the water out from the main river into an old slough."

High prices for hay and garden crops encouraged ranchers to dig many more ditches in the Carson, Humboldt, Truckee, and Walker River valleys. Between 1860 and 1880, ranchers built large private irrigation systems carrying water to thousands of acres of land. They were financed by the profits made from selling the hay or feeding it to cattle. A number of these ditches are still in use today, after more than one hundred years of service.

The irrigation ditches were a novelty — an intrusion upon the old way of doing things — but were so effective and profitable that they soon became an accepted technique of ranching. Canal irrigation made quite an impression on people who had never seen it before, such as Elizabeth Magee Murphy. Her parents and six sisters were travelling by wagon over the Simpson route when they entered Lahontan Valley during the summer of 1863. She was just a girl at the time, but her memory was clear when she testified more than sixty years later about early farming and irrigation in the area for the *Alpine* case:

> I remember the ditches more distinctly because we were going to California to dig gold, you know, and when the water was a little low, when the sun was shining little particles would glisten in the bottoms of the ditches, and we little barefeet waded in there and scooped up this sand, and put it in cans and things, and thought we were getting gold without going to California, out of the ditches; and they were particularly interesting to us because of that, and because we could paddle in them.

Sometimes, when the rivers were low, the ditches would not divert enough water into the fields. Ranchers solved this problem by building diversion dams made from dirt and brush to back the water into the ditches and force the water onto their fields. This innovation also made it possible to cultivate even more acreage, but the new cropland had to be cleared and broken first. The ranchers hired local Indians and others to grub up the sagebrush and make the land fit to grow hay. This allowed ranchers to harvest a bigger crop than ever before.

Recently, there has been another innovation in ranch life involving water: hydroponic farming. This technique allows plants to grow in a solution of water and nutrients, rather than in the soil. One of the first experimental hydroponic farms in the West was established at Fallon in the late 1960's.

Ervin Crane, a native of Vermont and a Washoe County pioneer, was the first rancher to raise alfalfa in Nevada. This agricultural innovation worked substantial changes in the livestock business, because it allowed ranchers to harvest several cuttings of hay each season, instead of the single crop of wild hay that they used to reap. Crane has also been given credit for being the first person in Nevada to successfully grow shade trees on sagebrush land.

From Angel's *History of Nevada*

New Crops

In 1863, two Washoe County ranchers, Peleg Brown and Ervin Crane, began growing alfalfa rather than the natural wild grasses of the region. They were the first to raise alfalfa in Nevada, which later became the most important source of food for livestock in the State.

As the amount of hay grown by ranchers increased, it became impossible to harvest it all with the old hand-held scythes. They were replaced at first by horse and steam-powered machinery and later, in the twentieth century, by gasoline-powered tractors. By using irrigation and mechanical harvesters, and by planting alfalfa, ranchers could get as many as three or four cuttings or harvests each year, instead of one crop of wild grass.

The most profitable ranches were the ones located closest to market, that is, ranches closest to well-traveled roads or prosperous mining camps. The mining camps needed fresh fruit and vegetables; otherwise, the townsfolk had to pay high prices to have canned produce hauled in from California or Utah. Ranchers were able to get good prices for grain, potatoes, onions, and other garden vegetables, as well as milk and butter. The ranchers drove their crop to market themselves or sold it to businessmen for reshipment by railroad.

During the late nineteenth century, many new settlers of Italian origin arrived in Nevada. They raised garden vegetables along Carson River, on Truckee Meadows, and along Walker River, using land they leased or rented from other ranchers. By saving their profits, these Italian-American ranchers were able to buy the land they were farming. Many of Nevada's prominent ranches were settled by these men, whose descendants still own a number of the original homesteads.

A high noon shot of Henry Lange, his family, and his workmen just before lunch break, during a Carson Valley summer in the 1890's. The Indian workmen at left and center have been pitching the hay from the stack into a wooden hay press (right), where it is compressed and bailed. The waiting oxen and flatbed wagon are there to take the bales away to be stored.

Courtesy of Special Collections, University of Nevada Reno Library

Heavily-loaded hay wagons transported the cut and dried alfalfa to the stacks, from which the hay might be stored or sold.

Courtesy of Special Collections, University of Nevada Reno Library

Steam-powered threshing machines of the Dangberg & Brockliss company at work during the 1906 harvest at Carson Valley. This kind of lucrative crop production encouraged the Virginia & Truckee Railroad to extend its tracks south to Minden from Carson City that year. A horse and buggy stands shoulder to shoulder with some of Nevada's first tractors, while workers sack and seal the grain.

Courtesy of Special Collections, University of Nevada Reno Library

Workmen pitch in to harvest the hay in this gas-powered operation near Fallon in the mid-1920's. The noon-time summer photograph illustrates how the internal combustion engine and inexpensive fuel changed ranching. Small crews could do the work of hundreds of men, as modern machinery went into action. The labor-saving result led to larger ranches and fewer ranchers, all but ending the age of family farms.

Courtesy of Nevada Historical Society

Fertilizing the melon fields with a mule-drawn manure wagon, this rancher improved the quality of his land and crop, and helped prevent late-spring frost damage.

Courtesy of Nevada Historical Society

Our State has been distinguished for years for its fine potatoes and other garden crops. The "Heart-O-Gold" cantaloupe, raised in the Lahontan Valley farming country around Fallon, is another crop which has made Nevada famous.

The Federal Government

The federal government has had a major effect on ranching in Nevada. This is no surprise, since the United States government controls 87% of the land in the State and is in direct competition with the State and private users for the right to the use of a scarce and valuable resource — water.

During the nineteenth century, Congress encouraged the new settlers who were ranching and farming on the public lands to use the water by enacting water laws in 1866, 1877, and 1891. However, the government position substantially changed after 1902, when Congress passed the Reclamation Act.

There was much public support for the Act, which created the United States Reclamation Service under the Department of the Interior. Many people thought that the government could make the deserts of the nation produce crops, if it only tried.

Many of the government's irrigation projects were expensive and controversial. This certainly was true in Nevada. Officials of the newly created U.S. Reclamation Service decided in 1903 to build, as one of their first projects, a huge irrigation system on the lower Carson River. It was designed to reclaim tens of thousands of acres of crop-land from the desert and was backed by Francis G. Newlands, the son-in-law of William Sharon. Newlands, an influential Congressman and later Senator from Nevada, helped President Theodore Roosevelt make the Reclamation Act of 1902 a law.

The original scheme included a plan to service over 400,000 acres of newly-reclaimed and irrigated fields in western and central Nevada. As first planned, the project involved the entire Truckee and Carson River Basins, as well as Lake Tahoe, with irrigation canals to cross the Forty Mile Desert to Humboldt and Carson Sinks. Government spokesmen predicted that within just ten years, 10,000 people would be

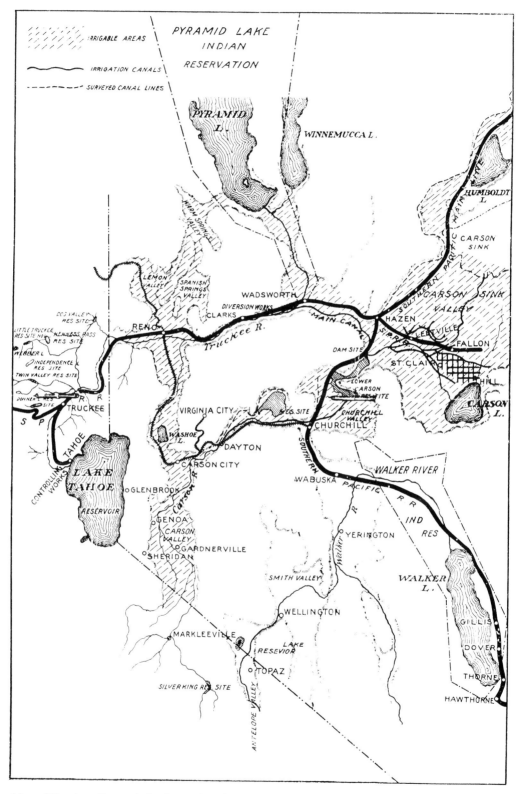

Map of Truckee–Carson irrigation project from government surveys.

From *Uncle Sam's Nine Million Dollar Nevada Farm*

Francis Griffith Newlands (1848–1917), born in Mississippi, married Senator William Sharon's daughter and inherited much of Sharon's wealth and influence. With the help of Senator William M. Stewart of Nevada, Newlands started his political career in the Silver-Democratic Party and was elected to Congress in 1892 and to the U.S. Senate in 1903. In 1902, he was one of the leading backers of the Reclamation Act, which ushered in a whole new era of economic development in Nevada and the West.

Courtesy of Special Collections,
University of Nevada Reno Library

Celebration of the Opening of Derby Dam and Canal, June 17, 1905. This was the first reclamation project ever undertaken by the federal government. The photograph shows Senator Francis Newlands and other dignitaries standing around the newly-completed structure on a very sunny day. The spillways at the left of the photograph will divert the waters backed up by the dam across the Truckee River into Derby Canal. In the background, an excursion train of the Southern Pacific waits to take the celebrities away.

Courtesy of Special Collections, University of Nevada Reno Library

living in Fallon, the center of the project, and that the irrigating works would serve 100,000 people.

U.S. engineers and workmen began to build a conveying canal across the desert in 1903, connecting the Truckee and Carson Rivers. The ditch, which was finished in 1905 and which still operates, carried water from a dam and diversion on the Truckee River at Derby past Fernley and Hazen to Carson Sink. The water carried in the unlined Derby Canal was to be used to irrigate new farmland on the public domain, which the government would open up for settlement in small parcels.

The Southern Pacific Railroad company published a pamphlet in 1907 about the Newlands or Truckee-Carson Project describing the irrigation system to prospective emigrants; it was called *Uncle Sam's Nine Million Dollar Nevada Farm:*

> Is he going to farm it himself? Oh, no; as soon as he has turned the water on it from the big reservoirs he has been building, he is going to give it away to the people of the United States.
>
> How can you get a part of it? Just as easy — if you are a citizen and he has not already given you a homestead in another place, you need simply tell the agent at the land office in Carson or the agent for the big farm at Fallon, that you want eighty acres of good land. Pick out the eighty acres first that you want and tell him just where it is. Then pay him eight dollars for papers showing that Uncle Sam has agreed to give you that land if you begin living on it within six months and make it a home for the next five years.
>
> Is that all Uncle Sam charges? That is all for the land — eight dollars. For the water he puts on the land to make things grow, he charges you $2.60 per acre every year for ten years. Then the water and land belong to one another and both belong to you. After the tenth year the only charge will be a few cents per month to keep up the ditches and reservoirs.

Only a portion of the massive reclamation project was ever built, and that at great expense. Many of the works were far less efficient than expected. This caused a number of problems, and poor planning also hampered the effort.

The government officials were unable to deliver on several of their promises to the new settlers. They could not guarantee adequate irrigation water. Many of the reclaimed plots had bad soil, and the ditches didn't completely drain the new fields, which left them muddy bogs.

The engineers for the federal Reclamation Service greatly underestimated how much water would be needed to irrigate the reclaimed lands and overestimated how much land could profitably be reclaimed. The new settlers on the land, who had been

The Derby or Truckee Canal outlet into lower Carson River, 1905–1914. The timber chute or flume carried the water right up to the cottonwood-lined banks, just below the present site of Lahontan Dam. From there, the water went to the Reclamation Project and other ranchlands in Lahontan Valley.

Courtesy of Nevada Historical Society

Lahontan Dam near completion in 1914. The timber chute was later replaced by a concrete structure emptying above the power house.

Courtesy of Special Collections, University of Nevada Reno Library

Aerial view of Lahontan Dam and Lake Lahontan on Carson River.
Courtesy of Special Collections, University of Nevada Reno Library

hoping for an early and profitable harvest, found that alfalfa took three to five years to produce a commercial growth. With these and other problems, many ranchers on the Truckee-Carson Project went out of business and abandoned their ranches, while others stayed and prospered.

The settlers in the area formed a water-users' association in 1912 and began to complain about the federal government's management of the project. In 1918, the local farmers formed the Truckee-Carson Irrigation District, and they took over management of the Reclamation Service Project in 1926. That year, a Department of the Interior report admitted that of $7,899,479 spent on the Newlands Project, more than half of that amount — almost $4.5 million — had been wasted.

In an attempt to provide more water to the Newlands Project's irrigating ditches, the government took two steps. The first was to build a dam and reservoir on the Carson River. Construction of Lahontan dam began in 1911. When it was finished in 1914, the backed-up waters of the Carson River formed Lahontan Reservoir. This provided water storage for the project but did not really increase the amount of water available to the federal authorities.

The rights of private persons to the waters of the Truckee and Carson Rivers were still unsettled, when the government took another step to save the Newlands Project. In 1913, the United States sued all of the water users and ranchers on the Truckee River in federal court, to determine their claims to the river and to allow the government to use more water for the Newlands Project. This lawsuit, called *U.S. v. Orr Water Ditch Company, et al.*, was supposed to be "friendly," but it turned into a costly thirty-one year battle for control of the River before it was settled in 1944.

Other federal reclamation and irrigation projects, such as those on the Truckee and Colorado Rivers, have been much more successful. However, shifting priorities and policies within the Department of the Interior and other branches of the government have kept these projects from being completely helpful.

Within recent years, the federal government has involved itself in lawsuits seeking to control the use of subsurface waters tapped by wells. In one well-publicized southern Nevada case, a federal court limited a rancher's right to pump water onto his land, where the pumping dropped the water levels in a cave on federal land, in order to protect an endangered species — the Devil's Hole Pupfish.

Of all the actions of the federal government affecting ranching in Nevada, the Taylor Grazing Act of 1934 was one of the most important. Congress ended its one hundred fifty-year-old policy of leaving the federal lands open to settlement and use. Instead, Congress began an entirely new policy in which the "scientific management" of the public lands was entrusted indefinitely to an administrative bureaucracy. At first called the Grazing Service, the agency became the Bureau of Land Management (B.L.M.) in 1946.

The B.L.M. restricts use of much of the public lands or forbids it entirely. It does this under the provisions of the Multiple Land Use Act of 1964, which gave the Secretary of the Interior this discretionary power. Most of Nevada's ranchers need access to the public lands to graze their livestock. Consequently, they pay the B.L.M. a lease fee to use the land from year to year, subject to government regulations. For the ranchers of Nevada, the administration of the B.L.M. has been a mixed blessing. Several of the federal land regulations have caused public protest. Other actions, such as the government's conservation efforts in the timberlands of the National Forests, have earned widespread praise.

THE GRAZING INDUSTRY

The mainstay of ranching in Nevada has been the raising of livestock, especially cattle and sheep. Of these, cattle ranching is the oldest. At first, the chief market for Nevada cattle was the mining camps of California, but the discovery of gold and silver in Nevada changed all that.

Cattle Ranching

The grazing industry in Nevada spread very rapidly, as settlers moved in and started ranching. Nearly every productive valley in the State was occupied within twenty years after John Reese built his house at Genoa in 1851, the year Carson and Eagle Valleys were first settled. Whites moved into Washoe Valley and the Truckee Meadows in 1852. Two years later pioneers began ranching in Clover Valley, the Humboldt River Valley, the Big Bend of Carson River, and Carson Sink (also called Lahontan Valley). In the south, Mormon settlers started farming Las Vegas valley in 1855. Ranchers took up land in Smith, Mason, and Ruby Valleys in 1859 — all before the rush began to the mines on the Comstock Lode.

Timothy B. Smith was one of the original settlers in Smith Valley. He came into the valley in August, 1859, with a band of his friends. They were buckaroos or cowboys; the word buckaroo comes from the Spanish *vaquero,* or cattle herdsman. Two of the group were named Smith, which is how the Valley got its name. In his *Recollections,* later published in the 1911–1912 Report of the Nevada Historical Society, Tim Smith recalled how he came to Walker River back in the summer of 1859:

> We had driven our herds from the west side of the San Joaquin River in California. The motive which had led to our making this change in herding grounds, taking us to a place as it seemed so far removed from the market, was the necessity of procuring feed for our stock. The previous winter had been an unusually dry one on the ranges of the west side, and feed became so scarce that something had to be done. We had learned of the Walker River country from some emigrants who had three or four years before crossed through to California by this route, and who gave glowing accounts of the abundance of meadow grass they had seen on the river bottom as also the quantities of bunch grass on the flats and hills back from the river.

Two of Smith's friends traveled over the Sierra Nevada, investigated the report, found it was true, and sent word back to California. The little band herded their cattle across the mountains to Smith Valley and made preparations to stay. This is how Smith told it:

> The grass on Walker River when we reached our destination was a fine sight. In the meadows it was standing practically undisturbed except where the Indians had made trails through it on their way to the river. The spot chosen for the camp was on the edge of a fine large meadow. . . . Corrals for the stock were constructed and a house for ourselves erected. As there was no sawmill within forty miles of the valley, the only building material for the house was tules. This house served very well for the first winter, and, there being very little we could do with the cattle, we spent most of our time within its walls. One morning it caught fire and considerable damage was done before the flames were extinguished. We patched it up as well as we could and made the best of it until the next summer.

The ranchers fattened their cattle on the lush, thick grasslands of the Carson, Humboldt, Truckee, and Walker River Valleys. The fattened cattle were driven to the slaughterhouses in the mining camps, where they were eaten by hungry miners. The milk, cheese, cream, butter, and other foodstuffs from cattle were also quickly sold. The number of ranchers increased in the valleys nearest the mines, resulting in small ranching communities all across western Nevada.

When important finds of gold and silver ore were made in central and eastern Nevada during the 1860's and 1870's, thousands of people started new ranches in the State. As in western Nevada, most of them were near the mining camps which furnished a ready market for ranch products. Settlers occupied Mound Valley after 1861, then moved into Smokey and Paradise Valleys in 1863. Ranchers took up land in Lamoille Valley in 1864, and in Halleck, Monitor, and Newark Valleys in 1866. The next year pioneers settled Huntington, Starr, and Railroad Valleys and in 1868, Steptoe Valley, and White Pine Valley in 1869.

Residence and Dairy Ranch of T. B. Smith, Smith Valley, 1881.
From Angel's *History of Nevada*

"Dugouts on the Plains Near Wells." Very simple accommodations characterize life on a new ranch in nineteenth-century Nevada, but hard work, good weather, and high prices for ranch produce could have the old homestead looking prosperous within a few years. This 1877 print is from Frank Leslie's Illustrated Weekly magazine.

The transcontinental railroad and its branch lines also caused changes in the ranching business. Because livestock can be transported rapidly by rail across great distances, at relatively low cost, it became profitable to take up ranching in valleys that were formerly remote from any market. The livestock could then be driven to the closest freight depot and shipped from there to distant cities such as Chicago or San Francisco.

In northeastern Nevada, the ranching business began to flourish after a prolonged drought in California. In 1871, as in 1859, dry conditions forced California cattlemen to look outside their state for range land. Many of them decided upon the sparsely populated valleys of Elko and Humboldt Counties.

The most successful cattle ranches were large operations. By 1880, perhaps only a dozen stockmen owned three-quarters of the cattle ranging north of the Humboldt River. This kind of consolidation was typical in Nevada. The owners of the larger ranches were called cattle kings or cattle barons. Even though their ranches were large, they owned only a fraction of the acreage on which their cattle grazed. Much of the land was public domain wasteland.

Cattle ranching is an exciting business; in fact, it is a way of life. Activities on a ranch are cyclical, that is, they are repeated with the passing seasons. The cycle was somewhat different in the nineteenth and early twentieth centuries, before the advent of the B.L.M. Ira H. Kent, a Churchill County ranchman, described the early system in 1926 for the federal court in the *Alpine* case:

> In the summer they took these cattle out in the various pastures that were available near the water, and in the winter they fed them hay. In the fall they brought the cattle back on the grass land that had been mowed for hay, and then when snow or storms came on and the weather got cold, they fed the hay to stock cattle.

In order to keep their own cattle from straying, and to keep stray cattle out of their fields, ranchers fenced their property. Until barbed wire was patented by Joseph Glidden in 1874, ranchers used whatever materials were handy to build their fences — rocks, logs, planks, and smooth wire. Churchill County ranchman William S. Bailey had an unusual fence at his home ranch near Fallon. According to John Sheehan, a Bailey Ranch buckaroo who testified in the *Alpine* case, it was:

> A wire fence made out of cables from Virginia City, they brought the cable out of those old mines, most of all of it was cable and put up on posts; some wire was regular fence wire, and some where there was three cables went on besides some smooth wire, one or two wire, I have forgotten.
>
> I kept that fence up; rode it every other day from the lake to the big corrals to see that the fence was up and the gates closed. At times stock used to go through it, and people would come along and tear the fence down, and knock the wire down so their stock could get on the inside and run with Bailey's; and every other day the first of the year I was there I rode that fence and repaired it and patched it with staples.

The ranchers put up fences to enclose their own fields. Some even went so far as to fence in federal land, but severe penalties discouraged this practice after about 1912. Today, a rancher must lease grazing land from the federal government or his neighbors if he doesn't have enough grassland to feed his herd.

In the springtime, the first order of business on a cattle ranch was the roundup or rodeo. Stockmen rode out all over the deserts and brushlands looking for the cattle they turned out to feed the winter before. Where there were several cattle ranches in the same vicinity, ranchers would generally cooperate to have one big roundup, after which the cows belonging to various ranchers could be sorted out by brand.

Catching the cattle could be hard, exhausting work. Joseph F. Triplett was in charge of a huge roundup in the spring and summer of 1862. A number of ranchers hired Triplett and about twenty other men to scour west-central Nevada for cattle. On May 3,

"Shipping Cattle on Board a Train From a Corral at Halleck," 1877. Frank Leslie's Illustrated Weekly's artist sketched this scene of seeming pandemonium at the loading pens of the Central Pacific Railroad Company's freight station at Halleck, while drovers loaded the train's cattle cars with beef.

"Settlers Building a Corral Near Wells, Nevada." *This Illustration from* Frank Leslie's Illustrated Weekly *magazine shows some of the early fencework in the days before barbed wire became available. The Elko County rangeland proved ideal for ranching, and the transcontinental railroad connections at Wells and elsewhere made shipping live or butchered beef and mutton a simple matter.*

he explained the situation with this entry in his diary: "Here I am on my way into the heart of a country known to be inhabited by hostile Indians, and all for the paltry sum of ten dollars a day, — and why: Because I have the misfortune to be broke. . . ."

Triplett's roundup lasted nearly two months, during which time his band of buckaroos found over 1300 head of cattle, not including calves. They nearly ran out of supplies, as Triplett noted on June 14:

> Took to the mountains with eleven men to search the country around Sand Springs and after a hard day's work reached camp on the east side of upper sink [of the Carson] with 172 more cattle. No bread — no sugar — beef and coffee strait. Can scoop up all the salt we want from the ground, — ten days without bread, getting ravenous, hard tack would taste to us like ginger cake to a school boy, — bound to get all the cattle in the country, bread or no bread.

Not all of the roundup was accomplished on horseback. The cattle could swim, and they had to be chased. This gave Triplett an opportunity to get acquainted with the tule swamps and draws of Churchill County, which he mentioned in his diary on June 22, 1862:

> Started up the lake for Carson river, saw a few cattle on an island in the lake supposed to be about one mile from the mainland, proposed to swim to the island and get them. A Cherokee joined me, — tied undershirts around our heads and plunged in: the longest mile I ever traveled was to that island. Found six gentle work oxen, got them onto a narrow point and forced them into the water. By swimming back and forth soon got them started to mainland. We each then mounted an ox and road ashore, — good thing we took our shirts or we'd been badly blistered. During our absence Mr. Benton was thrown from his

horse and had his arm broken — simple fracture — which I set, by measuring the well arm and using willow for splints.

Late storms on the range could also make the roundup dangerous business. In April, 1875, John Carling, a Lyon County rancher, became lost during a blizzard. His friends tracked him for days, according to a news report published in the Dayton *Lyon County Times:*

> On the morning of the fourth day the searching party emerged from the mountains upon the edge of Death Valley, and at a deserted cabin near Black Springs, having traveled over 200 miles. On entering they were overjoyed to find their lost comrade had recently been there, and were rewarded a few moments later by discovering both horse and rider a short distance away. Both were in a famished and almost dying condition, and had it not been for this opportune arrival of help yet another tragedy would have been added to the melancholy history of that Sahara of death. . . . When Carling first entered the cabin he found two pieces of tallow candle which he devoured. He had despaired of ever reaching home, and taking a piece of brown paper, in which the candles were wrapped, he wrote his will, bequeathing his property, worth $50,000, to his wife and children, and also recorded the date and circumstances of his adventure, that those who should find his body might also have a clue to its identity. Luckily for him his companions perservered in their search, his friends are spared that grief, and he lives to recount his most fortunate escape.

After the cattle were rounded up, the calves were branded by their owners. Today, brands are mandatory and must be recorded, as a result of a law passed by the State Legislature in 1915. In the early days some cattle were branded or were given earmarks by having their ears clipped, while other cattle went unmarked. When there were a lot of cattle around, it was prudent to brand those you owned, so they wouldn't become part of someone else's herd. Elizabeth Magee Murphy, in her *Alpine* testimony, described

Cutting out range cattle in Paradise Valley, these Humboldt County buckaroos had to move fast to corral this fleet-footed shorthorn steer and calf.
Courtesy of Nevada Historical Society

how her father started to brand cattle in Churchill County in 1868 for just that reason:

> It was the year that Mr. Bailey got possession of the Big Dobe and the Big Island, and brought his cattle down there by the thousands, and everybody that had from ten to a hundred head gathered their cattle in and branded them, because the big cattleman was entitled to all the unbranded cattle when the roundup came, and everybody branded cattle, and my father got a branding iron and branded our cattle; it was an iron with a ring around it; and we were angry, because we didn't want to see the cattle branded. I believe that was a law of the range, when the rodeo was over all the unbranded cattle went to the cattleman that had the rodeo. So all the men branded their cattle.

Although there had been brands on some of the first cattle to enter Nevada, the first brand wasn't recorded in the State until 1871, when E. Burner of Elko County registered his mark. Livestock brands have their own very interesting lore and figure prominently in tales of catle rustlers, how ranches got started, or personal stories about the ranchers themselves.

After the roundup and branding, some of the cattle would be driven to market. Ten year old John H. Sheehan of Gold Hill ran away from his home and parents by jumping on an ore train in 1874. He went to work on John Luce's horse ranch in Lahontan Valley and stayed four years. In 1878, he was hired by William S. Bailey, owner of the largest cattle ranch in Churchill County. Bailey ran about 5,000–10,000 cattle, 200–250 brood mares and colts, about 80 saddle horses, and 40–50 work horses on his ranch. When Sheehan testified in the *Alpine* case, he described himself as the kind of boy who at fourteen was doing a man's work and did two men's work from that time on. Here is what he had to say about his duties as a buckaroo and how the Bailey Ranch was run:

> Well I used to drive cattle from the ranch to Virginia City, to his slaughterhouse in Virginia City, and from the ranch to the slaughterhouse in Reno, and then I rode this country here looking out after his cattle; whenever he bought any cattle anywheres I almost always went with him, and brought cattle in and delivered them here for him.
>
> As I said before, Mr. Bailey was in the butcher business, selling cattle in Virginia City and also in Reno, and generally in the spring of the year, or

Cattle branding. As the long shadows show, the day is almost over for this tired crew of buckaroos, while spare branding irons smolder in the fire.

Courtesy of Special Collections, University of Nevada Reno Library

◄ *Nevada's first official brand, 1871.*

R L	
	crop
	upperbit of peak
	underbit
	round underbit, half-noose
	swallowfork
	slit
	uppercut
	undercut
	overslope
	underslope
	upper half crop
	under half crop
	fingermark, fingerprint
	slit and downfall
	sawtooth, or saw
	"M" punch
	punch (a hole through the ear)
	"L" slit
	kitchen slit
	cloverleaf, swallowtail or fantail
	figure seven
	lop
	double figure seven, paddle
	earrings
	stovepipe
	reef or hatchet
	keyhole
	jingle or jinglebob
	square swallowfork
	shoestring
	pennant
	stair or step

◄ *EARMARKS*
Cutting the ears of cattle is another way of marking the stock, and these earmarks must be recorded along with the brand. In Nevada, over 30 different types of earmarks have been recorded.

summer, later in the summer when the cattle began to get fat enough, we began driving cattle off the ranch to Virginia City for beef.

Well there would be times there when I would practically be on the road there all the time, just as fast as I would drive, and then times it would let up and I would not make a drive probably for two weeks.

At times I would deliver the cattle right to the slaughterhouse myself, and then there would be times that he wanted another drive at once, and he would come and meet me, come out to Six Mile Canyon, and he would take the cattle, or have men come and meet me and take the cattle, and send me right back to get another bunch of cattle and make another drive.

We would get them on the ranch, start them from what they called the Big Corrals over here across this pasture of the Big Bend. Johnnie Carling made that first day twenty-six miles. [The next day he would make] Cooney Ranch, Carson River, that was eighteen miles, and the next morning he aimed to get up at 2:00 o'clock and start them cattle and get them up Six Mile Canyon before daylight. They was all wild Spanish cattle, and mean to handle, and to get them by those houses and by the teams, he would get them up there and turned off and went up over the summit to the slaughterhouse.

He killed them cattle and sold them to different butchers, Reno and Gold Hill, besides having two or three butcher shops of his own. And then some of them cattle he would take to the Truckee Meadows. He had a slaughterhouse at Reno, and killed cattle there and shipped to San Francisco in his own refrigerator cars.

The first tame cattle entered Nevada with the Bidwell-Bartleson party in 1841. Other emigrants brought cattle with them, and many head were lost, stolen, or strayed as they traveled across Nevada. Cattle rustling in the State dates from this period when white men conspired with Indians to attack the overland travelers and steal their cattle. Cattle rustling was a chronic problem throughout the late nineteenth century. Sometimes, but not often, stockmen took drastic measures to punish cattle thieves. In the late spring of 1881, things got very drastic in White Pine County, as recounted by a newspaper article in the Ward *Reflex:*

There appears to be no longer any doubt about the hanging of Pete Megley and another man at or near Mud Springs, 45 miles north of Ward a short time ago. Archie Williamson, just in from that section, thinks it a pretty well established fact that Pete and another man pulled hemp without a foot hold. It is claimed that cattle stealing was their strong hold and not that of pulling hemp.

In order to protect themselves against rustlers and other dangers, the State's stockmen formed the Nevada Livestock Association at Winnemucca in 1884. This group began to circulate information about brands and offered rewards for the caputre and conviction of stock thieves. They also pressured the railroads for lower freight rates and exchanged information on areas of common interest. While stockmen continued to have

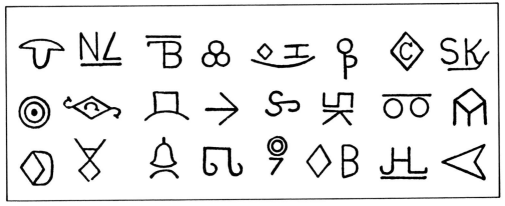

A variety of brands from our State show the imagination and romance of stock-raising in the Silver State. Most of these brands have interesting stories behind them, too.

Cattle Drive. A solitary buckaroo rides trail on his herd to make sure the heifers don't wander astray, as he moves the cattle away from their pasture in this Washoe County shot. The Mount Rose range dominates the scenic backdrop.

Courtesy of Special Collections, University of Nevada Reno Library

Breaking a wild horse. Exciting, dangerous work faces these buckaroos as they attempt to tame the desperate and muscular mustang. The first step was to get the animal to stop rearing and bucking, shown here.   Courtesy of Special Collections, University of Nevada Reno Library

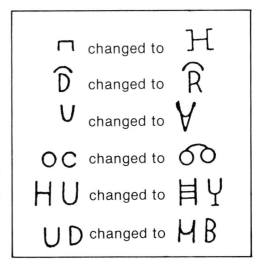

Cattle rustlers could skillfully alter a brand. Skinning the animal was sometimes the only way to prove a changed brand. When the inside of a hide is revealed, the old brand can be traced on the underside, the new one cannot. Following are some examples of rustlers' work, adapted from Velma Truett's On the Hoof in Nevada.

trouble with the railroads and natural disasters, the problem of cattle rustlers soon became all but nonexistent.

The first cattle driven into Nevada were longhorns; in the early days, fancy or purebred cattle were unknown. The first imported stock came into the State in the 1870's: shorthorns were introduced in 1874, Durhams soon afterwards, and Herefords in 1878. The hard winter of 1889-90 killed off many of the old longhorn cattle, which the ranchers replaced with better stock. The new breeds form the basis of almost all of Nevada's herds of cattle today, and the State's ranches have an excellent reputation as producers of fancy stock.

The cattle business has never been one to produce easy profits. The ranchers found prices severely depressed after harsh winters like those of 1879 and 1889-90, while poor market conditions prevailed in 1919-1925 and during the Great Depression of 1929-1937. However, the cattle business has been intermittently profitable notwithstanding government regulation, bad weather, and unstable prices, and Nevada is still one of the West's most prominent ranching states.

Sheep

Sheep ranching is the other main form of ranching activity in Nevada. Other than the wild mountain goats, the first sheep to enter Nevada came with the Workman-Rowland emigrant party which left New Mexico in 1841 on an overland trip to California. The emigrants carried 150 sheep with them to southern California by way of the Spanish Trail. The first commercial sheep drive took place eleven years later in 1852, when Richens Lacy "Uncle Dick" Wootton brought 9,000 head over the Humboldt River section of the California Trail. Wootton described the reasons behind the drive in his autobiography:

> In New Mexico, where the Mexicans had large flocks, fine sheep could be bought for one tenth of the price per head they were reported to be selling for in California and it looked to me as though a handsome fortune might be realized as profit on a large band of sheep driven through and disposed of at Sacramento or some other point on the coast. Up to that time nothing of the kind had been attempted, but I thought the scheme a practicable one and determined to try it. I knew it meant sixteen hundred miles of travel over mountain ranges, across barren plains and still more barren deserts, and in addition to this I knew that there was scarcely a mile of the road which was not beset by savages who were making it their principal business to rob and murder a white man or band of white men whenever opportunity offered. I did not think the undertaking more hazardous, however, than others in which I had engaged, and I began by making my arrangements to set out on the trip.

*Richens Lacy "Uncle Dick" Wootton of Virginia
(1816–1893) was a fur trapper, Indian fighter,
and pioneer who drove nine thousand sheep
overland to California in 1852.
He returned with a herd of mules, which he sold
for $40,000 profit, and became a legend
in his own time.*
From *Conrad's Uncle Dick Wootton.*

Wootton's drive was a commercial success and was followed in 1853 by a similarly successful drive, led by Kit Carson. H. T. P. Comstock, for whom the Comstock Lode was named, also made a sheep drive into Nevada in 1856, although not with the same kind of success as Wootton or Carson.

Sheep, like cattle, were shipped outside Nevada to markets serviced by rail. Not everyone in Nevada welcomed the sheep, which were thought to compete with cattle for the rangeland. By the late nineteenth century, however, ranches would often operate herds of both cattle and sheep. Sheep ranchers eventually gained an advantage over cattle ranchers, even though sheep required more supervision. Prices for mutton remained relatively stable, while beef prices had large fluctuations, and the profit was uncertain. Further, the wool on the sheep was an additional and valuable source of income which, unlike production of leather hides, didn't require killing the animal. The sheep were also better adapted to the extremes of climate and were prolific breeders.

In order to control the problem of tramp sheepmen — men who owned no land and grazed their sheep on others' property, using up the rangeland — the State Legislature passed a tax in 1895. It was levied on sheep but had an exemption for ranchers who owned land on which the sheep could be grazed. This act was successful in finally driving the tramp sheepmen from the range.

The Basques

Pedro Altube, a six-foot-eight-inch-tall Basque rancher, gave many of his fellow countrymen a start in Nevada. In 1870, the forty-three year old Altube began ranching in Elko County, where he operated herds of sheep and cattle. He employed Basque sheepherders who received their pay in livestock. Within four or five years a good sheepherder could acquire his own band of sheep and go into business for himself. Many sheep and cattle ranches in Oregon, Idaho, and Nevada got their start through Altube's activities. As a result, Altube gained the reputation of being "the Father of the Basques in America."

The Basque people live in the Pyrenees mountains on the border between France and Spain. They emigrated to this country in large numbers between 1860 and the 1920's, and many settled in Nevada. The Basques have made a rich cultural contribution to the State. One of the more spectacular contributions is their annual folk festivals held to celebrate the Basque heritage. These draw thousands of sightseers and revelers, adding color and vitality to Nevada's society.

The art of sheep shearing, shown before and after. The wool went to make clothing, rugs, and other manufactured goods for sale at home and abroad.

A Basque sheepherder and his
ever-vigilant dogs watch their
flock looking at them.
The nomadic ranchmen led
lonely lives wandering the hills
and valleys in search of grass
for their flocks. Sheepherding
first challenged the cattle
ranchers in the 1870's and
then surpassed it after 1890
as Nevada's principal
livestock industry.

Courtesy of Special Collections,
University of Nevada Reno Library

Basque dancers in their colorful traditional costumes revive ancient legends and folk memories in a
vigorous, spectacular festival of life.

Courtesy of Nevada Department of Transportation

RANCHING COMMUNITIES

Life on a nineteenth century Nevada ranch could be lonely and isolated at times, but it had its charms. The people were neighborly and took an interest in each other, which is characteristic of rural communities. When towns and cities formed, some of this spirit of kindred citizenship disappeared, as Andrew J. Newman stated during the *Alpine* case: "People were pretty close together those days; that is, if they was far apart they had a feeling for each other that they haven't got nowadays."

The pioneers were quick to form a society even in the first years of settlement. In his *History of Nevada,* Myron Angel described the first dance ever held by the State's first settlers:

> On the night of the last day of the year 1853, there was a dance in the log building over Spafford Hall's store, at the mouth of Gold Canyon. There were nine females, including little girls, that attended the party, and this number constituted three-fourths of all the fair sex in western Utah at the time. ... The miners, ranchers, and station-keepers, from all over the country, numbering possibly one hundred and fifty men, were there in or about the station; and while everybody was enjoying themselves, the Washoe Indians came and drove off their horses.

Horse racing and foot racing were also popular forms of amusement, as were gambling, drinking, and dog-fights.

Another fundamental aspect of pioneer life in old-time Nevada was the schools. The first one was taught in the State in 1854, by Mrs. Allen in Carson Valley. Every ranching community of any size had a school. The residents would join together in an informal school district, designate a ranch house where the pupils were to be taught, and hire a teacher to instruct the children.

Nevada's principal ranching communities are Elko, Fallon, Hawthorne, Lovelock, Minden-Gardnerville, and Yerington. These are not the only ranching communities in the State, but they are the most important. The story of Elko has been described more fully in the chapter on Transportation, so we will concern ourselves with the other towns here.

Fallon

The first permanent building in Lahontan Valley was Ragtown Station, on the Carson River. It began as a trading post for the overland emigrants at the southern edge of the Forty Mile Desert. At first, the men who kept the trading posts lived in tents; the ragged canvas gave the place its name, although there is another story that the drying laundry of the emigrants led men to call the spot Ragtown. In his overland diary entry for August 31, 1850, Byron McKinstry of Illinois described the station:

> When we first struck Carson River we found a village 8 or 9 stores (cloth tents). Flour sells at $2.00 per lb., Bacon $1., pies $1.25 to $1.75, small ones at that. Small biscuit at 50 cts. each, jerked beef at $1, coffee 12½ cts. per cup, a meal of vituals $3.00, and you are allowed at that only so much bread, beef and coffee. They tell a story of an emigrant that came in yesterday and eat and drank $25 worth at a single meal. They cut hay and haul it up from the sink of Carson River and sell it from 25 to fifty cts. per bundle, about as large round as a man's arm. It would take $5 to feed a hungry ox. Oxen sell here at from $5 to $25 per yoke and the emigrants complain bitterly that the traders steal their cattle and run them off. They certainly pick up a good many. One company lost all their oxen but found three of them in possession of a trader, branded. He would not give them up — they took them forcibly and packed their things on them to Cal., the rest of their stock they never found.

Asa Levi Kenyon settled there in 1854 and recorded his land claim with the settlers' government in Carson Valley. Kenyon dug a well on the Forty Mile Desert, about fifteen miles from Ragtown, and did an excellent business selling water to the thirsty emigrants.

Ragtown was just getting started as a transportation community when Captain James H. Simpson's survey of the central overland route changed the road in 1859, bypassing Kenyon's station. A new community started to the east of Ragtown at Stillwater in 1862. Stillwater began as a stagecoach station when the overland mail route was changed from the California Trail to the Simpson wagon road. It became the Churchill County seat in 1868. The few settlers in nineteenth century Churchill County did not have much money to spare for governmental operations. The County administrators had to take a practical approach to problems such as crime, as this 1875 newspaper article from the Austin *Reese River Reveille* indicates:

> NOVEL PRISON. — We are reliably informed that a man who was arrested for some offense at Stillwater, the county seat of Churchill county, was confined in a shaft, for lack of better jail accomodations. He was hoisted to the surface three times a day, and meals were placed at the edge of the shaft, and after he had eaten he was lowered back to his cell, and the rope hoisted out. The shaft in which he is confined is 200 feet in depth, so there was not much opportunity to escape. Who says that criminals are turned loose in Churchill county!

Ranchers settled in Lahontan Valley and sold their produce to the freighting teams which were traveling between railroad supply points and the mining camps at Belleville, Columbus, Candelaria, Belmont, and elsewhere. By the turn of the century, there were some ninety ranches in the area, and many of them had been operating for thirty or forty years. There was a substantial system of private irrigating ditches and dams in Lahontan Valley, carrying water to 15,000 acres of cropland and another 15,000 acres of pasture.

A boom started in the area when people realized that the U.S. Reclamation Service had big plans for the place. Stillwater was not destined to benefit, however. Nearly everyone moved to the more centrally located Fallon, a post office community named in 1896 for Mike Fallon, the owner. Leading Churchill County sheepman Warren Williams promoted the town, and many businessmen and settlers moved there from Stillwater. The S.P.R.R. built a spur line to Fallon, and the U.S. Reclamation Service set up its office in 1907. By 1908, the town had a chamber of commerce and a model volunteer fire brigade equipped with telephones in every fireman's house. By 1911, motion pictures were being shown triweekly in the town, and in 1912, an issue of

Ragtown Station, 1881. This view, taken from Angel's History of Nevada, shows some of proprietor Asa Kenyon's various activities — his horse-raising operation, several corrals full of cattle, a school, the station, store, saloon, ballroom, stables, and outbuildings, all inside a very neat and extensive fence.

Downtown Fallon on a cloudy day, about 1905. Other than the small groups of townsfolk chatting on the wooden sidewalks, there's not much traffic, but under the overhanging electric street lamps lie the dirt, dust, and ruts of a heavily-traveled road.

Courtesy of Special Collections, University of Nevada Reno Library

Governor Emmet D. Boyle occupied the place of honor at the Alfalfa Palace when he reviewed the 1915 Nevada State Fair parade at Fallon. Glamorous couples danced the starry night away in the Alfalfa Palace ballroom, just inside the portals. Forty-four tons of Nevada's principal agricultural product went into the building of this monument to ranching.

Courtesy of Nevada Historical Society

municipal bonds financed a town sewage disposal system and an electric power line from Lahontan Dam.

One interesting sidelight on Fallon's history was a socialist ranching colony established just outside of town in 1916. Named Nevada City, this cooperative society lasted only three years, but at one time had almost two hundred residents.

In addition to the Truckee-Carson or Newlands Project, Fallon's economy got a boost during the Second World War from the construction of the U.S. Navy Auxiliary Air Station nearby in 1942–44. United States Senator Patrick McCarran of Nevada was influential in bringing the federal facility into the State. Thousands of people arrived in Fallon, creating a housing shortage — the population doubled almost overnight. After the end of the war in 1945, the Air Station was placed on caretaker status, but in 1951, during the Korean War, it was reopened and has been operating ever since. In 1959, the base was named for a native hero of Fallon, Lieutenant Commander Bruce Van Voorhis.

For years, between 1915 and the late 1940's, Fallon was the site of the Nevada State Fair. The city has had its own high school since 1907, and in 1949, the Churchill County Hospital was built there. Today, Fallon is a prosperous and pleasant city, with green fields and shade trees. Hunting, fishing, and other forms of recreation are popular there and at the nearby Stillwater Wildlife Management Area.

Hawthorne

H. M. Yerington, the Superintendent of the Nevada railroad interests of the Bank of California, selected the town site of Hawthorne in early 1881. The scenic location on the south shore of Walker Lake also happened to be the place where the Carson & Colorado Railroad, then under construction, met the wagon road to the newly-discovered mines at Bodie, California. The wagon road was another Bank of California project, and its construction was supervised by William Hawthorne, after whom the town was named. Hawthorne was also the main division point of the railroad, where the C.&C.R.R.'s machine shops, roundhouse, and other facilities housed the locomotives, cars, and workmen.

There was an auction of town lots at Hawthorne held April 14, 1881. Governor John H. Kinkead was probably the most prominent of the eight hundred people who accepted free rides on a C.&C.R.R. excursion train to the townsite. Water was a problem; it had to be hauled four miles by wagon into town. However, Hawthorne got off to a brisk start, and by June, 1881, the Carson City *Appeal* noted that the town had thirty houses and eight tents.

Hawthorne merchants and freighters did a brisk business shipping goods brought in by rail out to the mines at Bodie and Candelaria. This in turn encouraged ranchers to grow hay to feed the teams and beef to feed the miners. Then, in 1883, Hawthorne became the Esmeralda County seat, replacing Aurora. All this helped to sustain the town, which remained a distribution center for the outlying mining camps.

In the late nineteenth and early twentieth centuries, Hawthorne suffered some reverses. The mines at Bodie and Candelaria stopped producing and were abandoned. As a result, the freighting business from Hawthorne suffered. The Southern Pacific Railroad bought the C.&C.R.R. and in 1905, built a new track which bypassed the town. The shops and workers, the trains and facilities were all moved to Mina. In 1907, the Esmeralda County seat moved to Goldfield, although in 1911, Hawthorne regained its status when it became the county seat of the newly-created Mineral County.

In 1926, Hawthorne was nearly destroyed in a disastrous fire. Fortunately, citizen volunteers and firefighters were able to save the historic courthouse. Another disaster that year, thousands of miles away on the east coast, caused Hawthorne's luck to change. The 1926 explosion of the U.S. Navy ammunition depot at Lake Denmark killed a number of people and destroyed much property near the heavily-populated New Jersey facility. Congress then began looking for a more remote location to store the Navy's shells and powder. United States Senator Tasker L. Oddie of Nevada used his influence to have the ammunition depot placed at Hawthorne.

The base was built between 1928 and 1930. The railroad connection between Hawthorne and the outside world was rebuilt to service the naval facility, which provided a major new source of revenue and population. The number of people living in Hawthorne increased from 244 in 1920 to 680 in 1930, and multiplied after the start of the Second World War. By 1944, according to a U.S. Department of Commerce study, Hawthorne had 13,000 residents.

Although the number of personnel stationed at the depot declined after World War Two, there were revivals of activity during the Korean War of 1950-53 and the Vietnam War of 1964-1972. In 1977, the U.S. Army took over operations at the ammunition storage depot, but since 1980, the facility has been managed by civilian contractors.

Today, tourism and recreation are popular activities at Hawthorne, especially fishing, boating, and camping at Walker Lake. Its motels, campgrounds, and spectacular scenery make it a favorite spot for visitors to the area.

Lovelock

Lovelock was originally a stagecoach station when it was founded by James Blake in the spring of 1861. George Lovelock, an Englishman, bought the place in September, 1866, and lived there until his death in 1907. He gave the community its name. The station became more important after the construction of the Central Pacific Railroad across Nevada in 1868-1869, when the C.P.R.R. set up a freight depot there. A little town grew up there to serve the outlying ranches and mining camps. Through most of the nineteenth century, Lovelock was a sleepy little community, although it had moments of excitement. In 1885, the townsfolk organized a local vigilance committee, called the "Association of 101," to deal with transients and cattle thieves. In 1887, the "101" ordered an Oregon rancher to get out of the country because he was suspected of rustling steers.

Another rare incident of local violence occurred in 1885, when the Humboldt River was in flood. The Oneida dam, a large earthen bulwark across the lower Humboldt River, backed up water onto the fields of a number of local ranchers. They donned masks and destroyed the dam with dynamite in order to reclaim their flooded croplands. But for the most part, the residents of Lovelock were peaceable, and the capture of the Nevada state baseball championship by the local team in 1887 was more characteristic of life in the nineteenth century community.

After the turn of the century, a mining boom began in the area and brought prosperity to the town. In 1904, Lovelock got telephone service, and soon Pacific Coast stockmen began sending cattle and sheep into Lovelock Valley for pasture and feeding. The First National Bank of Lovelock opened in 1905, and L. N. Marker brought the first automobile, an Oldsmobile, into town. That year, Allen C. Bragg, the newspaper editor of the Winnemucca *Silver State,* described the community for his readers:

> Lovelock is the center of a large and highly productive section of Humboldt County, which a generation ago was a barren waste. Hon. P. N. Marker and his brother, H. C. Marker, came to the valley and saw the wonderful productiveness of the soil and the great possibilities of the valley as an agricultural section and drove a stake on the banks of the Humboldt, four miles south of Lovelock and they were pioneers in the work of reclaiming this rich section. From those days in the '70's Lovelock has come up until today it is one of the best towns and stations on the whole line of the Central Pacific between Ogden on the east, and Sacramento on the west. The town is a town of homes, having at least 100, I should say, pretty little cottages, a good school house, employing two teachers during the school year; one National bank with a paid up capital of $25,000; a Catholic and Methodist church, wholesale and retail stores, drug store, bakery, hotels, saloons, blacksmith shops, roller process flour mill, lumber yard, coal and wood yard, two livery and feed stables and everything else that goes to make up a thriving community. The lawns, shade trees, orchards and pretty homes give the town a clean appearance.

Town improvements began in earnest in 1906. Lovelock got a central telephone exchange, a volunteer fire department, and a new water system. According to the local newspaper, the Lovelock *Tribune,* there were 20,000 cattle and 40,000 sheep feeding in the valley, and the stockyards near the railroad depot had to be enlarged. An electrical power plant was built in 1907, which provided power to residences and businesses. By

The High School and Court House at Lovelock, about 1930.
Courtesy of Special Collections, University of Nevada Reno Library

1908, there were 100,000 head of livestock in the valley, and Lovelock was supplying meat to the cities of the Pacific coast.

Motion pictures came to Lovelock in 1909, and in 1911, a second motion picture theater was built to cope with the demand for entertainment. At that time, a typical program involved three reels of cinema and a sing-along. Another innovation which appeared in 1910 was the tractor, at first called a self-propelled plough. According to a news story in the Lovelock *Review,* this tractor was the first in the State. By 1912, the town had 54 automobiles — 20 more than Carson City.

When Pershing County was created by the Legislature in 1919 out of southwestern Humboldt County, the seat of the new county government was at Lovelock. The courthouse is quite interesting from an architectural point of view, and many passersby pay it a visit. Today, Lovelock is still a ranching community. Its location on the S.P.R.R. and just off Interstate 80 makes it an ideal supply and distribution point for the Lovelock Valley area.

Minden-Gardnerville

Of the adjacent towns of Minden and Gardnerville in Carson Valley, Gardnerville is the oldest. It began as a hotel in 1878, on land owned by John Gardner, for whom the place was named. Promoter Lawrence Gilman bought the land, put up a hotel, saloon, and blacksmith shop. He enjoyed the patronage of heavy traffic moving from the V.&T.R.R. depots at Carson City along the road south to the mines at Bodie. A small village near the hotel was home for a number of Danish ranchers and their families.

Businessmen, merchants, and ranchers around the rich ranchlands of Carson Valley were anxious to get a railroad into the region. In 1876, a route was surveyed between Carson City and Genoa, but nothing came of the idea. There was talk about the Virginia & Truckee Railroad extending its tracks into Carson Valley in 1879, 1892, and 1901, but these proposals likewise came to naught. The ranchers and businessmen of Carson Valley were interested in getting railroad service and persuaded the management of the V.&T.R.R. to start construction in April, 1906.

The rail line went south from Carson City into the heart of Carson Valley. The V.&T.R.R. had planned to build its freight depot, station, and terminus at Gardnerville, but speculation in that town drove the price of land up. The V.&T.R.R. then accepted a donated site about a mile outside of town from the H. F. Dangberg Land & Live Stock

The Minden Flour Milling Company, about 1908. The large cylindrical silos at left are used to store the wheat, which is milled in the brick building by grinding until the grain is turned into flour. The final product can be seen sacked and stacked under the shelter of the roofed loading docks, while horse-drawn wagons stand ready to distribute the flour to local markets.
The V.&T.R.R. tracks immediately behind the mill allow the milling company to ship its output by rail to Reno and the rest of the world. Parallelling the tracks is the future U.S. Highway 395.
Courtesy of Nevada Historical Society

Company. Minden was founded there in the spring of 1906, and the first locomotive steamed into town on August 1st.

For years Minden was the distributing and shipping point for Carson Valley and the surrounding area. Livestock men shipped their cattle and sheep by rail to San Francisco and Chicago, while other livestock operators brought their herds into the Valley to feed. Competitive shipments by truck in and out of Carson Valley began in 1925, but the V.&T.R.R. continued operations to Minden until the railroad went out of business in 1950.

Minden was named for the Westphalian town in Germany near where H. F. Dangberg was born. It became the Douglas County seat in 1916, replacing Genoa. Today, Minden is in a state of transition. Thousands of persons have recently moved into Carson Valley, and the local economy is based on gaming and recreation at South Lake Tahoe, local manufacturing, and interstate travel on U.S. Highway 395, as well as ranching.

Yerington

Yerington got its start as the little town of Greenfield. Myron Angel described it in 1881 for the *History of Nevada:*

> Greenfield is a thriving little town in the center of the rich agricultural country in Mason Valley. In 1869 W. R. Lee settled upon 160 acres where the town now stands. In 1871 Dennis Higgins and E. W. Bennett came, and the year following

Mr. Higgins purchased the 160 acres of Lee, and had it patented in his own name. There was at that time the saloon of James Downey, the store of E. W. Bennett, and the blacksmith shop of Isaac Sims on the land. Geiger, of the Virginia Geiger Grade, kept store about two miles below the present site of Greenfield. He settled there about 1863. ... At present, the town is in a prosperous condition, having a population of 200, five stores, three hotels, two saloons, two restaurants, three livery stables, three blacksmith shops and four other places of industry. A tri-weekly mail goes there from Carson. ... Freights are received from Wabuska, twelve miles distant. They have a wood school house 20x30, with a seating capacity of forty. The regular attendance is twenty-two. The Methodists have a church building that will seat 200; also a Sabbath-school of twenty-five scholars. A good supply of pure water is obtained from private wells, and wood is procured from the mountains. The town is at an elevation of 500 feet, and is healthful the year round.

The liquor served in Greenfield was not entirely healthful, however. Some folks thought it was "pizen," or poisonous. From that opinion and the fact that the village was located at a crossroad, it became known as "Pizen Switch." The town was later renamed in honor of Henry M. Yerington, in the hopes that the Carson City railroad man would run the Carson & Colorado Railroad through the town. It never happened, but the place kept the name.

By 1907, the townsfolk elected a mayor and four city councilmen. In return for a fifty year franchise from the people of Yerington, the Truckee River General Electric Company ran a power line from Dayton, bringing electricity to the town. A water works and sewage system were built about 1908. The town fathers constructed a high school building in 1909 and an elementary school in 1912. In 1911, after the Lyon County courthouse at Dayton was destroyed by fire, the county seat was moved to Yerington.

The town owed its prosperity to the surrounding mining camps, for which Yerington served as distribution point and shipping center. Yerington was also the outfitting point for groups of prospectors wandering the surrounding hills in search of paying ore. The main reason for Yerington's marked increase in business was the copper mining boom that started in the area in 1901.

In 1909, the Nevada Copper Belt Railroad, built to link the copper mines at Ludwig with a smelter and the Southern Pacific Railroad's transcontinental connections at Wabuska, began laying its track. Work was completed into Yerington in January, 1910, when the town celebrated the arrival of the first passenger train. The tracks reached Ludwig at the end of 1911, and shipments of ore began almost immediately. The Ludwig mines intermittently went out of production after 1914, and the N.C.B.R.R. began to

Downtown Yerington, 1881. This view from Angel's History of Nevada *shows the beginnings of this Mason Valley community as a string of stores, shops, and stables along the road to Bodie, California.*

face stiff competition from gasoline-powered trucks and buses. The railroad began to abandon portions of the track after 1933 and ceased operations in 1947.

Anaconda Copper Company made another major discovery of copper ore in 1951 at Weed Heights, not far from Yerington, and proceeded to open up a large open pit mine. The mine produced copper for some twenty years until it was closed in the late 1970's. But while the intermittent but grandiose copper booms have enriched the town of Yerington, its most stable economic activity has been ranching.

CHAPTER 5

Government

IN THE BEGINNING

There was no government in the early days of Nevada. The white trappers, explorers, and overland emigrants were strictly on their own. There, in the mountains or on the prairies hundreds of miles from sheriffs and judges, the first intruders into the Great Basin had to protect themselves from lawless bandits and killers. Desperate criminals were able to avoid arrest in the unstable frontier regions, while determined citizens punished those they caught red-handed in crime.

The overland emigrants had the most problems. Where there's no one to administer the law, what happens when someone on the wagon train commits a murder? When this happened to the Donner Party of 1846, the members of the train formed a court and passed judgment upon the killer. He was banished from the wagon train to wander the prairies alone, with no weapons or food. (The man was able to reach California safely.) Other wagon trains crossing Nevada were faced with the same problem and used the same proceedings to condemn the killer to death.

The men who held trials and executed these criminals did not hesitate to identify themselves. They published letters in newspapers stating what they had done and signed their names. No one questioned what they did. At the time, most people thought the lynchings were necessary under the circumstances. Others thought they were fair since the judgment as well as the verdict were decided by a vote, made by a jury after hearing evidence. The right to a trial by jury, preserved even by these unofficial courts, is one of the fundamental principles of justice in our United States Constitution.

The Settlers' Government

The first settlers who decided to spend the winter in Nevada in 1851 were far from any place with an organized government, so they set up one of their own. That November 12th, there was a public meeting at Mormon Station in Carson Valley "to consider the necessity of providing for the survey of claims and subdivision of the Valley so as to secure each individual in their rights to land taken up and improved by them, to agree upon a petition to Congress for distinct territorial government, the creation of public officers for the Valley, and the adoption of by laws and fixed regulations to govern the community."

This meeting produced a local government which made laws relating to land claims. The newly established government consisted of a judge, his clerk, and a sheriff, supervised by a tribunal of twelve citizens — a kind of grand jury. It ruled over Carson Valley and surrounding areas until 1855.

Carson County

After Mexico gave up much of the far west to the United States under the 1848 Treaty of Guadalupe Hidalgo, the Great Basin area became a U.S. Territory. It had no government until 1850, when Congress created the Territory of Utah. Brigham Young was its first governor. At that time Utah Territory included not only Utah, but most of Nevada as well, and our State was called western Utah.

The residents of western Utah did not want to be ruled by authorities sent from Salt Lake City. They petitioned the legislature of California in 1853 and 1854 for that state to annex Carson Valley. They also sent petitions to Congress in 1851, 1857–58, and in 1859, asking for their own territorial government.

The authorities in Utah did not try to extend their rule to the eastern slope of the Sierra Nevada range until 1855, when U.S. Territorial Judge George Stiles, Carson County Judge Orson Hyde, and a group of other officials arrived in Carson Valley from Salt Lake City. Hyde, a Mormon Church official, had been ordered to establish LDS Church settlements in the area. He sent an exploring expedition south to Walker River to scout out areas for settlement and called for an election of county officers to be held in September, 1855. The voters decided the Carson County seat would be located at Mormon Station. Hyde named it Genoa "after the birth place of Columbus, the pioneer across the stormy deep, and discoverer of a country in which Heaven designed that man should worship his maker according to the dictates of his own conscience."

However, the attempt by the Utah Territorial officials to organize Carson County failed because of lack of local popular support. In 1862, Orson Hyde, remembering his unsuccessful mission, denounced the people who lived in Carson and Washoe Valleys:

> Not quite seven years ago I was sent to your district as Probate Judge of Carson County, with powers and instructions from the executive of this Territory to organize your district into a county under the laws of Utah — those valleys then being the lawful and rightful field of Utah's jurisdiction; but opposition on your part to the measure was unceasingly made in almost every form, both trivial and important, open and secret. Your allies in California were ever ready to second your opposition of whatever character or in whatever shape.

Orson Hyde left Genoa and returned to Salt Lake City toward the end of 1856. Within just a few weeks — on January 14, 1857 — the Utah Territorial Legislature passed a law which essentially moved the government of western Utah to Salt Lake City. By September, 1857, the LDS Church recalled its settlements in western Utah, and the area was once again without any local government — no judge, no sheriff, and no one to keep records.

Orson Hyde (1805–1878) of Connecticut established the first official local government in Nevada when it was still part of Utah Territory, in 1855. A senior official of the LDS or Mormon Church, Hyde set up Carson County in the shadow of the Sierra Nevada but left it with a curse. The settlements he founded were abandoned in 1857, but the LDS Church still propspers mightily in Nevada.

Courtesy of Nevada Historical Society

CAPTURE OF PERKINS

EXECUTION OF PERKINS

Vigilantes at Virginia City, 1871. These illustrations, taken from Dan DeQuille's The Big Bonanza, *show what happens when law enforcement breaks down. This is the execution of Arthur Perkins Heffernan by "The Association of 601," a group of masked and armed citizens. Vigilance committees, whose members were called "Vigilantes," formed when government crime suppression was ineffective or absent. Most large communities in Nevada during the nineteenth-century had vigilance committees, which were most active when the towns became crowded with transients.*

Isaac Newton Roop, first and only Governor of the unofficial, breakaway Territory of Nevada, 1859–1861. Roop settled near Susanville, California, in 1856 and became active in the movement to create a separate political unit out of western Utah Territory. Roop faded into obscurity after Congress created an official Nevada Territory in 1861, but our Legislature honored him, for a time, by naming a county after him.

Courtesy of Nevada Historical Society

John S. Child. Appointed Carson County Probate Judge in 1858 by Utah Territory Governor Alfred Cumming, Child battled vigilance committees and breakaway territorial movements to re-organize local government between 1859 and 1861 in what is now western Nevada.

Lynch Law in Carson Valley

Bandits flourished in the waste lands of Nevada during the 1850's. In the summer of 1851, an expeditionary force of California militia discovered the graves of six men supposed to have been murdered by outlaws on the California Trail on their way west from Salt Lake City. In the spring of 1852, Utah Territorial Indian Agent Jacob H. Holeman wrote to the Commissioner of Indian Affairs that there was "a company of white men and Indians who are stationed near Carson Valley, and that their object is to plunder and rob the emigrants." When a merchant was murdered at Volcano, California, in 1853, a posse tracked the killer over the mountains and into Carson Valley but couldn't catch him. According to an article published in the Sacramento *Union* in August, 1853:

> The party pursued the murderer to Carson Valley, in the vicinity of which they found him, but so strongly encamped as to render it utterly impossible to make any attempt to capture him. It seems the camp consists of a large party of Pah Utah Indians, and about 150 white men, principally robbers and murderers who have fled from justice. . . . They have an immense herd of cattle, estimated at $200,000. This camp is situated on the other side of the Valley, about thirty miles from the emigrant trail, and near the sink of the Humboldt. The position is well selected, and parties can sally out, and carry off the stock of the emigrants almost with impunity.

The overland emigrants reacted violently against the outlaws. In 1856, a group of white men disguised as Indians attacked a wagon train near the Deep Creek Mountains on the Utah-Nevada border and drove off a number of the emigrants' cattle. The overland travelers tracked them down, gave them a trial, convicted them, and shot six of them on the spot. In 1857, emigrants shot another man at the Sink of the Humboldt. He was recognized by his victims as a "white Indian" — one trying to blame his crimes on the Indians.

In Carson Valley, local ranchers formed a vigilance committee or "People's Court" in 1857, as the Mormon government and settlers withdrew. In 1858, this law and order group and the vigilance committee of Honey Lake Valley held a trial in which a gang of men were charged with the murder of a ranchman from the Honey Lake country and several other crimes. The vigilantes executed three men by hanging, banished another from the area for life, fined several, and acquitted several more. In other trials the "People's Court" acquitted the defendants, but on at least one occasion they cut off the ears of men who were convicted of stealing.

The inhabitants of the eastern slope of the Sierra Nevada didn't prefer things to remain that way. They petitioned Congress again and again to create a territorial government for Nevada. Congress, however, left the matter in the hands of the officials of Utah Territory at Salt Lake City.

In 1857–58, a bill in Congress to set up Nevada Territory failed to pass, and the ranchers of Nevada decided to create their own breakaway territory. Without the sanction of either Utah Territory or the United States, an election was called for delegates to a territorial convention, which met at Genoa on July 18, 1859. This convention drafted a constitution for the unofficial Nevada Territory. The residents of Nevada approved the new constitution on September 7, 1859. They also elected a governor — Isaac Roop of Honey Lake Valley — and representatives to a territorial legislature, which met for the first and only time on December 15, 1859. It was adjourned by Governor Roop, who declared in an address that the time was not right for the new territory's organization.

One major difficulty was the fact that Utah Territory decided to reassert its authority at the same time. There was an election for Carson County officers in October, 1858, in which only a few residents voted. Within three months, however, the Utah Territorial Legislature restored Carson County's representation in the Assembly and authorized the formation of a local government in January, 1859. This allowed the first court in over two years to be held at Genoa.

Even so, the residents of western Utah were not enthusiastic about their newly reorganized government. There were charges of vote fraud at nearly all of the Carson County elections. During the first year of the rush to Washoe, there were two different

Carson County Recorders holding office at the same time. Miners and others, not knowing who would eventually become the official recorder, had to file their papers with both. Time ran out for Carson County, Utah Territory, in 1861. The government of Utah Territory had just ordered the county seat moved from Genoa to Carson City when Congress finally established the Territory of Nevada.

NEVADA TERRITORY

Although the attmept to create a breakaway Nevada territorial government in 1859 was a failure, it had important consequences. It showed that large numbers of Nevadans wanted a government of their own and did not want to be ruled from Salt Lake City. Almost immediately, other important events led to Congress creating just such a territorial government.

The first of these events was the discovery of the Comstock Lode, which brought in thousands of settlers and added new importance to the region because of its mineral riches.

The impending war between the states was another critical event. After Abraham Lincoln was elected United States President in 1860, the southern states began to secede from the Union and formed the Confederate States of America in February, 1861. This removed many southern votes from the United States Senate, which had blocked the formation of Nevada and other territories because of the controversy over whether they would be slave or free states. Because Nevada's great mineral wealth could not be allowed to fall into the hands of the newly-formed Confederacy, Congress created Nevada Territory on March 2, 1861, from what had previously been western Utah Territory.

President Lincoln appointed the most important officers of the new territorial government. Most of these new officials were stalwart supporters of the Republican Party. The new Governor, James Warren Nye, was a Republican from New York, where he had helped deliver a sizable vote for President Lincoln in the 1860 national election. Other appointees had similar backgrounds. This assured Republican Party domination of the new territory for years to come.

Territorial Government

The territorial government created by Congress had the same system of checks and balances worked out by our founding fathers in the United States Constitution. There were three separate but equal branches of government — the executive, the legislature, and the judiciary.

The executive part of the government consisted of the Governor, appointed by the President and commissioned March 22, 1861. Other lesser officials charged with enforcing the laws of the territory were appointed and sworn into office on July 11, 1861.

The judicial branch of government amounted to a three-man Territorial Supreme Court. Each of the judges also held court in his own district of the Territory, riding a circuit through the various counties assigned to him. The judicial organization of the Territory was completed July 17, 1861.

The Legislature was organized as a bicameral or two-house system of elected officials. The people of Nevada elected Senators and Assemblymen from the various electoral districts on August 31, 1861. The first legislature met between October 1 and November 29.

The Territorial Legislature officially established its new capitol at Carson City on November 25, 1861. It had a problem finding somewhere to meet, however. Orion Clemens, the new Secretary of State for the Territory, had the responsibility of finding a hall, but couldn't find any place suitable for a reasonable rent. According to Mark Twain, Clemens' brother, "Everybody knew that Congress had appropriated only twenty thousand dollars a year in greenbacks for its [the Territory's] support — about money enough to run a quartz mill a month. And everybody knew, also, that the first year's money was still in Washington, and that the getting hold of it would be a tedious and difficult process."

Things looked bad until Abram Curry, one of the original founders and promoters of Carson City, stepped into the picture. Mark Twain told the story in *Roughing It:*

> There is something solemnly funny about the struggles of a new-born Territorial government to get a start in this world. Ours had a trying time of it. The Organic Act and the "instructions" from the State Department commanded that a legislature should be elected at such-and-such a time, and its sittings inaugurated at such-and-such a date. It was easy to get legislators, even at three dollars a day, although board was four dollars and fifty cents, for distinction has its charm in Nevada as well as elsewhere, and there were plenty of patriotic souls out of employment; but to get a legislative hall for them to meet in was another matter altogether. Carson blandly declined to give a room rent-free, or let one to the government on credit.
>
> But when Curry heard of the difficulty, he came forward, solitary and alone, and shouldered the Ship of State over the bar and got her afloat again. I refer to "Curry – *Old* Curry – Old *Abe* Curry". But for him the legislature would have been obliged to sit in the desert. He offered his large stone building just outside the capital limits, rent-free, and it was gladly accepted. Then he built a horse-railroad from town to the Capitol, and carried the legislators gratis. He also furnished pine benches and chairs for the legislature, and covered the floors with clean sawdust by way of carpet and spittoon combined. But for Curry the government would have died in its tender infancy. A canvas partition to separate the Senate from the House of Representatives was put up by the Secretary, at a cost of three dollars and forty cents, but the United States declined to pay for it.

The Counties

Among many acts of this first legislature, one of the most important was the organization of Nevada into nine counties — Churchill, Douglas, Esmeralda, Humboldt, Lake, Lyon, Ormsby, Storey, and Washoe.

How the counties were named and changed is interesting. Churchill County takes its name from U.S. Army General Sylvester Churchill, after whom Fort Churchill was named.

Senator Stephen A. Douglas of Illinois, the "Little Giant" who debated Abraham Lincoln in 1858 on the national issues of the day, gave his name to Douglas county.

Esmeralda means emerald in Spanish, and the colorful beauty of the region gave Esmeralda County its name.

James Warren Nye (1814–1876) of New York, Nevada's first Governor, studied law and was elected a judge in New York by the age of thirty. He joined the Republican Party in 1856 and became an influential politician in New York City, where he campaigned strongly for his friend Abraham Lincoln's election in 1860. Beginning in 1864, Nye served two terms as U.S. Senator from Nevada.

Courtesy of Special Collections,
University of Nevada Reno Library

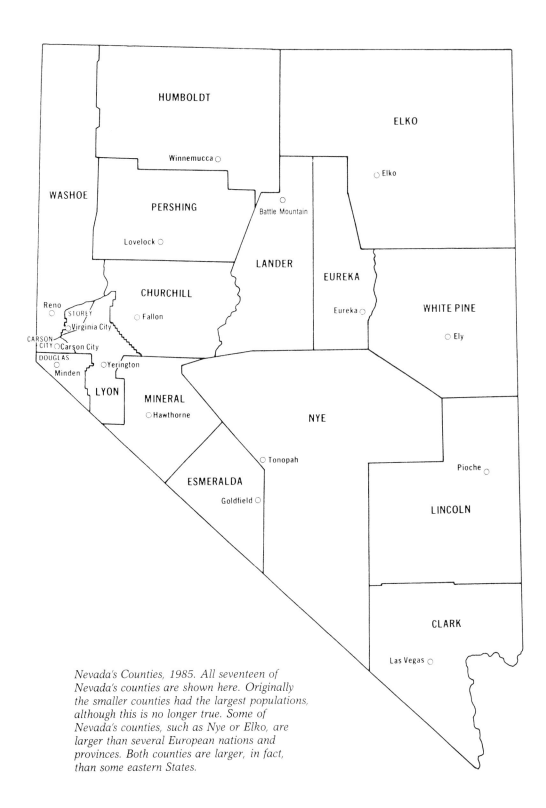

Nevada's Counties, 1985. All seventeen of Nevada's counties are shown here. Originally the smaller counties had the largest populations, although this is no longer true. Some of Nevada's counties, such as Nye or Elko, are larger than several European nations and provinces. Both counties are larger, in fact, than some eastern States.

Humboldt County, like the river, was named for the German geographer Alexander von Humboldt (1769–1859).

The large number of lakes within its boundaries gave rise to the name Lake County; it contained Pyramid, Winnemucca, and other lakes. In 1862, Lake County was renamed Roop County after the 1859 Governor of Nevada Territory, Isaac Roop. In 1883, it was merged into Washoe County.

Major William M. Ormsby, killed at the battle of Pyramid Lake on May 12, 1860, during the Pyramid Lake Paiute War, was honored by having Ormsby County named after him; in 1969, the administrative unit was renamed the City and County of Carson, after "Kit" Carson.

Another casualty of the 1860 Paiute War, Captain Edward Storey, gave Storey County its name. He was killed at the second battle of Pyramid Lake June 2, 1860.

Washoe County, the last of the original nine, takes its name from the Washo tribe of Indians.

Today Nevada has seventeen counties. Of the new additions, Elko County got its name from the county seat, named by C.P.R.R. officials for obscure reasons. One story says that Charles Crocker, one of the Central Pacific's "Big Four," called it after the elk which lived thereabouts, with an "o" added to make the name sound better. Another version has "elko" as being Shoshoni for "white woman;" the name was supposedly given by the local Indians to the place where they first saw a white woman.

Eureka County's cognomen comes from the Greek word which means "I've found it!" The saying was repeated by miners discovering rich ore in the County. The original remark is attributed to the Greek mathematician and inventor Archimedes (B.C. 287?–212), when he discovered the first method for determining the purity of gold.

Created by the Legislature on February 1, 1908, Clark County was named for the railroad promoter and U.S. Senator from Montana, William A. Clark, who built the second transcontinental railroad across Nevada.

Frederick W. Lander, the chief engineer for the National Wagon Road of 1856, who was killed at Paw Paw, Virginia, while serving as a General for the Union forces during the Civil War, lent his name to Lander County, created December 19, 1862. He negotiated an armistice with the Northern Paiute Indians in 1860 which effectively ended the Pyramid Lake Paiute War.

Lyon County was probably named for a General in the Union Army during the Civil War, Nathaniel Lyon, who was killed at Springfield, Missouri, during the Battle of Wilson's Creek on August 10, 1861. Other historians believe that the name honors Captain Robert Lyon, an overland emigrant and Indian fighter.

Mineral County, created February 10, 1911, takes its title from the rich ores that can be found there.

Lincoln County is so called in honor of President Abraham Lincoln, who had recently been assassinated when the County was named.

Nevada's first Governor, James Warren Nye, is responsible for the name of the State's largest county, organized in 1864.

United States General of the Armies John J. "Black Jack" Pershing was honored for his part in the allied victory in World War One by having Pershing County named for him on March 18, 1919.

White Pine County, named for heavy stands of coniferous trees around the Treasure Hill mines, was created by the Legislature out of Lander County March 2, 1869.

The counties are run by a board of County Commissioners, who combine legislative and executive powers. The County Sheriff keeps the peace and arrests law-breakers, who are charged and prosecuted by the County District Attorney. Deeds and records are registered by the County Recorder, and taxes are assessed and collected by the County Assessor. The County Surveyor lays out the boundaries of claims to real estate. The County or District Judge hears criminal and civil controversies and is assisted by the County Clerk and the bailiffs of the Court. These are the basic functions of county government, but even in the nineteenth century counties often maintained "poor farms" for the relief of the needy, hospitals, libraries, and fire departments.

Within the counties there are independent, self-governing local political units — incorporated cities and towns. These have their own mayor or city council, a city attorney, a chief of police or constables, a municipal court judge (or in outlying townships, a justice of the peace), and other officials.

Almost all of these features of territorial government formed the basis for the political organization of our present-day State, although today they have been improved and enlarged.

STATEHOOD

It took Nevada just a little over three years to change from a United States territory to a State. There were several reasons for this, mostly political.

Many people in Nevada were dissatisfied with the territorial judges, who had a reputation for corruption. Under a State constitution the judges could be popularly elected or defeated and thus kept in check.

To achieve statehood, there first had to be a State constitution, ratified by the voters of the territory, which Congress would approve. The territorial legislature called for a constitutional convention, which met in November, 1863. The proposed constitution which this convention produced, however, was defeated by popular vote in January, 1864.

This did not change the powerful arguments in favor of statehood, however, and a new enabling act was passed by Congress and signed by President Lincoln on March 21, 1864. A new constitutional convention met during July of that year, and their constitution was approved by popular vote September 7th. Nevada then became the 36th State, admitted to the Union on October 31, 1864.

William M. Stewart, first U.S. Senator from Nevada, commented on one of the reasons Nevada became a State in his *Reminiscences:*

> When the Enabling Act was passed by Congress on March 21, 1864, authorizing Nevada to enter the Union, it was understood that the Government at Washington was anxious that Nevada should become a State in order that her Senators and Representatives might assist in the adoption of amendments to the Constitution in aid of the restoration of the Southern States after the Union should be vindicated by the [Civil] war.

When Stewart was elected U.S. Senator in December, 1864, he traveled to Washington, D.C. to attend his first session of Congress. Once there, he met President Lincoln:

> The morning after I took my seat in the Senate I called upon President Lincoln at the White House. He received me in the most friendly manner, taking me by both hands, and saying:
> "I am glad to see you here. We need as many loyal States as we can get, and, in addition to that, the gold and silver in the region you represent has made it possible for the Government to maintain sufficient credit to continue this terrible war for the Union. I have observed such manifestations of the patriotism of your people as assure me that the Government can rely on your State for such support as is in your power."

The wealth of Nevada helped secure the victory of the North in the Civil War and thus helped preserve the United States.

The Right to Vote

At first Nevada's constitution established the electoral franchise (the right to vote) only for adult white males. In 1880, that rule was abolished in a State election, which extended the right to vote to all adult males.

People who thought that adult women ought to be able to vote were active in Nevada politics from the early days of statehood. In 1883, 1885, and 1897, Legislators introduced bills to give women the right to vote, but they all failed to pass. In 1895, a women's suffrage movement was organized at Reno, after a convention. The Nevada Equal Suffrage Association had bills introduced in the Legislature during the 1895, 1897, and 1899 sessions, but these also met with defeat, and adult women did not gain the right to vote until 1914.

Anne Martin (in the front passenger's seat), a native Nevadan, was president of the Nevada Equal Franchise Society, and it was largely through her efforts that women won the right to vote in Nevada. She was the first woman to be nominated for the U.S. Senate, in 1918.

Courtesy of Nevada Historical Society

At first, political representation in the State Legislature was the same as that used in the United States Congress and most of the other states. One house, the Senate, had its members elected from districts drawn according to political boundaries. The other house, the Assembly, had its members elected from districts drawn according to population. This scheme ended in 1965, when the Legislature, following the 1964 United States Supreme Court decision of *Reynolds v. Sims,* changed its apportionment plan to the one man, one vote system. When the Legislature apportioned political representation on the basis of population rather than political geography, it effectively ended rural control of the government. This re-apportionment plan, accepted by the U.S. District Court in 1966, is largely the same system used today.

State Boundaries

Nevada is a political unit formed by Congress without reference to the natural physical features of the region. Our northern boundary is the same as that set by the Adams-Onis Treaty of 1819 between Spain and the U.S. — the 42nd Parallel, then the dividing line between U.S. and Spanish territory after the Louisiana Purchase. It has not been changed since.

The southern boundary of Nevada was set by both the territorial and State constitutions at the 37th Parallel, but in 1867, the State Legislature took advantage of a Congressional act passed the year before to extend Nevada's boundary south to the point where the Colorado River intersects the 35th Parallel.

The eastern boundary was originally established at the 116th West Meridian but was moved twice, expanding Nevada at the expense of Utah Territory. The first change

By the President of the United States of America

A Proclamation.

Whereas the Congress of the United States passed an Act which was approved on the 21st day of March, last, entitled, "An Act to enable the people of Nevada to form a Constitution and State Government, and for the admission of such State into the Union on an equal Footing with the original States';

And Whereas, the said Constitution and State Government have been formed pursuant to the conditions prescribed by the fifth section of the Act of Congress aforesaid, and the certificate required by the said act, and also a copy of the Constitution and ordinances have been submitted to the President of the United States;

Now, therefore, be it Known that I, Abraham Lincoln, President of the United States, in accordance with the duty imposed upon me by the Act of Congress aforesaid, do hereby, declare and proclaim that the said State of Nevada is admitted into the Union on an equal footing with the original States.

In witness whereof, I have hereunto set my hand, and caused the seal of the United States to be affixed.

Done at the city of Washington this Thirty-first day of October, in the year of our Lord one thousand eight hundred and sixty-four, and of the Independence of the United States the Eighty-ninth.

Abraham Lincoln

By the President:

William H. Seward
Secretary of State.

On October 31, 1864 — during a time when the United States government sorely needed Nevada's silver to help finance its war against the Confederate States — President Abraham Lincoln signed this proclamation admitting Nevada to the Union as a full-fledged state. Every year since, Nevadans have celebrated that historic occasion on the last day of October — Nevada Day.

came in 1862, when the line was moved eastward to the 115th Meridian, and the border was moved again in 1866, to the 114th Meridian.

The western boundary has the most complex history. It is set by the eastern boundary of California, which became a state in 1850. The California constitution placed the boundary not along the natural boundary, which is the summit line of the Sierra Nevada mountains, but along a meridian believed roughly to correspond with the summit. The terrain was so rugged that no one could really tell where the boundary was. California made its first survey in 1852, and there was a second survey by California and Utah territorial officials in 1855. Neither of these surveys fixed the line with any exactness. Settlers in Honey Lake Valley, claiming that they were in Nevada, refused to pay taxes to the California government. In February, 1863, a gun battle began at Susanville between sheriffs' posses from California and Nevada, each claiming to be the legitimate authority in the area. There was a similar situation, without the violence, in Esmeralda County, Nevada, and Mono County, California, where rival sets of State officials attempted to exercise their powers in the town of Aurora.

The problem was supposed to be settled by the Nevada legislature in 1864, which agreed to recognize California's eastern boundary as Nevada's western border. This particular boundary was surveyed by Houghton & Ives in 1863, but in 1872–1873, California commissioned another boundary survey by A. W. von Schmidt, which found

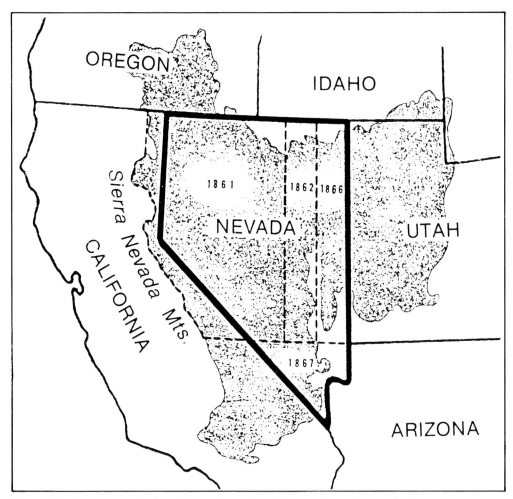

The political and geographic boundaries of Nevada. This map shows the political boundaries of the State and the dates of its territorial enlargements, superimposed over a map of the Great Basin region. Unlike most borders, the Nevada-California state line does not run along the summit of the mountains. Note that the entire watershed of the Sierra Nevada mountains, and with it the mountain passes, lie within the State of California.

that the border should be moved further east. The diagonal delineation, made by the U.S. Coast & Geodetic Survey (U.S.C.&G.S.), took place between 1893 and 1899. In 1977, California claimed that more accurate astronomical methods required another move to the east and brought a lawsuit against Nevada to acquire more land. Nevada countersued to have the border returned to the 1863 Houghton & Ives survey line. The case was finally settled by the U.S. Supreme Court in 1980, with a ruling that the von Schmidt and U.S.C.&G.S. lines would constitute the permanent boundary.

State Buildings

The Legislature decided to provide for a State capitol building in 1869. The Legislators chose an unlikely spot to build it, according to pioneer Allen Bragg, who recalled the site in a 1915 newspaper article for the Carson City *News:*

> The Capitol grounds was an unsightly place called the Plaza, without a blade of grass or a tree of any kind, but a little sagebrush in spots. The place was fenced with unpainted six by six timbers, two timbers high and for years a half burned wooden structure called the pavilion, which was never finished, stood by where the capitol now stands. Later in the [eighteen-]sixties the plaza was used by the Silver Star Baseball Club.

The grounds were cleared, the design was approved, and the contractor selected by the time the cornerstone celebrations took place on June 9, 1870. The stone was cut at the Nevada State Prison and hauled to the site. The workmen finished construction by the end of the year, and the Legislature of 1871 was the first to get to use the building. It was extensively reconstructed in the 1970's.

The new legislative building southeast of the capitol was built in 1970, one hundred years after the first. The Legislature of 1971 was the first to meet there.

The Governor's Mansion dates from 1908–09. Governor Denver S. Dickerson and his family were the first to occupy it. Before that time the Governors lived in their own private houses.

Great Seals of Nevada

Both the Territory and State of Nevada have official seals — a device which makes a raised impression on wax or paper, and which symbolizes the authority of the State. By law the design of the Nevada Territorial Seal was specified as:

> Mountains, with a stream of water coursing down their sides, and falling on the over-shot wheel of a quartz-mill at their base; a miner leaning on his pick, and upholding a United States flag, with a motto expressing the two ideas of loyalty to the Union, and the wealth to sustain it. *"Volens et Potens"* ("Willing and Able.")

The State Seal, adopted in 1866, is more elaborate:

> In the foreground, there shall be two large mountains, at the base of which, on the right, there shall be located a quartz mill, and on the left a tunnel, pene- trating the silver leads of the mountain, with a miner running out a carload of ore, and a team loaded with ore for the mill. Immediately in the foreground, there shall be emblems indicative of the agricultural resources of the state, as follows: A plow, a sheaf and sickle. In the middle ground, there shall be a train of railroad cars passing a mountain gorge and a telegraph line extending along the line of the railroad. In the extreme background, there shall be a range of snow- clad mountains, with the rising sun in the east. Thirty-six stars shall encircle the whole group. In an outer circle, the words, "The Great Seal of the State of Nevada" shall be engraved with these words, for the motto of our state, "All for Our Country."

State Flags, Songs, and Symbols

Nevada did not have a state flag until the turn of the century. The Legislature approved a design in 1905 which was the first official flag ever designated in the State. It was replaced by another flag in 1915, and by our current flag in 1929, which was originally sketched by Louis "Don" Shellback III. An attempt to change the State flag in 1953,

The State Capitol of Nevada at Carson City, shortly after its construction in 1871. The successive Legislatures of the State met here for one hundred years, deciding what to do about Nevada's problems and special advantages. The Governor of the State also had his offices inside this building, which now stands like a relic from a different age of small government and low taxes.
Today, the structure which formerly housed all of the government of the State is too small for many administrative departments.

Courtesy of Special Collections, University of Nevada Reno Library

The Legislative Building at Carson City.

Courtesy of Nevada Historical Society

passed by both houses of the Legislature, was vetoed by Governor Charles H. Russell. The words "Battle Born" on our State flag recall our vital role in the Civil War.

The State adopted an official State Song, "Home Means Nevada," in 1933. The song, written by Mrs. Bertha Raffetto of Reno, goes like this:

HOME MEANS NEVADA

'Way out in the land of the setting sun,
Where the wind blows wild and free,
There's a lovely spot, just the only one
That means home sweet home to me.
If you follow the old Kit Carson trail,
Until desert meets the hills,
Oh, you certainly will agree with me,
It's the place of a thousand thrills.

"Home," means Nevada, "Home," means the hills,
"Home," means the sage and the pines.
Out by the Truckee's silvery rills,
Out where the sun always shines,
There is a land that I love the best,
Fairer than all I can see.
Right in the heart of the golden west
"Home," means Nevada to me.

Whenever the sun at the close of day
Colors all the western sky,
Oh, my heart returns to the desert grey
And the mountains tow'ring high.
Where the moon beams play in shadowed glen
With the spotted fawn and doe,
All the livelong night until morning light
Is the liveliest place I know.

Nevada also has an official State Tree, the single-leaf pinon pine (Pinus monophylla), established by the Legislature in 1953; in 1959, the Legislature adopted the shrub sagebrush (Artemisia tridentata) as the official State Emblem. It is also our State Flower.

The Governor's Mansion at Carson City.
Courtesy of Nevada Historical Society

Nevada Territorial Seal.
Courtesy of Nevada Historical Society

State Seal of Nevada.
Courtesy of Nevada Historical Society

1905 State Flag.
Courtesy of Nevada Historical Society

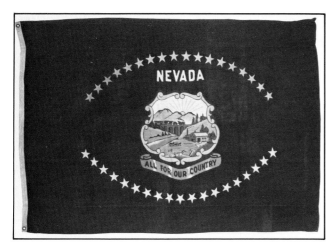

1915 State Flag.
Courtesy of Nevada Historical Society

1929 State Flag.
Courtesy of Nevada Historical Society

State Agencies

Nevada has a number of administrative agencies, sometimes called bureaucracies. These agencies take care of recurring problem areas or types of conflicts which cannot be conveniently settled by the criminal code or judges. Typically the areas being regulated by the administrative agencies require special expertise, or the Legislature wants to keep direct popular electoral control out of the picture.

The first administrative agencies were for the general health and welfare of Nevadans: the State Orphans' Home was established in 1870, the State Insane Asylum in 1881, the Board of Health in 1893, the Board of Dental Examiners in 1895, the Board of Medical Examiners in 1899, and the Board of Pharmacy in 1901. Most of these were consolidated in 1963, when the Legislature created the Department of Health and Welfare. Many other state regulatory agencies have since been created, of course, and today the State employs a considerable number of administrative office-holders and secretaries.

Other agencies were created to promote or assist public education, although at first this was considered a local and not a state government function. The Legislature created the University of Nevada in 1873, the Indian School Commission in 1887, the State Board of Education in 1895, and the Textbook Commission that same year. For years the situation remained the same, until the appearance of the State Teachers' Employment Bureau in 1923, but no major changes went into effect until the Legislature created the Department of Education in 1956. New sources of revenue, derived from the State sales tax and gaming revenues, allowed the expansion of the State system of education to its present level. This includes a greatly expanded University of Nevada, with campuses at Las Vegas as well as Reno, and several junior colleges across the State.

One Room Schoolhouse and Class, Somewhere in Nevada, about 1890. In Nevada's sparsely populated rural communities, one room classes were the rule and not the exception. Here, a mixed collection of students and their dapper instructor are frozen in time by the photographer.

Courtesy of Special Collections, University of Nevada Reno Library

University of Nevada at Elko. Established by the State Legislature in 1873, Nevada's university system was a monument to the State's committment to education. In 1885, the University was relocated to Reno. Since that time, the Legislature has added a campus at Las Vegas, and in 1970 it created a system of State community colleges.

Courtesy of Nevada Historical Society

State Taxes

The State government pays for its operations out of the taxes it collects in Nevada. There are all sorts of taxes, direct and indirect.

Sales taxes, room taxes, the gasoline tax, and other similar taxes are good examples of how the State raises money by the direct approach. The State also raises money by charging license fees for persons or corporations doing business within Nevada. Doctors, lawyers, dentists, pharmacists, and other professionals have to pass a skills test and pay an annual fee for their professional licenses. Owners of motor vehicles and trailers also have to have a license to operate their property on the State's road system.

There have been heated political battles in Nevada over taxation. The first such controversy took place in the 1850's, when local ranchers in Carson Valley and western Nevada refused to pay taxes to the Carson County officials of Utah Territory. In fact, they wouldn't pay taxes to California either, a situation "Snowshoe" Thompson mentioned to the editor of the Sacramento *Union* in early December, 1856: "The Utah and California assessors have both assessed the property, and the consequence is that the owners will not pay taxes to either."

Another such battle took place over taxes on the mines. Right from the start of deep tunnel mining on the Comstock, the industry had a spokesman in attorney William M. Stewart, a member of the territorial legislature and later U.S. Senator from Nevada (1864–1875 and 1887–1905.) Mark Twain, then a reporter for the Virginia City *Territorial Enterprise,* parodied Stewart's tireless efforts on behalf of the mining interests. In an 1863 article on an imaginary meeting of the Territorial Legislature, Mark Twain has himself "elected President of the Convention, and Messrs. Small and Hickok appointed to conduct him to the Chair, which they did amid a dense and respectful silence on the part of the House, Mr. Small stepping grandly over the desks, and Mr. Hickok walking under them." Not far into the fanciful proceedings, Twain poked fun at Stewart's usual speech:

> The question being on Section 4, Article 1 (free exercise) of religious liberty.
>
> Mr. Stewart said — "Mr. President: I insist upon it, that if you tax the mines, you impose a burden upon the people which will be heavier than they can bear. And when you tax the poor miner's shafts, and drifts, and bed-rock tunnels, you are NOT taxing his property; you are NOT taxing his substance; you are not taxing his wealth — no, but you are taxing what may become property some day, or may not; you are taxing the shadow from which the substance may

William Morris Stewart (1827-1909), Nevada's first U.S. Senator. Born in New York, Stewart served as Nevada's U.S. Senator for almost thirty years. A teacher, prospector, lawyer, and politician, Stewart dominated the Senate's politics for years. In the Senate, Stewart put Nevada first in his efforts to stabilize the economic structure of the Silver State.

Courtesy of Nevada Historical Society

eventually issue or may not; you are taxing the visions of Alnaschar; which may turn to minted gold, or only prove the forerunners of poverty and misfortune; in a word, sir, you are taxing his hopes, taxing the aspirations of his soul! — taxing the yearning of his heart of hearts! Yes sir, I insist upon it, that if you tax the mines, you impose a burden upon the people which will be heavier than they can bear. And when you tax the poor miner's shafts, and drifts, and bed-rock tunnels, you are NOT taxing his property; you are NOT taxing his substance; you are not taxing his wealth — no, but you are taxing what may become property some day, or may not; you are taxing the shadow from which the substance may eventually issue or may not; you are taxing the visions of Alnaschar; which may turn to minted gold, or only prove the forerunners of poverty and misfortune; in a word, sir, you are taxing his hopes, taxing the aspirations of his soul! — taxing the yearning of his heart of hearts! Ah, sir, I do insist upon it that if you tax the mines, you will impose a burden upon the people, which will be heavier than they can bear. And when you tax the poor miner's shafts, and drifts, and bed-rock tunnels — "

The President — "Take your seat, Bill Stewart! I am not going to sit here and listen to that same old song over and over again. I have been reporting and reporting that infernal speech for the last thirty days, and want you to understand that you can't play it off on the Convention any more. When I want it, I will repeat it myself — I know it by heart, anyhow. You and your bed-rock tunnels, and blighted miners, blasted hopes, have gotten to be a sort of nightmare to me, and I won't put up with it any longer. I don't wish to be too hard on your speech, but if you can't add something fresh to it, or say it backwards, or sing it to a new tune, you have simply got to simmer down for awhile."

Stewart gave talks up and down the State opposing adoption of the State Constitution of 1863, which contained a clause allowing a tax on "the poor miner's shafts and drifts and bed-rock tunnels." Stewart's complaints about this unjust tax were, according to Myron Angel in his *History of Nevada,* one of the reasons that the constitution was defeated in an 1864 election. The fight continued. In the next, successful proposed State constitution, taxes were designed to favor the mining industry. After the discovery of major ore bodies on the Comstock, lobbyists for the mining companies tried to reduce mining taxes even further. According to Angel:

> The unprecedented prosperity of mines all over the State combined to help give owners an overshadowing influence upon legislation; and they sought, as preponderating capital always seeks, to shift the burden of taxation as much as possible on to the properties and industries less fortunate and able to bear it.

This law was changed in 1867 and 1871 to allow for a tax discrimination only in favor of Storey County mines. This was quite an advantage for the shareholders and directors of the mines of the Comstock Lode, as Myron Angel explained:

> Under this new regime, the owner of a horse valued at $100 paid to Storey $1.50 in tax, while the owner of a ton of ore yielding $100, first deducted eighteen dollars out of it, if the same was free milling ore, and then paid twenty and a half cents tax on what remained; but if the ore had to be either roasted or smelted to reduce it, then forty dollars was first deducted, leaving only sixty dollars to be assessed that was taxed only fifteen cents.

There was strong popular feeling against these subsidies to special interests. In 1875, the Legislature repealed the law and provided for mining properties to be taxed at the same rate as other property.

Another political problem of taxation and regulation in the nineteenth century was that of railroads, especially taxes on their property and freight rates. For fifty years voters and legislators of Nevada struggled over the issue, in campaigns that often shed more heat than light upon the issue. In his *History of Nevada,* Myron Angel didn't mince any words about the early policies of the railroads:

> From the first a system of freight and passenger tariffs was introduced that, although low enough to prevent competition by teams or stages, yet worked a serious damage to the State. It was for the interests of the company to increase its freight traffic to the utmost extent. . . . The prices charged were governed by

FREIGHT DISCRIMINATIONS.

BY THE CAR LOAD.	From New York ——— miles to San Francisco	From New York to Reno, Nevada, 306 less number of miles	From New York to Winnemucca, Nevada, 475 less number of miles.	From New York to Battle Mountain, Nev., 535 less number of miles	From New York to Palisade, Nevada, 587 less number of miles	From New York to Elko, Nevada, 619 less number of miles
Coal Oil.	$300	$ 536	$ 716	$750	$780	$800
Candles	300	536	716	750	780	800
Machinery	600	818	996	------	------	------
Dry Goods	1,200	1,436	1,616	------	------	------
Clothing.	1,200	1,446	1,796	------	------	------
Iron	300	454	576	------	------	------
Liquors	500	736	916	------	------	------
Fine Machinery.	1,000	1,246	1,596	------	------	------
Nails and Sipkes	300	536	716	------	------	------

This schedule of exorbitant freight charges clearly illustrates the burden imposed on the merchants and consumers of Nevada by the Central Pacific Railroad Company.

a rule that permitted the existence of traffic, and took for such a permit the principal profits.

By 1874, there was considerable political opposition to the railroad's shipping rates. Local taxes had not affected the railroad's activities at all, since the company could increase its freight rates within the county to make consumers pay for any tax that county could levy. In an 1881 speech before the U.S. House of Representatives, Nevada Congressman Rollin M. Daggett denounced the situation in emphatic terms:

> Is comment necessary upon these terrible rates? Do they not speak trumpet-tongued of impositions unparalleled in the annals of railroad ruffianism? . . .
> Nevada is an orange which for ten years these railroad vampires have been sucking in silence.

John Kinkead, Governor of Nevada during the same period, also made a strong protest against the freight rates of the Central Pacific Railroad in his last speech to the Legislature, in 1883:

> We are the victims of an injustice in the matter of transportation charges by this railroad company which is well nigh intolerable. The energies of our people have been fettered, the growth of the State retarded, and the development of its resources hampered by the outrageous exactions imposed upon us by this corporation.
> We are bound hand and foot; our industries languish, and the State which should be prosperous, is struggling on the verge of retrogression.

Daggett and Kinkead were talking about railroad reprisals against counties that attempted to raise taxes on the company. When this happened, the railroad directors would either raise the freight rates in that county or drop the rates on competing items from California, which ruined local producers and manufacturers.

Things changed late in the nineteenth century. The Southern Pacific Railroad Company purchased the Central Pacific in 1899, acquiring millions of dollars worth of land, tracks, rolling stock, equipment, and buildings in Nevada. Then, in 1907, the State Legislature created the State Railroad Board and Commission to regulate shipping rates and work conditions. The federal Interstate Commerce Commission backed up Nevada in its battle for reasonable rates and ended the problem after 1910.

The scope of State government (the number of activities regulated by the government) has greatly increased since the time of the settlers' government of 1851. The State government, created by successive acts of the Legislature, increased by fits and starts. At first, its function, like that of the earliest informal governments, was to provide a system of land claims, to settle disputes civilly, and to keep the peace. Later, the Legislature tried to encourage economic development, sometimes with very uncertain results. One of these results was monopolies — business corporations which had almost no competition in vital areas of public interest. These monopolies became regulated in the late nineteenth and early twentieth centuries, and the regulation of trades affecting the public safety began at about the same time. The State then built highways which contributed to Nevada's prosperity by encouraging commerce and tourism.

THE FEDERAL GOVERNMENT

Changing policies of the federal government have had a tremendous effect on life in Nevada. Since Nevada's political borders do not correspond with the natural terrain features, its economic base has always been fragile. In distant Washington, D.C., men make decisions vital to Nevadans from thousands of miles away. Their policies to encourage or discourage certain business activities and settlement can be and have meant the difference between prosperity and ruin to thousands of people. As a result, the federal government's actions have both good and bad effects upon the people of Nevada.

The overwhelming majority of the land in Nevada — about 87% of it — is owned and controlled by the United States government. Exercising that control, Congress and the President made Nevada first a Territory and then a State. The Congressional policy of settling and using the public land, established in the West since the Homestead Act of 1862, provided Nevada with a stable population. By virtue of the land it owns, the federal government possesses great power in and over the State.

Some federal policies, such as those favoring transcontinental transportation, are stable and have been maintained for over one hundred and fifty years. The transcontinental mail service, the transcontinental telegraph, the transcontinental railroad system, and the interstate highway system are good examples of this national promotion.

The Interstate Highway System

The federal interstate highway system is important to the economy of modern Nevada. Millions of people come to or pass through Nevada every year, and most of them travel on the freeways which cross our state.

Tasker L. Oddie was one of those responsible for getting the federal government involved in building interstate auto highways. The former Tonopah pioneer and Nevada governor was elected United States Senator from our State in 1921. That year Congress passed its first law to encourage national highway construction, the Federal Highway or Phipps-Townsend Act, which provided financial help to states to build interstate highways. Senator Oddie realized what a boon a modern highway system would be to Nevada, and after his re-election in 1927, he began building support in Congress for a federally-funded interstate highway program. On May 21, 1928, Congress passed the Oddie-Colton Highway Act, which provided for a sliding-scale increase of federal aid to states building interstate highways over public domain land. Oddie was also able to get federal aid for state road projects after Congress passed the

Tasker Lowndes Oddie (1870–1950), born in Brooklyn, New York, went to Nevada to practice law in 1898. In 1900, he was one of the original partners in the great Tonoaph ore bonanza discovery. An attorney, Oddie became Governor of Nevada in 1911–1914 and served the State as U.S. Senator between 1921 and 1935. Oddie, acting with the advice of important Nevada interests, brought the interstate highway system to the United States.

Courtesy of Nevada Historical Society

Oddie-Colton Forest Highway Act and the Oddie-Colton Public Domain Highway Act in 1930. By 1931, the Nevada Section of the federal highway system was completed and gravel-surfaced.

The modern system of interstate highways was greatly improved in 1956, when Congress passed and President Dwight D. Eisenhower signed the National Defense Highway Act. In a series of construction programs spread over many years, the federal government enlarged, improved, or created large sections of the interstate routes. Travelers and the Nevada cities along these freeways have also benefitted, as have businesses in the warehousing, tourist, and recreational industries. The last major United States highway project in Nevada was the 1964 opening of Interstate 80 as an all-weather highway between Reno and Sacramento over Donner Pass.

Boulder Dam

Another successful government project is Boulder Dam in southern Nevada. The story of Boulder Dam began early, as ambitious businessmen, engineers, and government officials considered what could be done by damming the 1,450 mile long Colorado River. In 1921, the State Legislature created the Colorado River Development Commission to coordinate plans to exploit the river with six other States — Arizona, California, Colorado, New Mexico, Utah, and Wyoming. Nevada and all of the other states except Arizona signed an interstate compact on the Colorado River reclamation system in 1928, and that same year Congress passed the Boulder Canyon Project Act, which President Calvin Coolidge signed into law on December 21st. A second act by the same name, signed in 1930 by President Herbert Hoover, authorized construction of the immense dam and hydroelectric plant across the Colorado River.

The spot selected for the dam was Boulder Canyon, a desolate place on the Colorado River. The government allowed private companies to bid for the contract to build the dam, but no single business was large enough to handle the work. A coalition of corporations formed Six Companies, Inc. to undertake the project. This huge combination built a road from the U.P.R.R. line near Las Vegas to the dam site and also built a branch railroad to transport supplies to the spot. Six Companies, Inc. also ran an electrical transmission line to Boulder Canyon over two hundred miles from San Bernardino, California, to provide power for the work.

The dam was built between 1930 and 1935. Thousands of workmen came into the area, creating a new town, Boulder City — one of the most charming communities in

The original site of Boulder Dam before the start of construction. This U.S. Bureau of Recalamation photograph shows Boulder Canyon, looking upstream to the north. The long-term effects of water on rock can easily be seen in the narrow gorge, cut by the Colorado River through centuries of erosion.

Courtesy of Special Collections, University of Nevada Reno Library

Boulder Dam. This radiant beacon of technological achievement tamed the turbulent Colorado River and harnessed its energy for generations to come. Completed between 1931 and 1935, this dam became a symbol of constructive uses of national power. A truly heroic engineering project, the dam provided inexpensive power to southern Nevada and benefitted all of the surrounding States.

Courtesy of Special Collections, University of Nevada Reno Library

Nevada. During the construction some eight thousand people lived there. The immense dam—727 feet high, 660 feet thick, and 1,244 feet long at its base—brought inexpensive electrical power to the region. This power allowed relatively inexpensive refining of ore, resulting in a mining boom in southern Nevada. It also allowed men to cool the torrid climate with air conditioners and powered the neon signs which light up the night skies around Las Vegas.

The dam gave a strong economic impetus to southern Nevada and brought together men who stayed and built up the region. Boulder Dam, officially called Hoover Dam after the President who authorized its construction, provides flood control and water for irrigating farmland in three states. It has been called the single greatest victory achieved by man in his fight to reclaim desert waste lands, while Lake Mead, a vast artificial lake formed by the dam, gives pleasure and recreation to tens of thousands of people each year.

All For Our Country

Not all of the decisions of the federal government have been particularly wise or helpful to the people of Nevada. Sudden shifts in government policy have been particularly harmful. For example, the Newlands or Truckee-Carson reclamation project brought long and costly lawsuits, one of which—the *Alpine* case—was the longest active case ever heard in the federal court system.

Another area of tension in Nevada is the extent and quality of federal government land ownership. The U.S. government holds title to about 353 million acres, not including federal lands in Alaska, Hawaii, and outside the United States. These holdings amount to about 18% of the mainland U.S. Most of this land held by the federal government is in the West, where the percentage of land controlled by the Department of the Interior ranges from a low of about 30% in Montana to a high of almost 87% in Nevada.

Of the 13% of Nevada which is not owned by the federal government, the major portion of the land is held by the Southern Pacific Railroad, as a result of land grants made by Congress when the Pacific Railroad bill was passed in 1862. Only about 2% of the land area of the State is owned by private parties.

The original Congressional policy was to encourage homesteading and settlement on these lands, but that policy was reversed in 1934, after it had been in effect for over one hundred and twenty-five years. That year Congress passed and President Franklin Roosevelt signed the Taylor Grazing Act, which established the U.S. Grazing Service (later the Bureau of Land Management) and authorized the Secretary of the Interior to withdraw millions of acres of grazing land from public use or sale. In Nevada, the Bureau of Land Management controls almost 48 million acres and is by far the largest land holder of the various federal agencies.

The death blow to settlement on the public lands in Nevada came when Congress passed two bills which President Lyndon Johnson signed into law on September 19th, 1964. The Multiple Use Act of 1964 gave the Secretary of the Interior the power to withdraw land from the public domain "for multiple use." The Act also allows the Secretary, if he sees fit, to prohibit any sale, lease or entry on the public lands. The second Bill—the Public Sales Act of 1964—gave the Secretary of the Interior the discretion to sell or withhold from sale any public lands. Before this time any sale, use, or entry of the public lands was not a matter of anyone's discretion but was regulated by law. After these acts were passed, the United States Department of the Interior ended almost all sales and stopped any further settlement of the public land. In 1976, Congress passed the Federal Land Policy and Management or Organic Act. This law allowed the federal government to retain public domain lands indefinitely.

The mining industry has been particularly hard hit by changes in federal policy. When the silver and gold of the Comstock Lode were discovered, the federal government used gold and silver coins as money rather than paper. Because the United States bought and minted bullion every year to use in the coins, the price of gold and silver stayed relatively high. In 1873, however, Congress decided to stop making nearly all silver coins and switched to an all-gold national currency. This act, called "the Crime of 1873" by politicians from the Western mining states, had a devastating effect upon

"The Author of Hard Times." The Silver Knight, a nineteenth-century magazine devoted to the cause of currency reform, published this cartoon blaming U.S. Senator John Sherman for the economic problems which plagued silver miners and the nation after Congress passed Sherman's Coinage Act, also called "The Crime of 1873."

Nevada. After the Coinage Act took effect in 1875, silver prices slumped, and a depression set in for the mining industry in the United States. Nevada was especially hard-hit, since its economy depended on silver mining. After 1880, mines began to close all over Nevada, and whole communities were abandoned. The State's population in 1880 was 62,266, but by 1890 it had fallen to 47,355, and in 1900 only 42,335 persons lived in Nevada.

William M. Stewart described the effect of the Coinage Act in his *Reminiscences:*

> The depreciation of silver as compared with gold during the twelve years from March, 1875 to March, 1887, was a great calamity to the people of my State, and more injurious to the people of the civilized world than famine, pestilence and war combined.

Western Congressmen tried hard to bring some relief to the mining industry. In 1878, the Bland-Allison Act was passed by Congress. The law provided that the United States would purchase and coin a relatively small amount of silver each year. This amount was doubled in 1890, when Congress passed the Sherman Silver Purchase Act. Within just two years, there was a national financial panic which was blamed on the Sherman Silver Purchase Act, and the law was repealed in 1893. This left the silver miners in the same position they had been in during 1875–1878, when the government bought almost no silver.

Silver coinage became an important political issue in Nevada. By 1885, both the Republican and Democratic parties in Nevada were calling for the United States

"Senatorial Courtesy." This 1893 cartoon from the humor magazine <u>Puck</u> shows that not everyone was sympathetic to the cause of silver. Here, Nevada Senator William M. Stewart declaims the merits of silver coinage, while his fellow Senators snooze.

Treasury to issue silver coins again. When William M. Stewart was elected to the U.S. Senate in 1887, he started a vigorous campaign in Washington, D.C., for the return of silver coinage.

Supported by William Stewart and Francis G. Newlands, Winnemucca banker George S. Nixon began organizing Silver Clubs all across Nevada. These groups formed a separate political party, the Silver Party, in 1892. That year Francis G. Newlands was elected U.S. Representative, Stewart was re-elected U.S. Senator, and the Silver Party candidates swept the State. In the next election, held in 1894, the "Silverites" gained complete control of Nevada. They formed an alliance with the much weakened Democratic Party organization in the State. The combination called themselves "Silver-Democrats" and controlled Nevada politics until after 1906.

The silver issue became a national concern in the 1896 election, but the silver-backed Democratic Party candidate for the Presidency, William Jennings Bryan, was defeated that year by William McKinley. The silver cause flourished during the hard times of the 1880's and the 1890's, when prices were down and credit was hard to find. By the turn of the century, however, new gold discoveries in Alaska, Colorado, and elsewhere, along with more efficient ore reduction methods, increased the supply of gold coinage. Increased business activity and prosperity followed, especially after the Spanish-American War of 1898. With this prosperity, people became less interested in the cause of silver coinage, and the Silver Party faded into history.

Key Pittman, elected United States Senator from Nevada in 1913, helped the mining industry in 1918, when Congress passed the Pittman Act. Like the Bland-Allison

The United States Mint at Carson City. This nineteenth-century photograph shows the structure where the silver and gold produced by the State's mines was minted into coins by federal government employees. Today, this imposing building houses the Nevada State Museum, with its wonderful collection of exhibits and information.

Courtesy of Special Collections, University of Nevada Reno Library

Key Pittman (1872–1940) of Mississippi left his native State for Alaskan gold fields before he settled in Nevada. When U.S. Senator George S. Nixon died in office in 1912, the State Legislature chose Pittman to replace him. Re-elected to the Senate four times, Pittman spent much of his career fighting to stabilize silver prices.

Courtesy of Nevada Historical Society

*Patrick Anthony McCarran (1876–1954)
of Nevada served his native State for twenty-two
years as U.S. Senator. He had previously been a
justice on Nevada's Supreme Court. McCarran
fought President Franklin D. Roosevelt's
attempts to pack the U.S. Supreme Court and
often opposed "New Deal" measures in
Congress. He was responsible for a good deal of
important national legislation, including the
Civil Aeronautics Act, the Internal Security Act
of 1950, and the McCarran-Walters
Immigration Act. His life was dedicated to an
unrelenting fight against communism.*

Courtesy of Nevada Historical Society

and Sherman Silver Purchase Acts, this law was a promise by the federal government to buy a certain amount of silver each year, in this case until 1923.

Other western states helped Nevada in its fight to renew silver coinage and restore it to its pre-1873 value. Senators from Arizona, Colorado, Idaho, Montana, New Mexico, and Utah helped Senator Pittman to form a "Silver Bloc" or group of votes in Congress. When the Pittman Act expired, they banded together to try and pass new silver purchase agreements. They were unsuccessful, however. All through the 1920's, many major foreign governments stopped producing silver currency, and the price of silver fell.

The Great Depression, which began in 1929, gave new strength to the movement to remonetize silver. Many Senators wanted to restore silver coinage, hoping that this would help the national economy. Franklin D. Roosevelt, elected President in 1932, agreed. As a result, on December 21, 1933, President Roosevelt accepted an international silver agreement negotiated at the London Economic Conference earlier that year. The Treasury Department eliminated gold coins and began to purchase and coin all silver mined in the United States into dimes, quarters, half-dollars, and silver dollars. Senator Pittman helped lead the fight in Congress to pass a silver purchase act in 1934, increasing the number of silver coins in circulation.

The United States minted silver coins for more than thirty years. This ended after 1965, when Congress passed the Coinage Act of 1965 and stopped making silver dimes and quarters. In 1970, the last of the silver coins, the half-dollar, went out of circulation when Congress stopped minting silver coins altogether. These acts had a devastating effect on the mining industry in Nevada, and ended a 195–year policy of value-backed currency.

NEVADA'S STATE CAPITAL

Nevada has a number of communities which owe their existence to government, among them Mercury and Boulder City, but the oldest and best-known is our State capital, Carson City.

Carson City

The future seat of government for the Territory and State of Nevada got its start in 1851, when it was first settled. Myron Angel's *History of Nevada* provides the details:

> Early in November of that year a party, consisting of Joe and Frank Bernard, George Follensbee, A. J. Rollins, Frank Hall, and W. L. Hall, came from Bents Bar, Placer County, California, for the purpose of mining in western Utah, but finding the pay was not sufficient to warrant them in doing so, they took up, in December, the celebrated Eagle Ranch, where now stands the State Capitol. They built a log house there for a station. . . . An eagle soaring over the heads of the builders was shot and killed by Frank Hall, and the skin stripped from the bird was stuffed and nailed upon the station. This incident furnished a name for the station that was transferred to the ranch, and eventually to the valley that surrounded it.

Early in 1858, Abram Curry came into Carson Valley — the same man as Mark Twain's *"Old* Curry – Old *Abe* Curry."* He was immediately disappointed, as Angel, quoting an 1876 *Nevada Tribune* newspaper story, relates:

> A traveler, weary with riding over the Sierra from California, arrived at the ancient village of Mormontown (Genoa), where a town site had been laid off, the owners expecting to make a great speculation in the sale of lots therein. Curry was in pursuit of an eligible location to build a store for general merchandising. He examined the town site, and soon selected a corner lot to build upon. The price, $1,000, and no less, must be paid. Only one of the partners plead for reduction, the other was unflinching in his demands for the sum, or no sale. His stubbornness was excelled only by his inability to estimate the strength and determination of his man, in consequence of which the trade was never consummated. The stranger mounted his horse, asked for the last time for a reduction of terms. The cold, unrelenting answer was returned as before. Our hero replied, "Well, then, I will build a city of my own," and, suiting the action to the word, pressed his spurs to the flanks of his already restive steed, and, before the sun had settled into the lap of the west, Abram Curry was in Eagle Valley for the purpose of redeeming his promise of the morning.

Curry bought Eagle Ranch for the same $1,000 the Genoa developers had asked, and laid out a town site in September, 1858.

Like many promoters, Curry encouraged people to move to his new city by selling his lots cheaply. Sometimes he even gave them away. Major William M. Ormsby, for whom Ormsby County was named, had a store at Genoa, but he relocated his business in Carson City. He also built a hotel. Curry and his partners, F. M. Proctor, B. F. Green, and J. J. Musser, sold two blocks for $25 and a pair of boots, while a ¼ interest in the Warm Springs was sold for a pony which was afterwards traded for 25 pounds of butter.

Carson City had a modest beginning. In October, 1858, Richard N. Allen, writing under the pen name of "Tennessee," informed the readers of the San Francisco *Herald:*

> I am told that it is about fifteen miles from Genoa, in a northeasterly direction. I also learn that, although only a few months have passed since its site was selected, a house is already built and occupied by a white man, and numerous wigwams of Indians can be found in the mountains nearby.

The new town had problems with law and order, like most frontier settlements. The problem was aggravated by the lack of any effective local government in western Utah. In the summer of 1859, a Carson City correspondent to the Placerville *Observer* complained:

> Such things as cutting and shooting are of too frequent occurrence here, and a stop should be put to them. Offenders ought to be placed in confinement until we shall have courts legally organized. It is true some time may elapse before we are blessed with such institutions, but criminals are the persons who should suffer for this delay. They ought to be kept even for forty years, and if they survive the present generation of men and still no courts are organized, we should hand them down prisoners to posterity.

Civilization came quickly to Carson City, however. In late 1859, the *Territorial Enterprise* moved its newspaper offices from Genoa to Carson. Settlers stayed in Carson City and avoided Genoa, whose population then began to dwindle. According to contemporary accounts, Carson had a more favorable climate and was better located as a stopping point on the roads to the mines of the Comstock. Even today the town stands at the crossroads of two major interstate routes, U.S. Highways 50 and 395.

By 1860, Carson City was the most important town in western Utah. The Carson County seat was moved from Genoa to Carson City early in 1861, and Abram Curry's dream city started its career as a government community.

William M. Stewart was largely responsible for locating the capital at Carson City. He was elected a member of the first Territorial Legislature, representing Carson.

Abram Z. Curry, founder of Carson City, Warden of the Nevada Territorial Prison, and first superintendent of the U.S. Mint at Carson.
Courtesy of Nevada Historical Society

Atomic Bomb explosion at the U.S. Atomic Energy Commission's Nevada Proving Grounds. Established in December, 1950, at the Frenchman's Flat area of southern Nevada, the nuclear test site saw its first A-Bomb burst on January 27, 1951. Much of the nation's nuclear testing moved underground after 1957, and after 1961, the United States discontinued above-ground testing of nuclear devices. The town of Mercury was founded there in 1957 to house scientists and workers in the research and testing of nuclear propulsion for spacecraft, as well as for the nuclear testing program.

Stewart worked very hard in the town's interest, as he described in his *Reminiscences.* As a result the Legislature made Carson the Territorial capital:

> Knowing that I had been elected for the purpose of locating the capital at Carson, I remained at home during the time the members of the Legislature were coming in from different parts of the Territory. I inquired of each how he wanted his county bounded and where he wanted the county-seat. Each one told me, and I framed a bill dividing the Territory into counties and making Carson the capital.
>
> Virginia City lacked a few votes of half the Legislature. A large delegation came down, confident that they would locate the capital at Virginia City, and it was understood that any change in the programme would be disastrous to them in arranging their county boundaries. The Virginia delegation debated the question in a very enthusiastic manner, but we on the outside kept quiet until the vote was reached, when our programme was carried by three votes, the number that we anticipated.

There are many other stories about Carson City — too many to be repeated here. Its history is as long as any other community in the State. Only Genoa is an older settlement, by about four or five months. Today, Carson City is a bustling place. It is home for State government offices, the county administration, and a number of fascinating museums, including the Nevada State Museum, housed in the old U.S. Mint building, and the State Railroad Museum.

CHAPTER 6

Gaming

In Nevada, gaming and tourism have combined to form the State's richest and most powerful industry. Gaming and tourism have provided a relatively stable economy, compared with mining where "rushes" and "booms" brought rapid but temporary increases in population and wealth.

Gaming is just as important for the number of jobs it provides for those who have come into the State to work. In his 1975 testimony before the United States Joint Congressional Committee on the Review of the National Policy Toward Gambling, Governor Donal "Mike" O'Callaghan spoke of the significance of gaming today:

> The latest surveys reveal approximately twenty-five percent of Nevada's total labor force are employed in the gaming industry and related tourist-oriented businesses, for example, motels, gas stations, and so on.
>
> It is estimated that an additional twenty-five percent of Nevada's businesses are indirectly dependent upon the gaming industry. This means that one-half of Nevada's total labor force is dependent either totally or in part on the legalized gaming industry in Nevada.

TOURISM

Tourism has been a part of our State's history from the earliest days of settlement. The first tourist in Nevada was probably Lola Montez, the Countess of Landsfeldt, an internationally famous actress and celebrity living in Grass Valley, California. Her excursion to Donner Lake and the Truckee Meadows in the summer of 1854 is the first such sightseeing jaunt to Nevada recorded in the early newspapers of the Pacific Coast.

Nevada's first hotel was built at Genoa in 1857 by William B. "Lucky Bill" Thorington and William D. "Uncle Billy" Rogers, to take advantage of the increase in travelers brought over the trans-Sierran stagecoach routes which opened that year. It was also known as the "White House" hotel, where many a card game was played.

When intruders first came into Nevada, they were just passing through to get to someplace else — California or Oregon Territory, or back to the trans-Mississippi east. After the discovery of gold and silver in Nevada, there was an entirely different situation. The prospect of sudden wealth fired the hearts of a restless class, and many people began to travel to the State and not just across it. There were all sorts of travelers on the road in the middle of the nineteenth century: teamsters, bankers, miners, lumbermen, stock-drovers, engineers, railroad workers, businessmen, and tourists.

The first accommodations in the booming mining camps were primitive. The miners often lived in tents or dugouts. The teamsters freighting cargo to and from the mining camps needed places to eat, sleep, and be merry. Within just a few years of the discovery of the Comstock Lode, hotels and stations were operating all along the routes leading to the mines. The teamsters' wagons moved very slowly along the dusty, windswept dirt trails to the mining camps; they usually only made 8–15 miles each day, and sometimes less. This meant that they were often out on the road for days.

Tourists visited nineteenth century Nevada as the mines of the Comstock

Lola Montez, Countess of Landsfeld (1818–1861). This Irish-born celebrity blazed the trail to Nevada for tens of millions of tourists when she and a party of friends and guests visited the Truckee Meadows on a sightseeing trip in July, 1854.

Courtesy of Nevada Historical Society

Nevada's First Hotel. The Rogers & Thorington House, built at Genoa in 1857, provided lodging for travelers on the California Trail and especially for passengers on the transcontinental stagecoaches which began operating that year. This Douglas County photograph, taken some years later, shows the California Trail (Genoa's main street), the overland telegraph, developing shade trees, and a new wing added to the back of the freshly-painted hotel. As road traffic increased, so did the hotel business.

Courtesy of Nevada Historical Society

The International Hotel at Virginia City. This morning scene from the 1870's depicts the finest eating, drinking, and sleeping establishment in nineteenth–century Nevada. Everything about it was modern and up-to-date, from its richly-furnished rooms illuminated by gaslight to its shining brass elevator. A hotel of this class provided special areas or rooms for its patrons who cared to gamble.

Courtesy of Special Collections, University of Nevada Reno Library

prospered. Some travelers, like Emperor Dom Pedro II of Brazil, were of royal blood. Others, such as ex-President Ulysses S. Grant, had been heads of state. Mark Twain and Oscar Wilde were two of the best-known literary figures to have toured Nevada, but there were many more. Famous publishers like Frank Leslie and wealthy financiers such as Darius O. Mills stayed in luxury hotels in Reno and Virginia City, giving the tourist industry of the time an elegant tone.

During the nineteenth century the International Hotel in Virginia City had a reputation to match its name. It was the most sophisticated and cosmopolitan hotel in Nevada. A towering skyscraper in its day, the six story International Hotel for years had the only elevator between the Mississippi River and the Pacific Coast. President U. S. Grant and General William T. Sherman were guests there, and many foreign dignitaries and financial kingpins spent the night in the tastefully finished, gas-illuminated rooms.

The early Nevada hotels and restaurants set a pattern for later days. Mary McNair Mathews, a resident of Virginia City, remarked in her 1880 book *Ten Years in Nevada:*

> Every restaurant table groans with food of every kind gathered from every kingdom of the globe. From eight to twelve different kinds of vegetables and nearly as many kinds of meat, are on the table three times a day. Cakes, and

every kind of pastry and puddings you will find; there are also fruits from every country and clime.

Nevada's first resort was opened in 1862 by David Walley, at the hot springs in Douglas County which bear his name. Still in operation today, the original resort has been reconstructed and improved. The establishment was impressive in 1881, as Angel described in his *History of Nevada:*

> Near Henry Vansickle's at the base of the mountain spurs which jut into the valley from the west, two miles south of Genoa, are some large thermal springs, now known as Walley's Hot Springs. Here is a large hotel building containing forty rooms, with bath-houses adjoining. There are eighty acres of land belonging to the property, and the improvements were made at a cost of $100,000. These springs have a great reputation for the cure of rheumatic and scrofulous affections, and have become a noted place of resort. The location is extremely pleasant, the scenery grand, and the climate in summer invigorating and healthful.

For local residents looking for something less medicinal, there were parks and gardens which, although owned by private persons, were open to the public for a fee. Some of the better-known parks were in Washoe and Eagle Valleys. One of the most famous of these, Bowers Mansion, is now a State park.

Although the first tourists came to Nevada by horse, mule, and wagon in the early years, and later by train, the modern tourist industry as we know it only became possible with good highways and the widespread popularity of the motor car. The construction of gravel-surfaced and paved roads after World War I, described in the chapter on transportation, made it possible for millions of people each year to visit Nevada by automobile.

Another spur to Nevada's twentieth century tourist industry has been its world-famous sports events. Racing of all sorts has been particularly favored. In 1908, the course for the New York to Paris transcontinental auto race crossed Nevada, and more recently the State has hosted high-speed hydroplane racing matches at Lake Tahoe. At Reno, the National Championship Air Races are an annual event, as are speed contests involving flotillas of hot air balloons. On the Comstock, camels and ostriches race

Nevada's First Resort. Opened in 1862 on the California Trail near Genoa, Walley's Hot Springs offered a well-appointed hotel, curative mineral springs, and a superior climate to persons seeking healthful relaxation. Many of Nevada's natural hot springs have provided the site for a resort hotel.

Savage Action at the Johnson-Jeffries Fight, July 4, 1910. Jack Johnson (right) conclusively defeated Jim Jeffries (left) in this world heavyweight boxing championship match, which attracted tourists from all over the Pacific coast.

Courtesy of Nevada Historical Society

Downtown Reno During the Johnson-Jeffries Fight, 1910. The streets are crowded with some of the thousands of reasons why popular national sport promotions are good for business. Just before and during the fight, Reno's hotels were full to capacity, and rooms were nowhere to be had.

Courtesy of Nevada Historical Society

annually through the center of Virginia City. In southern Nevada, the arid deserts outside of Las Vegas are the scene of nationally famous motorcycle races as well as the Las Vegas Grand Prix and Can-Am automobile races. Automobile racing in the area dates from the early 1900's.

For over one hundred years, ski racing has been popular in the Lake Tahoe region. "Snowshoe" Thompson's pioneer activities gave rise to the fast-moving sport. Skiing in the Sierra Nevada range started to draw large numbers of tourists after a local ski resort, Squaw Valley, California, was chosen as the site of the 1960 Winter Olympic Games.

Nevada is especially well-known for having hosted some of the most exciting world championship boxing matches ever held. In the late nineteenth century, few states allowed public boxing matches. In 1895, World Heavyweight Boxing Champion James J. "Gentlemen Jim" Corbett and Robert Fitzsimmons wanted to have a prize fight. First Texas and then Arkansas refused to allow the match. Nevada was willing to permit the show, however; in 1897, the Legislature passed and Governor Reinhold Sadler signed a law specifically authorizing prize fights.

The bout was held at Carson City on Saint Patrick's Day of that year. It was a spectacular fight, with the underdog Fitzsimmons knocking out Corbett in the 14th round. A film made of the fight grossed three-quarters of a million dollars.

George L. "Tex" Rickard, a Goldfield saloon-keeper, decided to try to recreate the same excitement in 1906, when he put up the largest prize or purse ever offered at that time for a boxing match — $30,000 — to bring famous lightweight boxers Oscar M. "Battling" Nelson and Joe Gans together in the ring. Amidst unprecedented publicity, the fight was held in Goldfield on Labor Day, 1906. There was extensive betting on the match, which Gans won in the 42nd round when Nelson was disqualified for foul blows.

Rickard went on to become an internationally famous sports promoter and gambler. After the Gans-Nelson fight, his next big move was arranging a World Heavyweight Boxing Championship match at Reno. James J. Jeffries, a retired but undefeated former World Champion, met John Arthur "Jack" Johnson, the reigning champion, in the ring on July 4, 1910. Johnson, the underdog in the contest, defeated Jeffries in the 15th round. Rickard made more money from selling tickets to the match than did all that year's World Series baseball games.

"Tex" Rickard then began to promote spectacular sporting events at Madison Square Garden in New York and elsewhere. When he left, big-time boxing left Nevada and did not return for more than fifty years. All of that changed in 1963, when Las Vegas

George Lewis "Tex" Rickard — a portrait of the man who made millions of dollars for himself and his backers promoting national sports events. Rickard, a Texas cowboy, rancher, town marshal, and gambler, got his start in Goldfield, Nevada, and went on to become an international-class sports promoter.

Courtesy of Nevada Historical Society

hosted a World Heavyweight Boxing Championship match on July 22. Sonny Liston retained the title with a knockout victory in one round over Floyd Patterson. Two years later, Mohammed Ali, boxing under his given name Cassius Clay, came to Las Vegas as the new Champion. In another World Heavyweight Boxing Championship match in Nevada's largest city, on November 11, 1965, he defeated former champion and perennial challenger Floyd Patterson after a twelve round bout.

Ten years later and still Champion, on May 16, 1975, Ali defeated challenger Ron Lyle by knocking him out in the 11th round at Las Vegas.

In another World Heavyweight Boxing Championship match three years later, on February 15, 1978, Ali lost his crown as the world's greatest heavyweight boxer to Leon Spinx after 15 rounds in Las Vegas. Of the next six World Heavyweight Championship matches held around the United States, four took place in Las Vegas. These bouts brought tens of thousands of tourists to the State.

GAMING

Gaming is almost as old as man himself. There are basically three types or classes of games: guessing games, games of chance, and games which mix chance and skill. All of these are said to have originated in the efforts of mankind to foretell the future. The urge to place a bet or wager on the result of the game is also nearly as old as man himself. The earliest histories and myths mention gambling as a common pastime in almost every known culture.

In Nevada, the Paiute, Shoshone, and Washo Indians have played and bet on games since prehistoric times. Legends of these tribes mention wagers and betting among the earliest inhabitants and mythological figures.

When the first fur-trappers and explorers came into Nevada, they reported that many of the Indians they met liked to gamble and bet. In *The Big Bonanza,* Dan DeQuille mentioned it also:

> Young Winnemucca [Numaga] never gambled, but Old Winnemucca was an inveterate gambler — that is, among his own people. The Paiutes do not gamble

Poker-playing Paiutes gamble their earnings on the turn of a card in a camp outside Rhyolite. Wagers played an important part in Indian society, where even mythical characters liked to play games of chance.

Courtesy of Nevada Historical Society

with white men. Old Winnemucca has been known to lose all his ponies, all his blankets and arms, and, in fact, everything he possessed, down to a breech-clout, at a single sitting.

The white intruders brought their own games with them — mostly games of cards and dice. They liked to gamble and bet, too, especially when they had nothing better to do. For example, in a letter to the Virginia City *Territorial Enterprise*, Mark Twain described how he passed the time while stranded by the Carson River flood of 1861–62:

> I was 15 days on the road back to Carson on horseback, with Colonel Onstein and Captain Pfersdorff, 9 of which were spent at Honey Lake Smith's, when there was but two hundred feet of dry ground around the house, and the whole desert for miles around was under water. The whole place was crowded with teamsters, and we wore out every deck of cards on the place, and then had no amusement left but to scrape up a handful of vermin off the floor or beds, and "shuffle" them, and bet on odd or even. Even this poor excuse for a game broke up in a row at last when it was discovered that Colonel Onstein kept a "cold deck" down the back of his neck! He would persist in cheating, and so we played no more. Take it together, that was the funniest trip I ever made.

One of Nevada's most famous gamblers of the Utah Territorial or preterritorial period was William B. "Lucky Bill" Thorington. In 1851, Rollin F. Daggett, later U.S. Congressman from Nevada and Ambassador to Hawaii, saw "Lucky Bill" at Sacramento. He described the game of thimblerig (also known as the shell game) to the readers of the San Francisco *Golden Era* in "Lucky Bill"'s own words:

> Here, gentlemen, is a nice, quiet little game conducted on the square, and especially recommended by the clergy for its honesty and wholesome moral tendencies. I win only from blind men; all that have two good eyes can win a fortune. You see, gentlemen, here are three little wooden cups, and here is a little ball, which, for the sake of starting the game, I shall place under this one, as you can plainly see — thus — and thus — and thus: and now I will bet two, four or six ounces [of gold] that no gentleman can, the first time trying, raise the cup that the ball is under; if he can, he can win all the money that Bill, by patient toil and industry, has scraped together.

"Lucky Bill" was a "sure-thing" gambler — that is to say, he cheated. He didn't always keep it all for himself, however. There are many stories about "Lucky Bill"'s charity and his skill at thimblerig; this one is from Angel's *History of Nevada*:

> In 1854 a couple of California bound emigrants stopped at Mormon Station, and had a falling out, and it transpired that they were partners, one of them owning the wagon and the cattle that hauled it, while the other, who had a wife, supplied the provisions. The expense of this provision supply and incidentals along the route had exhuasted the husband's finances, and the owner of the train refused to take the bankrupt emigrants any further. Lucky Bill passing, saw the woman weeping disconsolately by the wagon, and his sympathies were at once aroused. Upon inquiry he learned the state of affairs, and told the husband and wife to borrow no further trouble, for he would see that they reached the Sacramento [River] without further delay.
>
> That night the owner of the outfit was induced to bet against Lucky Bill in his "thimble-rig game," and in the morning he had neither an outfit nor a dollar in money left. The winner gave him back fifteen dollars of the money, bought him a new pair of boots to travel in, told him to 'lite out' for California on foot, and never after that to bet against any one who was playing his own game. To the bankrupt family he gave a cow, spent the loser's money in buying them provisions, etc., and then hired a man to drive the team with them to California.

Unfortunately, "Lucky Bill" came to an unhappy end. He was tried and convicted of murder in 1858 by the Carson Valley "People's Court" or vigilance committee. Thorington and two other men were hanged for the crime.

In the early days of government, gaming was illegal in Nevada. In November, 1861, the first Territorial Legislature rejected a bill to permit licensed gambling. Instead, they prohibited gaming altogether by passing a law providing criminal penalties for gaming operations and betting. This first act of the Legislature on the subject made the conducting of gambling games a felony punishable by up to two years' imprisonment and a fine of not more than $5,000. Betting on the games was a misdemeanor and could be punished by a fine of up to $500 and incarceration in the county jail for up to six months.

The laws didn't work and didn't prevent gambling, especially as Nevada boomed. When people came to Nevada following the discovery of the Comstock Lode, the number of gamblers and gambling games also increased. Since there were ten or fifteen men for every woman in the Territory, drinking and gambling were rife.

Every mining camp had a collection of saloons and gaming parlors for the amusement of the townsfolk. The most popular games were those involving cards or the roulette wheel. Faro, a card game which has all but disappeared today, was an old favorite; playing it was called "bucking the tiger." These games went on unregulated by the State, and some were dishonestly run. In 1863, William Brewer visited Aurora, then in its heyday as a mining camp, and described his impressions in his *Journal:*

> Aurora of a Saturday night — how shall I describe it? It is so unlike anything East I can compare it with nothing you have ever seen. One sees a hundred men to one women and child. Saloons — saloons — saloons — liquor — everywhere. And here the men are — where else *can* they be? At home in their cheerless, lonesome hovels or huts? No, in the saloons, where the lights are bright, amid the hum of many voices and the excitement of gambling. Here men come to make money — make it *quick* — not by slow, honest industry, but by quick strokes — no matter *how,* so long as the law doesn't call it *robbery.* Here, where twenty quartz mills are stamping the rock and kneading its powder in bullion —

Mining Camp Social Center — the Northern Saloon in the newly-founded tent town of Tonopah, 1902. This bar and gambling hall has a prosperous look to it, with its large sign and frame-construction, in a place where most citizens played and slept under canvas. Jim Butler, discoverer of Tonopah's silver mines, stands in front of the open door. The proprietor of the Northern, legendary western lawman and gunfighter Wyatt Earp, is just to the right of the sign and behind the lady on horseback. The saloon was usually one of the first permanent buildings to be constructed in a new town or camp.

Courtesy of Nevada Historical Society

here, where one never sees a bank bill, nor "rag money," but where hard silver and shining gold are the currency — where men are congregated and living uncomfortably, and where there are no home ties or social checks, no churches, no religions — here one sees gambling and vice in all its horrible realities.

Here are tables, with gold and silver piled upon them by hundreds (or even thousands), with men (or women) behind, who deal *faro*, or *monte*, or *vingt-et-un* [twenty-one] or *rouge-et-noir*, or who turn *roulette* — in short, any way in which they may win and you may lose.

The fact that the law was ineffective didn't make a difference. After Nevada was admitted to the Union in 1864, the first State Legislature continued the Territorial ban with another act which also made gaming operations and betting criminal acts. The situation was a compromise. The people who didn't like gambling could take satisfaction that the law prohibited it. The people who enjoyed gambling could feel secure in the knowledge that the law was almost never enforced.

In 1869, eight years after gaming was forbidden by the Territorial Legislature, the State Legislature passed a law over the veto of Governor Henry Blasdel which made gaming legal in Nevada. The new law required a quarterly license fee for the privilege of running a gambling business. The license cost $1000 per year in counties with a population of under 2,000 votes, and $1600 per year in the more populous counties. The State split the licensing revenues with the counties, 50-50. It was forbidden to operate a gambling game in the front room of a saloon or to admit minors under 17 years of age. Towns were not allowed to ban gaming establishments or restrict their operations.

The system was improved by the Legislature in 1879, when it passed a bill which

A Bunch of the Boys Were Hamming It Up. Squinty-eyed, card-playing cowboys smoke and joke for the photographer in a Goldfield saloon, about 1908. Illustrations and the photographic calling cards of their favorite persons decorate the walls. They keep the guns around just in case somebody might try to cheat.

Courtesy of Nevada Historical Society

banned cheating in any licensed game. Before that time, cheating was a problem which was usually settled privately.

Many prominent Nevadans opposed legalized gambling. In 1889, the State Legislature approved a special election to decide, among other things, whether the section of the Nevada Constitution prohibiting state lotteries should be repealed. A number of influential citizens fought the plan for a state lottery system. One of them was District Court Judge R. R. Bigelow of Humboldt County, who later became Chief Justice of the Nevada Supreme Court. In a letter written to the Winnemucca *Silver State,* Bigelow denounced the special election as a fraud called especially for the occasion to pass the lottery bill:

> The real reason is to enable the lottery schemers by concentrating all their money and efforts in Virginia City and other populous centers, and by excluding as many as possible of the votes that would be against it, to give the lottery amendment a seeming majority and get returns in time to enable this legislature to disgrace itself and every man, woman and child in the State by giving state recognition to a lottery — a plan to enable a few rich gamblers to grow richer through the unfortunate mania for gambling that possesses so many people — a vice second only to drunkeness in its home-destroying and character-ruining tendencies.
>
> Think of it! The State of Nevada, not content with being known as the 'rotten borough' is now to descend to the very depths by becoming part owner in a gambling game.

Another correspondent, who wrote in 1889 under the name of "Index" to the Reno *Evening Gazette,* predicted dire consequences if the State got into the gambling business by legalizing the lottery:

> If this proposition ever carries it means good-bye to the last vestige of political liberty in Nevada. It will dominate this State as no bonanza kings or railroads or cattle association ever did before, and with our small population and large floating element, it will never be in the power of the people to throw it off in the world; and while it will control the state it will have no motive except to wreck it.
>
> Instead of bringing in an industrious class of prospectors and small farmers to build up the community by honest industry, they would encourage a swarm of fast people, sharpers, would-be sharpers and victims, bad women and worse men, who would have no more regard for the state or its citizens than the vulture has for the sheep camp where it steals its lamb.
>
> Weak men who love to gamble and commit other follies have a right to claim that temptation not be put upon them by the State that is supported by them and others to suppress crime and promote prosperity.
>
> But more than all the rising generation have claims of this sort. They should not be forced to face this evil genius of gaming with the sanction of their fathers and mothers backing it up. Children should not be taught that it is a good way to earn a living or spend their wages. They will have temptations enough and difficulties enough to overcome in order to succeed in life without being born gamblers.

A number of prominent Nevadans — among them Judge Bigelow, newspaperman Robert Fulton, cattlemen George Russel and J. R. Bradley of Elko, Jerry Moore of Ruby Valley, J. H. Thiess of Lovelock, E. G. Stevenson of Gold Hill, and future Governor John Sparks of Elko County — signed a pamphlet opposing the lottery system and circulated it throughout the State. On election day, the lottery proposal was defeated by popular vote.

There were problems with legalized gaming in nineteenth century Nevada. The most serious difficulties then were: where gambling games were permitted; admitting minors; calculating the populations of the counties to set the licensing fees; the hours of the day when gaming was proper; cheating games; and whether it was proper to allow gambling by persons who had no right to bet the money.

During the period between 1869 and 1907, the Legislature made a number of changes in the law to deal with these problems. Decreased revenues from gaming may have helped convince the Legislature to legalize "nickel-in-the-slot" machines in 1905.

Gambling Parlor in the Goldfield Merchant's Hotel. Electric lamps have replaced the gaslight fittings of yesteryear, as well-to-do players while away the hours and their wages playing craps (right front), faro (left front), and roulette (left rear). On the wall, Otto Becker's 1895 print "Custer's Last Fight" celebrates the Indian-fighting foundations of a now-vanished frontier world.

Courtesy of Special Collections, University of Nevada Reno Library

The falling taxes resulted in a two-class tax, passed in 1907, which gave the State the right to claim a percentage of the slot machine revenues while the counties retained all of the revenues from all other gaming operations.

After forty years of legal gaming in Nevada, the Legislature decided to make a change. In 1909, it once again passed a law prohibiting all forms of gambling in the State. The prohibition took effect on October 1, 1910. Crowds of curious and sentimental people packed Reno's gambling halls, but wagering stopped promptly at midnight. The new law was not widely respected. Within a few weeks, the Reno *Nevada State Journal* reported:

> If you are properly armed with the high sign and the counter sign, and the address, it is said that there is a place in town where the roulette wheel spins nightly and where the faro bank is dealt of old.

There was a great deal of opposition to the 1910 law banning gambling in every form of game — many people liked to place bets on cards, for example. As a result, the people in favor of allowing limited forms of gambling lobbied the 1911 legislative session and were successful in passing a law allowing bets to be made on card hands. In 1913, the next Legislature once again prohibited all forms of gambling, and the law stayed that way until 1931.

The total ban on gambling in the State was ineffective. Law enforcement agencies found it difficult to enforce the prohibition. Since the people who chose to break the law and gamble did so willingly, there were few complaints about gaming, unless it involved obvious cheating. Sheriffs' departments and city police ignored illegal gambling games or enforced the law unevenly. As a result, the State's gambling

This is the sort of combination that has made Nevada famous—an alliance of government, gamblers, and entertainment. Reno gaming figures Bill Graham and Jim McKay flank Governor Fred Balzar (left center) and heavyweight boxing champion Jack Dempsey in the early 1930's. Governor Balzar, under whose administration gambling was legalized in 1931, shows the new-found respectability of gaming as he rubs elbows with men who ran illegal betting operations for years.

Courtesy of Nevada Historical Society

Elegant society women amuse themselves by gambling at Nevada's most sophisticated casino of the 1920's, Graham and McKay's The Willows. It was a favorite spot for out-of-state divorcees waiting to satisfy Nevada's residency requirements for a "quickie divorce." This fashionable trio are having mixed reactions to their fortune. They are playing "chuck-a-luck" as a poker-faced croupier stands in the shadows.

Courtesy of Nevada Historical Society

Reno by Night, about 1940. Harrah's casino and the Nevada Club are visible in this neon-lit view south on rain-slick Virginia Street. Legalized gambling was still relatively small-time in Nevada, in the days before national advertising and automobile tourism began to bring millions of visitors to Nevada.

Courtesy of Special Collections, University of Nevada Reno Library

operations produced no revenue in licenses and taxes, while clandestine games flourished and made a mockery of the law.

In 1931, after much discussion over the question of whether to allow legal gaming in Nevada, Assemblyman Phil Tobin of Humboldt County introduced a bill into the State Legislature. Termed "a wide-open gambling bill," Tobin's proposal drew strong criticism from religious, temperance, and other groups in public hearings on the subject. Women's groups, many civic organizations, and the clergy all were against the legalization of gaming. In a meeting called in January, 1931, by the Democratic and Republican Party national committeewomen and held in the Reno Chamber of Commerce, the antigambling element seemed to be in charge. One woman speaker said that "Reno should not seek the riffraff of the world." Another stated, "We do not legalize murder, highway robbery or other unlawful practices and we should not legalize gambling." However, notwithstanding this opposition, Tobin's bill passed both the Senate and Assembly, to be signed into law by Governor Fred Balzar on March 19, 1931.

One of the major factors behind the legalization of gaming in Nevada was a desire to regulate the industry. Gaming was a factor in Nevada life all through the nineteenth and early twentieth centuries. It was illegal for only two brief and widely separated periods in the State's history. Hence, the 1931 bill legalizing gaming was more of a continuation of the past, rather than a sharp break with it.

The Legislature also hoped that legalized gaming might encourage the local economy. The Great Depression, which started at the end of 1929, had ruined many businesses in Nevada, and tourism almost stopped. No one seemed to have any money, and the Legislature bet that legalized gaming might pay off.

The 1931 gambling bill set up a system of license fees to be collected by the county, based on the number of games operated. The revenues were then distributed to the State, county, and local governments. The license fees provided an additional source of government revenue and gave relief from other taxes. This was a realistic concern in the Legislature, which a January, 1931 article in the Reno *Nevada State Journal* mentioned: "There is strong sentiment, particularly in Southern Nevada, that some state or municipal revenue should be derived from the games which now run on every hand with the apparent sanction of public sentiment."

MODERN GAMING REGULATION

In modern hotel-casinos, 95 percent of all money bet is said to be played on five different games: craps, which is played with dice; the card game of black-jack, also called twenty-one; baccarat or chemin-de-fer, another game of cards; roulette; and slot machines.

The games played with cards and dice are very old, but the slot machine is a much more recent intrusion into the field of betting on numbers. Charles Fey, a twenty-nine year old mechanic, designed the first "one-armed bandit" in San Francisco in 1895. At that time it was called a "nickel-in-a-slot machine," later "slot machine" for short. By 1910, slot machines could be found in every state in the Union. Today, tens of millions of Americans play slot machines each year, getting a sort of hypnotic satisfaction from the rhythm of play and betting on the spinning wheels.

Cheating is always a problem in gaming. It always has been and always will be. That is one of the main reasons that the industry is regulated in Nevada. Many cheaters are ingenious, as "Lucky Bill" was. This nineteenth century article from Austin's *Reese River Reveille* shows just how tricky cheating can get, even in a simple game of cards:

> A short time ago, a couple of Paiutes went to a store on Main Street and purchased the entire stock of playing cards. They took them to their camp, and having secretly marked each one, came back to the store and offered to sell them back for one-fourth of what they had paid. The pasteboards were purchased on these terms and were subsequently sold, one pack at a time, to the Shoshones.
>
> The Paiutes knew that the Shoshones made their purchases at this particular place; and the guileless Shoshones, unaware of manipulation, played poker with the wily Paiute, without a suspicion that all was not 'on the dead squar.' The result was that there is weeping and wailing and gnashing of teeth in the camp of the Shoshones.

The problem of cheating became more serious in modern times, when infinitely more money was at stake. The reputation of the games for honesty became a matter of State concern, since the State would be blamed if it permitted dishonest games, and the State's economy would suffer.

Benjamin Siegel and a number of Nevada gaming pioneers were gangsters. In 1951, the Report of the Special Senate Committee to Investigate Organized Crime in Interstate Commerce (also known as the Kefauver Committee after its chairman, United States Senator Estes Kefauver of Tennessee) stated what Congress knew about the man who established the first modern hotel-casino:

> Before he was shot to death in 1947, Benjamin "Bugsy" Siegel was undoubtedly the gambling boss of Las Vegas, Nev. Siegel, who had carried on gaming operations in California and elsewhere before coming to Nevada, had been associated with "Lucky" Luciano, Frank Costello, Joe Adonis, Meyer Lansky, and other influential members of the eastern underworld.
>
> It seems clear to the committee that too many of the men running gambling operations in Nevada are either members of existing out-of-State gambling syndicates or have had histories of close association with the underworld characters who operate these syndicates. The licensing system which is in effect in the State has not resulted in excluding the undesirables from the State but has merely served to give their activities a seeming cloak of respectability.

Stung by these accusations, the State Legislature undertook a thorough-going reform of gaming licensing in Nevada. After the Nevada Legislature legalized gaming in 1931, the regulation of individuals in the gambling business was left up to the counties. That changed in 1945, when the State imposed a 1 percent tax on gross revenues, and in

1947, when the Legislature doubled the tax. Not long after that, the State began to increase the controls or conditions on obtaining a license to run gambling games. Background investigations of applicants for gaming licenses started in 1949 but became much more comprehensive after 1955, when the Legislature created the Gaming Control Board and financed the new agency by raising the gaming tax to a sliding scale of 3 to 5 percent, depending on how little or how much money the casino made.

The State Gaming Control Board is a group of three men, appointed by the Governor, who serve full time investigating applicants for gaming permits, enforcing the gaming laws and regulations by prosecuting offenders, and collecting all gaming taxes and fees.

The Legislature added the Gaming Commission in 1959, to oversee the operations of the Gaming Control Board. There have been other slight changes, but that is basically how gaming is regulated in the State.

The Nevada Gaming Commission is a five-man bi-partisan commission appointed by the Governor. The Commissioners are not full-time State employees, but meet one or two days each month to act on matters affecting gaming. The Commission establishes its policies by its power to grant or deny licenses, take disciplinary action against licensees, and make rules and regulations.

The State Gaming Policy Committee, created by the Legislature in 1961, conducts hearings on policy issues and makes recommendations to the Gaming Commission and Control Board.

One of the most important changes in gaming regulations came in 1967, when Governor Paul Laxalt signed a bill into law which allowed public corporations to own gaming facilities. Before that time, each stockholder of a licensee of the State had to be investigated and approved individually. In his 1975 testimony before the Commission on the Review of the National Policy Toward Gambling, Laxalt stated:

> So, we finally, with the cooperation of the legislature decided that our whole licensing framework should be completely overhauled. Whereas previously each person within a gaming establishment who had any form of interest had to be individually investigated and subsequently licensed, we felt that the solution to the problem would be to establish a licensing framework whereby public companies could be licensed *per se*. And after a great deal of heated debate within the state, within the halls of the legislature, there was eventually passed what is now the existing corporate licensing law. And the rest is history.
>
> That then enabled major hotel chains and major public companies to come in and now be licensed. In my judgment that has helped tremendously in improving our ownership image throughout the whole state.
>
> In addition, it has proved a means whereby we could get substantial financing which again was a problem. It is no easy task to go into the money markets of this country and attempt to get any kind of a loan from any of the established financing institutions. They are scared to death of investing in Nevada gaming. Less so now, but still scared to death. In any event, the public companies brought with them the framework of public financing through issues, debentures and state mortgage financing. Had that not been available at that time

Warren Nelson sneaks a peek at the pack before playing his next card in a game of solitaire, about 1938. Nelson, a Nevada gaming pioneer and co-founder of the Club Cal-Neva in Reno, came to Nevada in the mid-1930's from Montana. He is credited with having introduced the game of keno, one of the more popular forms of gambling today, to the public at large.

Courtesy of Greg Nelson

Paul Laxalt (b.1922) of Nevada had just been elected Governor when he signed the law allowing corporate gaming in the State. The son of an immigrant Basque rancher from France, Laxalt built the Ormsby House hotel-casino, the first major hotel to be built in Carson City in nearly a century, and over the past twenty-five years, he has served Nevada as its Lieutenant Governor, Governor, and United States Senator.

Courtesy of Nevada Historical Society

The Biggest Hotel-Casino in the World. Bally's Grand Hotel-Reno, formerly the MGM, towers over its surroundings in this twilight photograph. The twenty-seven story all-weather resort skyscrapper employs 3,500 people to care for and entertain its patrons, who can be housed in the hotel's 2,001 guest rooms and suites. The corporate hotel-casino business dominates modern Nevada's economy and gives employment to tens of thousands of workers.

Courtesy of Bally Corporation

through the corporate framework, what you see in Las Vegas now would certainly not be here. And you could go through every one of these major developments which have substantially expanded and who are going well and invariably they bring you to the door of public stock ownership.

Today, there are about 1200 licensed gaming or casino operations in Nevada. More than 90 percent of the State's income from gambling, however, is produced by just eighty casinos and hotels. Gaming taxes are a very important part of Nevada's government revenues, amounting to about one-third of the total annual take of the State tax collectors. Of these revenues, the vast majority goes to health, education, or welfare agencies.

Today, the vast majority of money from Nevada's combined tourist and gaming industry comes from three areas: Las Vegas, Reno, and Lake Tahoe.

Reno

Nevada's gaming industry did not dramatically increase just because the State Legislature legalized betting and games of chance. In 1931, more than two years into the Great Depression, few people had the money to do any interstate touring. The gambling clubs in Reno were small and patronized mostly by local players and a few wealthy people from out of state.

In 1936, Harold Smith, Sr. opened a gambling place in Reno which he called Harold's Club. Smith and his family originally operated bingo games and other forms of gambling in California, but came to Nevada when the Bear Flag State began a crackdown on people operating games of chance for profit. In 1941, Harold's Club began an

The Smith Family — three generations of gaming innovators who didn't ask what their country could do for them. President John F. Kennedy coolly surveys the scene as Harold Smith Sr., Raymond I. "Pappy" Smith, and Harold Smith Jr. ponder the pros and cons of gambling at Harold's Club. The casino was posted with signs which said, "No one can win all the time. Harold's Club advises you to risk only what you can afford."

Courtesy of Special Collections, University of Nevada Reno Library

Publicity put Nevada Gaming on the Map. Raymond I. "Pappy" Smith and his son Harold Smith Sr.
started a publicity campaign in 1941 to promote the fun of gaming, which was spread by soldiers
during World War II. After Harold's Club began to provide free evenings to graduates of the nearby
United States Air Force Survival School, the servicemen reciprocated by putting up Harold's Club
signs as far away as the Congo and both the North and South Poles. Millions of people saw the
signs posted in combat zones, along the highways, and in newsreels, which helped legalized gambling
to become acceptable. Every casino in Nevada benefitted from the publicity generated by
the Smith family.

Courtesy of Nevada Historical Society

Distinctive casino architecture developed as tourism and gaming became big business in the years following World War II. For the older casinos with modest storefront beginnings, the large profits meant expansion. Harold's Club has taken over several adjoining shops and buildings in this view of the intersection of Virginia Street and Commercial Row, Reno, in the mid-1950's. The largest signs emphasize the historical link between the modern casino and the gambling saloons of the Old West. Over the main entrance to the original club, there is a large mural showing the overland trek of the pioneers by covered wagon, "Dedicated in All Humility to Those Who Blazed the Trail."

Courtesy of Nevada Historical Society

advertising campaign that made the casino internationally famous through its slogan "Harold's Club or Bust." For the first time, large numbers of people began to come to Nevada just to gamble.

Harold Smith did pretty well for himself, but his club didn't make millions of dollars overnight. In his autobiography *I Want to Quit Winners,* Smith talked about the turning point:

> Until 1941 we were to draw our trade from local residents and a few venturesome tourists who tackled the games skeptically. Then in the early months of '41, suddenly, we began to boom. California seemed suddenly to awaken to Reno's legal gaming (Vegas was nothing) and people came pouring over the mountains with their money. We added games and machines and expanded upwards, downwards and sideways through the old building in that block of Virginia Street.
>
> The advertising campaign we started that year was to make our name known on every continent of the world. Now that we'd got our feet wet, we weren't happy with Nevada's reluctance to promote its legal gaming. We started building roadside billboards extolling the FUN of playing at our club. The 25 signs we put up within 500 miles were to grow in the years ahead to more than 2,000 scattered over much of the civilized world. (I understand one even was raised inside the Antarctic Circle.) As the crowds poured in, we would have had to be geniuses not to make money. We made it and expanded the club more. It was still a pretty rough gem, however, to sightseers expecting a deluxe casino. As Daddy admitted: "It took us five years to catch up with our advertising."

Another California gambler, William F. Harrah, moved his operation to Reno in 1937. Like Harold Smith, Harrah became disgusted with government harassment and decided to try his luck in a State where gaming was legal. Almost forty years later, Harrah recalled the early days of Nevada's casino industry for the Commission on the Review of the National Policy Toward Gaming:

> I came to Nevada in 1937 from Venice, California where my father . . . had been Mayor, . . . he ran a very small game which was similar to Bingo. That game, I remember very distinctly opened on July 4th, 1932; and I ran the game for my father.
>
> I was impressed with the way his customers played the game to escape the harsh realities of those depression days. And, I think I began to form my own

William Fisk Harrah (1911–1978) of California got his start at the age of twenty, when he ran a commercial bingo game. Attracted by Reno's legalized gambling, he relocated there in 1937, telling a friend, "That's a place! Look at that; they don't close the bars and they don't close the games. They leave you alone." Harrah was the first casino owner to use modern sociology and psychological studies to attract tourists, and he built a multi-million-dollar empire with advertising and charter buses.

Courtesy of Nevada Historical Society

attitudes about gaming as a form of recreation and entertainment at that time. It was an escape.

I bought my father out for $500 and consciously or unconsciously applied many of the same principles to the running of the game as we considered to be basic to our operations today — scrupulous honesty — a great variety of opportunities for their entertainment value — the development of a clientele through friendliness and courtesy and extra little amenities.

Our arrival in Reno — six employees from Venice and myself — was a rather insignificant event in the history of Reno. We opened a Bingo parlor, and it immediately failed. We tried at another location — and the statement says existed, but we did a little bit better than that. We made a few dollars.

So it went for the first few years. I did not foresee Nevada industry as it is today; nor did I picture anything like the business Harrah's is today. Yet, I believed that the same practices, ethics, principles which make any business successful would work for gambling as well. I have never had anything but a positive view of Nevada gaming, realizing that it is subject to the same mistakes, misconceptions and misdirections as any other business.

And, as a new industry, with nothing to precede it or model it after, we expected it would make more than its share of mistakes. The concept of a completely controlled industry was, to say the least, very bold.

I gambled on Nevada in its infant days. I borrowed some money to buy our first casino location on Virginia Street in 1946, with no background in casino gambling. We gambled on buying a quonset hut at Lake Tahoe in 1955 called George's Gateway Club.

We gambled on staying open in the winter at Tahoe, when anyone in his right mind knew that the day after Labor Day, only the squirrels were around, and they were getting ready to call it a year. They still run cattle right down Highway 50 in the spring, and still reminds me of those early days.

But, what I'm saying is that in a new industry, any new industry, a certain amount of gamble is necessary. We did not enter the business with any preconceived ideas on what made it work. We were novices, and we all learned the business while we were building the business.

Reno at Twilight, 1986. The ski resorts and scenic attractions of Slide Mountain (left) and Mount Rose (right) overlook the commercial district of Reno in this recent photograph of the Biggest Little City in the World. The expansion of Reno, like that of Las Vegas, has been largely the result of gaming and tourism.

Courtesy of Nevada Historical Society

Reno began a boom period immediately after the end of the Second World War. The Mapes Hotel was Nevada's tallest skyscraper when the twelve-story edifice opened in 1945. Built by Gladys, Gloria, and Charles Mapes, the business was the first major hotel to be constructed in the U.S. after the defeat of Germany and Japan.

The next year, 1946, Lincoln Fitzgerald opened his Nevada Club casino in downtown Reno. The place has become a landmark in the town and in Nevada's gaming history, and it helped finance the construction of one of Reno's major hotel-casinos, Fitzgerald's, which opened thirty years later, in 1976.

One well-known Reno hotel-casino, the Riverside, has another claim to fame. Nevada's pioneer television transmitter sent the first TV signal in the State from Mount Rose to a receiving set in the Riverside in 1952.

In 1969, William F. Harrah, taking a chance that the improvement in business would last, built the 24-story high-rise hotel-casino which bears his name. It was Reno's first high-rise structure but not its last.

Harrah's gamble was already paying off in 1973, when the Carano family built the Eldorado Hotel-Casino and started an epic building boom. In 1974, the Holiday Inn and Reef Resort opened. In 1975, the Sundowner was built, and construction on Fitzgerald's began that same year. During the United States bicentennial (1976), workmen started to erect the MGM Grand at Reno. Finished in 1978, it is one of the biggest buildings in the State. The boom peaked in 1977, when work began on no less than five hotel-casinos: the Sahara (now the Reno Hilton), the Circus Circus, the Colonial, the Comstock, and the Onslow.

With all this expansion, Reno is more bustling than ever. The town has prospered through gaming, but there's more to modern Reno than that. The city is well-known for its cultural achievements, especially the formation and success of the Nevada Opera guild. Museums, parks, festivals, and the arts also prosper in Reno, which is still the "biggest little city" in the world.

Lake Tahoe

Lake Tahoe has been a tourist attraction since territorial days. Its magnificent scenic beauty brings people from all across the world to see it. Mark Twain loved to look at "the fairest picture the whole earth affords" and described the effect of his trip to Lake Tahoe in *Roughing It:*

> Three months of camp life on Lake Tahoe would restore an Egyptian mummy to his pristine vigor and give him an appetite like an alligator. I do not mean the oldest and driest of mummies, of course, but the fresher ones. The air up there is very pure and fine, bracing and delicious. And why shouldn't it be? — it is the same that angels breathe. I think that hardly any amount of fatigue can be gathered together that a man cannot sleep off in one night on the sand by its side. Not under a roof, but under the sky; it seldom or never rains there in the summertime. I know a man who went there to die. But he made a failure of it. He was a skeleton when he came, and could barely stand. He had no appetite and did nothing but read tracts and reflect on the future. Three months later he was sleeping out of doors regularly, eating all he could hold, three times a day, and chasing game over mountains three thousand feet high for recreation. And he was a skeleton no longer, but weighed part of a ton. This is no fancy sketch, but the truth. His disease was consumption. I confidently commend his experience to other skeletons.

Twain's works and lectures made Lake Tahoe familiar to millions of people in the United States and abroad, and many of them took the trouble to see the spot.

When J. Ross Browne visited Lake Tahoe in 1864, he got some idea of the potential the area had and told the readers of *Harpers Monthly Magazine* about it:

> Within the past two years the people of California and Washoe have begun to discover the beauties of this charming region, and its rare advantages as a place of summer resort. Situated in the bosom of the Sierra Nevada mountains, 6,000 feet above the level of the sea, with an atmosphere of wonderful purity; abounding in game; convenient of access, and possessing all the attractions of retirement from the busy world, amid scenery unrivalled for its romantic

Looking south across Lake Tahoe on a sunny afternoon during the 1920's, the camera has caught the graceful lines of the recreational steamer "Tahoe" gliding through the water, past the shady pines on the shoreline. Sailing on the lake has been a favorite activity of tourists and locals alike.

Courtesy of Nevada Historical Society

Stateline, Lake Tahoe, about 1956. This view of U.S. Highway 50, looking north from the California border, illustrates the area in the years before big-time gaming began in the 1960's and 1970's. The Wagon Wheel casino and restaurant (left) was opened by Harvey Gross in 1946, who added a resort hotel in 1963. The collection of small clubs on the right became Harrah's Tahoe.

Courtesy of Nevada Historical Society

The State Line Country Club, on the south shore of Lake Tahoe, was purchased by William Fisk Harrah and combined with the Gateway Club next door to form Harrah's Tahoe. In 1957, the Harrah's Tahoe hotel-casino stayed open all year, ending seasonal gaming at the lake and establishing all-weather recreation at Stateline.

Courtesy of Nevada Historical Society

The Cal-Neva Lodge on the north shore of Lake Tahoe appears well-patronized in this photograph from the early 1950's. The Cal-Neva Lodge was one of the first of the Lake Tahoe hotels to offer cosmopolitan gaming along with the other pleasures of the region.

Courtesy of Nevada Historical Society

beauties, there can be no doubt it will soon become the grand central point of pleasure and recreation for the people of the Pacific Coast.

Stateline, where the Tahoe skyline bears the silhouettes of most of the Lake's large hotel-casinos, has been a place for parties since prehistoric times. The Washo Indians used to hold a yearly festival at the site, where they danced and feasted for days.

Stateline, on the South Shore, is also the home of the first hotel on the Nevada side of Lake Tahoe. W. W. Lapham built the place in the summer of 1860 as a landing and fish market, as well as a hostelry to serve the teamsters hauling freight between Sacramento and the Comstock Lode. When the transcontinental railroad was completed in 1869, much of the road traffic moved north, away from Lapham's hotel. Lapham countered by catering to the tourists. In 1872, he had Lake Tahoe's first large luxury steamer, the *Governor Sanford,* built to carry mail, freight, and tourists between his establishment and the four other major resorts then existing at Lake Tahoe.

Lapham's hotel had another distinction: the dividing line between Nevada and California ran right through the living room. The hotel burned in 1876, and the site was deserted until the spring of 1892, when a new owner built the Lakeside House. By 1895, a small community existed there, and got its own post office in 1901.

The owner also established a campground at Stateline for the more rustic-minded tourists, which was a success for years. Since that time, camping has become extremely popular in Nevada. Since World War II, the tourist who pitches a tent or rents a small cabin has been joined by the traveling families who bring their own camp, in the form of trailers, mobile homes, and recreational vehicles. Today, recreational vehicle parks, state parks, and national campgrounds offer increased opportunities for people who want to see our scenic beauties within a comfortable setting.

Another well-known station offering rooms, meals, and other entertainments in the South Lake Tahoe area was Friday's, named for station keeper G. K. "Friday" Burke. It opened in the spring of 1860 as a stopping-place for Pony Express riders racing between Placerville and Carson City. Burke operated the western section of the Kingsbury Grade toll road and made a great deal of money in the days before the transcontinental railroad was built. Almost everyone going to the Comstock mines from northern California traveled over the route. This station still stands today, preserved by its owners.

By the end of the Second World War, there were a number of gambling clubs at Stateline. Many of these clubs began to imitate the format of the Flamingo Hotel-Casino in Las Vegas, though on a smaller scale. Brothers Nick and Eddie Sahati, who operated Sahati's Stateline Country Club, combined high-stakes gambling with big-name entertainment, well-known bands, and a chorus line. Harvey Gross opened the Wagon Wheel there in 1946, and other small club-owners also prospered.

In 1955, William F. Harrah bought the Gateway Club, which first opened in May of 1949 in a quonset hut. Located at Stateline, the Gateway Club was later combined by Harrah with the Stateline Country Club to form Harrah's Tahoe Hotel-Casino. Year-round operations at the hotel began in 1957 and have continued since then. Before that year, tourism at Lake Tahoe was strictly a summer business.

Harrah's gamble, like so many other gambles connected with the gaming business, paid off. Year-round tourism soon became an established fact and brought increased revenues to South Shore. Harvey Gross, using profits from his Wagon Wheel Casino, built Harvey's Hotel-Casino there in 1963, and in 1965 the Sahara Tahoe Hotel-Casino opened. New casino and residential construction at South Shore and at other points on the Lake has been minimal since the 1970's. A special bi-state commission to administer the Lake Tahoe basin, the Tahoe Regional Planning Agency, has effectively stopped any further large-scale development in the area.

The North Shore of Lake Tahoe, long populated only by loggers, was opened to tourist and commercial visits in 1892, when a road was built between Reno and Incline. Today it is called the Mount Rose Highway.

Tourism at North Lake Tahoe took a new turn when gambling casinos were built there. One of the first of these was the Cal-Neva Club at Incline. Originally constructed in 1927, it burned ten years later and was rebuilt as a hotel-casino. Its owners built a high-rise hotel there in 1969.

A second large gaming establishment and hotel, the Tahoe Biltmore, opened at North Shore in 1946. There are other hotels and casinos which were built around Crystal Bay, such as King's Castle (now the Hyatt Tahoe) which began business in 1970. The area has not been as well-frequented as the South Shore casinos, but still presents a fair face to tourists. The community there, Incline Village, is a planned residential area which offers extensive recreational opportunities to its property-owners.

Las Vegas

In Nevada, one city predominates — Las Vegas. The area contains about half of the State's population and generates nearly three-fourths of the gaming industry's total gross revenues. Much of its earlier history appears in the chapter on transportation, but the story of Las Vegas' golden years, following the Second World War, is one of the most astonishing tales of success ever to appear on the pages of history.

There are many reasons why Las Vegas is a winner. One of the most important is the fact that the modern hotel-casino industry started there. Las Vegas pioneered the hotel-casino concept, which led to a multi-billion dollar empire and served as a model for other, smaller ventures in other states and other lands. But when it was first tried in Las Vegas, it was a remarkable innovation. It radically changed the hotel and gambling saloon business in the State and made Nevada what it is today.

The Flamingo Hotel-Casino was not the first gaming establishment in Las Vega:. Betting had been going on since prehistoric times, and the intruding nineteenth-century settlers and miners brought their own assortment of gaming pastimes. Card rooms and gambling saloons were common in downtown Las Vegas, or "Glitter Gulch," all through the first three decades of the twentieth century. Things changed in a small way in 1940 with the construction of El Rancho Vegas, a motor court and roadhouse with gambling attractions located on the highway which connected Los Angeles with Salt Lake City and other points north and east. The Last Frontier, built in 1942–43, was an establishment similar to the El Rancho, but featured an additional attraction: an amusement park in the form of an Old West-style village. Both the El Rancho and the Last Frontier were designed to attract the business of travelers passing through Las Vegas on their way to other places. The Flamingo, on the other hand, was an entirely new and different concept in the history of Nevada gaming. Built in 1946–47, it was conceived as a destination resort — a place with legal gambling, top-name entertainment, distinctive architecture, and opulent and relaxing accommodations which would draw an affluent clientele solely for the purpose of staying and playing there.

The Flamingo Hotel-Casino was the brain-child of Benjamin "Bugsy" Siegel, a New York gangster who came to the West Coast in the late 1930's to organize a national wire service reporting sports events for bookmakers. He was interested in getting a share of the bets placed on those events, and in other gambling operations in California.

Early in 1947, Siegel told world-famous gaming authority John Scarne why he had

A lineup of early recreational spots in downtown Las Vegas, about 1906. Eating, drinking, and gambling were the main diversions in the newly-built town.

Stormy skies over Las Vegas. Neon signs light up the night along Fremont Street in this scene from the late 1930's, when the construction of Boulder Dam brought electricity, progress, and prosperity to the region. At that time, most of the gambling in town took place along these two blocks — an area known as "Glitter Gulch." The Hotel Apache (right) later became Benny Binion's Horseshoe Club.

Courtesy of Nevada Historical Society

The El Rancho Vegas hotel-casino was opened in 1940 by Thomas E. Hull, south of Las Vegas on the highway to Los Angeles. This was the first hotel-casino to be built along the Las Vegas Strip, which has become internationally famous as a symbol of legalized gaming. Tourists relaxed and gambled in a swimming pool and bungalow atmosphere. The success of the El Rancho Vegas and the Last Frontier convinced Benjamin "Bugsy" Siegel that he could attract enough "high rollers" to make a multi-million dollar hotel-casino resort operate profitably for years.   Courtesy of Nevada Historical Society

The Fabulous Flamingo. High-rolling tourists from southern California stroll into the main entrance of the world's first modern hotel-casino, against a backdrop of orange and purple twilight. Built on the Las Vegas Strip in 1946 by gangster Benjamin "Bugsy" Siegel, the Flamingo was the prototype of the multi-million-dollar gambling resort and set the standard for all hotel-casinos which followed.

Courtesy of Nevada Historical Society

Poolside at the Fabulous Flamingo. A cloudless sky, shady tables, beautiful girls, and cool drinks made tourists feel wanted when they stayed at the Strip's premier resort in the late 1940's. "Bugsy" Siegel's penthouse rises above the rest of the architecture — it's just above the young woman chatting pleasantly on the house phone. Courtesy of Special Collections. University of Nevada Reno Library

come to Las Vegas to build his resort hotel-casino. Scarne recounted the tale in his *Complete Guide to Gambling:*

> He grinned. "I had a little trouble with Governor Earl Warren. I owned a piece of all those gambling ships that were getting plenty of action three miles off the coast of Southern California. Business was so good we had plans to add a dozen more boats. And just when I thought I had it made, Governor Warren came along and closed gambling up tight as a drum, not only in the state [of California] but on the boats too. Overnight my dream of a Monte Carlo in the ocean is killed.
>
> So I'm thinking about where I can find another spot away from any other casinos — a place like the ocean so that when people come to gamble they can't go any place else but have to stick with me. There were too many sawdust joints in Vegas, Reno, and other Nevada towns, but I figured it this way. If people will take a trip out into the ocean to gamble, they'll go to a desert, too — especially if its legal and they don't have to worry about getting pinched. So one day I drive into Nevada looking for a nice desert spot and I picked this one because the price is right and its on the main road to L.A. Then I took a trip around the country and tried to interest some of the boys in the proposition. Some of them thought I was nuts. But I dug up the dough, and here I am with a five-million dollar hotel and a casino full of customers."

The successful example of the Flamingo Hotel-Casino was soon imitated. A large building boom began in Las Vegas during the Korean War (1950–53). By that time the hotel-casino industry in southern Nevada was "on a roll" which was to make Las Vegas the biggest city in Nevada. Tourist excursions to Las Vegas by car made these gambling emporiums and night spots immensely profitable, and a number of casinos were built through 1955.

Only a few more casinos were built in Las Vegas over the next ten years. In 1966, there was another boom in the hotel-casino business, coinciding with the Vietnam War.

A number of new gaming establishments were built, and Howard R. Hughes decided to invest extensively in Nevada. Hughes had inherited the Hughes Tool Company from his father in 1923, and immediately began to reinvest his profits in that company, the aviation business, and the motion-picture industry. His investments made Hughes one of the world's richest men, with a fortune estimated at well over one billion dollars. An aviation pioneer, Hughes was awarded the Congressional Medal of Honor in 1941, but was nearly killed in the 1946 crash of an experimental airplane he was flying as test pilot. When Hughes sold his controlling interest in Trans-World Airlines in 1966 for $546.5 million, he decided to invest much of the money in Nevada hotel-casinos.

Hughes also purchased considerable real estate holdings around and in Las Vegas, some 2,700 mining claims scattered across the State, a television station, and two airline companies. In all, Hughes spent about $300 million in Nevada, becoming the State's largest employer (of some eight thousand employees), biggest landowner, and most important single gaming figure in the world.

Hughes explained some of the reasons for his heavy investments in a statement prepared by his Summa Corporation in 1975, for the Commission on the Review of the National Policy Toward Gaming:

> The Corporation did not look upon Las Vegas or Nevada as a gaming Mecca, but rather as a total environment, of which gaming was one part. The recreation industry represented a short vacation-oriented, get-away resort area whose attractions included outdoor sports, an attractive climate, high-quality entertainment, luxury hotel accommodations, fine food and a unique attraction — gaming. Nevada was also close to a large metropolitan customer population; and properly developed, could expand from the close-proximity California market to draw from the entire world, particularly with the increased facility made possible by the jet airplane. This assessment continues to be verified each day. Experience also confirms our belief that Nevada represents a unique, already-established circumstance for a legalized-gaming involved industry, locally-controlled and well-regulated (as in Nevada), which can be an entertainment activity of increasing and growing interest to larger and broader segments of the population.

Howard Robard Hughes (1905–1976) of Texas stands in front of his specially modified Northrup Gamma racing plane in this 1936 process shot. That year, Hughes broke all existing speed/distance records for Los Angeles–New York and Miami–New York flights. He had inherited the Hughes Tool Company and the patent to a revolutionary oil drill when his father died in 1923. Hughes parlayed his holdings, originally valued at less than one million dollars, into a billion dollar fortune. By the time of his death, he was one of the richest men in the world. Shy as a youth, he became reclusive during the 1950's and never appeared in public again. Hughes invested hundreds of millions of dollars in Nevada casinos and other holdings between 1967 and 1970. At one time, he was the State's largest employer.

Courtesy of Summa Corporation

McCarran International Airport at Las Vegas. This newly-expanded transportation facility, with its own customs-free port zone, is the largest airport in Nevada. The immense terminal, the runways and gates, parking lots, and visiting jet transport aircraft are all clearly visible in this aerial view. Scores of large airplanes land here every day of the year, bringing tourists, travelers, and products from all around the world to Las Vegas.

Courtesy of Las Vegas News Bureau

The Legendary Las Vegas Strip. Fortunes are made and lost every night in the casinos along this three-and-a-half-mile stretch of highway, which draws paying customers from every quarter of the globe.

Courtesy of Las Vegas News Bureau

Another reason for the success of Las Vegas is the idea that other people have of the place — its "image". Las Vegas has always had a very active promotional program for the city, as General R. G. Taylor, President of the Chamber of Commerce, testified in 1975:

> The promotion of gambling, the promotion of tourism as it is called today, is and always has been a civic enterprise of the people of Las Vegas. It is the major activity of the greater Las Vegas Chamber of Commerce. A little bit of the background and history. The Las Vegas Chamber of Commerce was founded in 1912 when the population of our city was only 1,500 people. The major concern at that time was the pavement of streets and the building of a passable highway between here and Los Angeles and here and Salt Lake City.

> Later on the Chamber conducted programs to retain the population which had been involved in the construction of Hoover Dam. Many persons attracted to the area by this construction remained here, became leading citizens and have contributed much of its growth.

> The Chamber was instrumental in bringing the Henderson industrial plants to the area during the war and retaining those facilities and operations for peacetime purposes.

> The Chamber was in the forefront of the development of a large permanent Air Force installation, Nellis Air Force Base, just outside our city.

> A most significant change occurred in the community in 1944 and 1945 when World War II came to an end.

> A civic movement headed by the Chamber of Commerce was undertaken to promote Las Vegas as a tourist attraction with legalized gambling; the greatest entertainment in the world; other recreational facilities, including swimming, boating, fishing, skiing; and scenic beauty of the area.

> Gambling along with entertainment and the excitement of a 24-hour town was adopted at that time as our major industry.

> In 1945 our population of 20,000 people raised $85,000.00 to promote Las Vegas in a successful conversion to a peacetime economy. The contributors of the $85,000.00 were called Las Vegas "Livewires" and the "Livewire" fund still exists today and is used for the same purpose.

> We believe that a major factor bringing millions of visitors to Las Vegas each year is the incomparable entertainment available here — from the shows featuring superstars to the lavish production spectaculars. In this modern jet age the traveler has a choice of casinos throughout the world, yet only in Las Vegas can be found the unsurpassed entertainment offered around the clock.

> I am sure that you would agree from all of this that our visitors are thoroughly preconditioned for the impact of Las Vegas. On the impact, another question which you posed, for many visitors we believe that Las Vegas is a therapeutic recreational experience, a 24-hour fun place where they can lose track of time. We believe that this, for most visitors, certainly not all, is a healthy experience. Las Vegas has a unique image as the entertainment capital of the world, and its name carries an aura of glamour wherever it is mentioned. This has caused some to speak of Las Vegas as a phenomenon. I have never thought of Las Vegas in that respect, for a phenomenon can be without real substance and often disappears as suddenly as it came. The international reputation and respect Las Vegas has attained could not have been realized without the integrity of self-discipline it has demonstrated within county, state and national governments, and without the solidarity of community life that has been the basis of its progress and growth. It is in that sense that we are proud to be a part of the Las Vegas community and have invested so much in its future.

Index